EYEWITNESS COMPANIONS

Scuba Diving

MONTY HALLS &
MIRANDA KRESTOVNIKOFF

"WE FORGET THAT THE
WATER CYCLE AND THE LIFE
CYCLE ARE ONE."

Jacques Cousteau

DK

LONDON, NEW YORK,
MUNICH, MELBOURNE, DELHI

Project Editor	Richard Gilbert
Project Art Editor	Mark Cavanagh
Managing Editor	Stephanie Farrow
Managing Art Editor	Lee Griffiths
Publishing Director	Jonathan Metcalf
Art Director	Bryn Walls
DTP Designer	Vania Cunha
Production Controller	Melanie Dowland

Produced for Dorling Kindersley by

cobaltid

The Stables, Wood Farm, Deopham Road,
Attleborough, Norfolk NR17 1AJ
www.cobaltid.co.uk

EDITORS	ART EDITORS
Marek Walisiewicz,	Paul Reid, Lloyd Tilbury,
Jamie Dickson, Maddy King,	Claire Oldman, Darren Bland,
Kati Dye, Steve Setford	Rebecca Johns

Commissioned photography by Dan Burton

First published in Great Britain in 2006 by
Dorling Kindersley Limited
80 Strand, London, WC2R ORL

A Penguin Company

2 4 6 8 10 9 7 5 3

Copyright © 2006 Dorling Kindersley Limited

This companion guide is intended to help you understand the key
principles that enable divers to practise their sport enjoyably and safely.
It is not a training manual, and it is recommended that you read this
guide in conjunction with an accredited course of diving tuition and
official training literature. Diving centres around the world will ask to see
evidence of formal qualifications before allowing you to hire equipment,
have your cylinder filled, or join a diving trip. The authors and publishers
have made every effort to ensure that the information in this book is
correct at time of going to press. However, they accept no responsibility
for any injury, accident, or inconvenience sustained by any person using
this book, or following advice presented in it.

A CIP catalogue record for this book is available
from the British Library.

ISBN-13: 978-1-40531-294-
ISBN-10: 1-4053-1294-

Colour reproduction by GRB, Italy.
Printed in China by Leo.

Discover more at
www.dk.com

CONTENTS

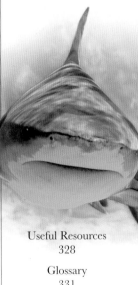

THE IDEA THAT PEOPLE COULD BREATHE UNDERWATER WAS ONCE A FANTASY. BUT TODAY, DIVING HAS LEFT THE REALMS OF IMAGINATION AND GROWN INTO A WORLDWIDE SPORT WITH MILLIONS OF FOLLOWERS. THOSE WHO TAKE PART IN IT ARE GRANTED PRIVILEGED ACCESS TO A MYSTERIOUS YET BEAUTIFUL WORLD, AND EVERY DIVE IS AN ADVENTURE INTO THE UNKNOWN.

Since prehistoric times, people have been drawn to explore the incredible world that lies underwater – whether in pursuit of food, lost riches, or from sheer inquisitiveness. There is evidence, for example, that people were holding their breaths and diving for shellfish by about 3,000BCE (*see p.22*).

Despite this long relationship with the undersea world, the human body is not designed to remain underwater for prolonged periods of time. Only comparatively recently, with the development of rudimentary diving bells and helmets from the Middle Ages onwards, did it become possible to stay

THE DAWN OF AN ERA
Diving pioneer Jacques Cousteau (*right*) models early scuba equipment.

submerged for longer than a single breath allows. During the 18th and 19th centuries there were remarkable advances in diving technology, such as full diving suits supplied by air pumped from the surface. These advances, which were often spurred on by the lucrative rewards of salvage work, extended dive times and gave access to ever greater depths.

The invention of the Aqua Lung in the mid-20th century permitted divers to explore the depths of the world's oceans freely for the first time. This truly remarkable apparatus enables people to take their own air supply with them when they dive, eliminating the need to be connected to the surface by an airline. The system that evolved from it – scuba – is today widely used in recreational and professional diving.

GLOBAL APPEAL

As scuba technology became cheaper, diving opened up to the general public. What was once the realm of experts and professionals gradually became a sport with global appeal. Even in countries

WRECK DIVING
Divers inspect a wreck in tropical waters. Such underwater relics offer a glimpse into maritime history, and are home to colonies of sealife.

A NEW GENERATION
Trainee instructors receive a group briefing at a dive centre in Egypt. For many, a job in diving represents the ultimate career move.

without a coastline you will find divers who spend time underwater at inland sites, such as lakes and rivers, or who travel abroad to experience the beauty of the oceans. Once you are qualified, you can dive virtually anywhere in the world. Language is no barrier underwater, since divers use standard hand signals that are understood internationally.

It is difficult to estimate how many divers there are worldwide, but well over a million people qualify each year. Since its inception in 1966, over 13 million divers around the world have been certified by PADI (the Professional Association of Diving Instructors), and PADI is just one of many training agencies. Diving is one of the fastest-growing hobbies in the world today.

SILENT ODYSSEY
Clown fish shelter in an anemone while a diver swims by. The underwater world can be a uniquely serene environment.

THE WORLD'S OCEANS

Covering approximately 71 per cent of the Earth's surface, or 361 million sq km (140 million sq miles), the vast size of the world's oceans is difficult to comprehend. The total volume of sea water is about 1,347,000,000 cu km (322,300,000 cu miles), equivalent to around 97 per cent of all the Earth's water – the rest exists as glaciers, rivers, lakes, groundwater, and atmospheric vapour. The average depth of the world's oceans is 3.8km (2.3 miles), with the deepest point being in the Pacific Ocean's Mariana Trench, where the seabed plunges down to a depth of nearly 11 km (7 miles). With only about 5 per cent of the ocean floor having been mapped in detail, we know more about the surface of the Moon than the bottom of our oceans.

The oceans teem with wildlife, from giant kelp and the mighty blue whale (the largest animal alive) to microscopic plankton that form the basis of the oceanic food chain. Scientizsts estimate that there may be between 500,000 and 10 million marine species yet to be discovered. While much of the oceans' biological wealth is concentrated between continental shelves and coastal margins, the open sea also abounds with life. Even the mud on the floor of the Mariana Trench is home to single-celled organisms called foraminiferans.

NATURAL WONDERS
Diving can lead to encounters with many intriguing and beautiful marine creatures, such as this leafy sea dragon.

GETTING READY
Buddy pairs prepare for a beach dive. By working in pairs, donning awkward kit becomes considerably easier and safer.

EXPLORING THE UNDERWATER WORLD

What will I see? What will it feel like? Will I feel claustrophobic? These are all questions you will ask as a novice diver entering the underwater world for the first time. Everyone feels different about being underwater; some people take to it immediately, but others need more training and experience before they feel at ease. Either way, it is an unforgettable experience. There is the initial thrill of being able to breathe underwater, and also the novelty of moving freely in three dimensions, thanks to the buoyancy provided by the water, which is a denser medium than air. This same buoyancy can enable those with mobility problems on land to feel relaxed and move more easily in water, and give what some divers call a "womb-like" experience.

Imagine the thrill of being the first person to see a sunken ship or coral reef, or of coming face to face with a wild dolphin, or diving under ice. Whatever excites you – whether it be encounters with fascinating creatures, investigating shipwrecks, or just diving into the unknown – you will not fail to be satisfied by what the oceans have to offer.

CAPTURING THE MOMENT
Underwater photography is an absorbing activity in its own right, and offers the chance to record your dive experiences for posterity.

CONSERVATION WORK
A diver notes down his observations of marine life at a conservation site. Divers can play an active role as "stewards of the seas".

BUT IS IT SAFE?

Many people new to the sport worry about the safety aspect. It is true that a small number of divers die every year whilst pursuing their sport. The majority of these incidents are not due to equipment failure, as some people might suppose, but rather to inadequate training, diving in extreme conditions, or diving beyond the limits of safe practice.

Diving today is safer than it has ever been. If you undertake the correct training and adhere to recommended safety procedures, you will rarely encounter problems. Dive training is thorough, and a great emphasis is placed on rescue skills and the importance of diving in a buddy pair (*see pp.110–11*). Good communication with your buddy is essential, as most minor difficulties can be easily resolved with the help of another diver.

NEW SKILLS, NEW DIRECTIONS

You may find that you enjoy diving so much that you want to pursue it beyond the hobby level. Some people use their underwater knowledge and skills for voluntary or charitable work, or in a full-time career. The directions in which diving can take you are endless, from environmental projects,

RECOGNITION GUIDE
A pair of divers consult a species identification slate. Becoming familiar with marine life, in all its fascinating variety, is part of the fun.

marine archaeology, historical research, and working with disabled divers, to filming and photography, and even training to be a diving instructor yourself.

RESPECT AND RESPONSIBILITY

Ask any group of divers what inspired them to take up the sport and you will hear a range of different answers, from a love of the sea to a desire to challenge their personal limits. One thing they all have in common is the fact that they return again and again to the water – the magical environment that Jacques Cousteau (*see p.26*) described as the "Silent World". Divers should be custodians of the world's oceans, and respect what they contain: "take only pictures and leave only bubbles" is a good maxim for low-impact diving.

Many of the marine ecosystems around the world are today in decline. Hopefully education and investment will help to reverse this trend, so the divers of tomorrow will have healthy oceans to explore. By taking part in conservation work and diving responsibly, you can become a force for the good in preserving the oceans' natural treasures.

DISCUSSING A DIVE
Diving is a social sport and the diving community is a supportive one. Experienced divers are often willing to offer advice to novices.

MARINE LIFE
A diver examines a beautiful and delicate sea pen – a colonial polyp organism – growing out of white sand next to the Great Barrier Reef.

GLIMPSE OF A GIANT
Anticipation of a dive can be almost as thrilling as the dive itself. Sighting large animals, such as rays, from the boat adds to the excitement.

UNDERSEA GARDEN
Coral thrives in clear, shallow water, because it needs plenty of light to live. Such reefs are an ideal environment to explore whilst snorkelling.

REEF SAFARI
Coral reefs are home to diverse marine species, offering sheltered areas for sedentary animals, and feeding grounds for predators and foragers.

CRYSTAL WATERS
Exploring the shallows above reefs is a perfect pastime between dives. Many thousands of fascinating marine species live in these areas.

CLOUDS OF FISH
Shoals of orange antheas are a common sight on the reefs of the Indo-Pacific. They appear to move as one when startled.

FROM WRECK TO REEF
In tropical waters, a wreck provides a firm platform for coral growth. Wrecks are swiftly colonized by marine life, creating eerie reefs.

LONE VOYAGER
If approached cautiously and respectfully, turtles will happily tolerate the presence of divers. Many species migrate for thousands of miles.

History
of diving

Diving through the ages

The search to free divers from the limitations of breath-holding began in ancient times with the use of reed snorkels. Developing from diving bells and diving suits supplied with air from the surface, it evolved into modern scuba, in which divers carry their own air supply.

EARLY DIVERS AND DIVING BELLS

It is hard to trace the origins of diving, but mummified human remains dating back more than 5,000 years have been found in Chile alongside fish bones and mussel shells. Small growths in the humans' ears, resembling the modern condition called surfer's ear, suggest that these people may have been divers.

Hollow reeds or breathing tubes that extended to the surface were used in ancient times to enable divers to stay submerged for longer. Herodotus recorded that in 500BCE, a Greek diver named Scyllias used a reed snorkel to swim unnoticed and cut the moorings of Persian ships. Salvage diving was well known in the ancient world, and laws regulating those who dived for treasure were in operation in Greece as early as the 1st century BCE.

An important milestone in helping divers to overcome the restrictions of breath-holding was the invention of an apparatus to hold air underwater. At the siege of Tyre in 332BCE, Alexander the Great reportedly used such a device, descending beneath the waves in a glass barrel. In the 4th century BCE, Aristotle described a bell-shaped diving chamber that took the form of an upturned cauldron filled with air, in which divers made trips to retrieve objects from the seabed. From the Middle Ages onwards, diving equipment became more sophisticated. During the Renaissance, speculative designs for diving suits began to appear, although

ALEXANDER'S GLASS BARREL
Surprisingly, Alexander the Great used his glass barrel to make observations of fish, rather than as an aid to his military campaigns.

KEY DATES

*c.*3000BCE Early divers collect oysters from the sea bed, developing a bone deformity caused by frequent exposure to cold water; a condition today known as "surfer's ear".	9th/8th century BCE Homer's *Iliad* refers to the use of military divers in the Trojan War, *c.*1250BCE.	*c.*4th century BCE Aristotle records the first use of a diving bell, made from an upturned cauldron filled with air. The diver within could venture out for short periods before returning for air.

3000 BCE   **1000 BCE**   **0**

*c.*2800BCE A Sumerian epic detailing the exploits of King Gilgamesh reports that he used weights to sink to the seabed in search of a plant granting immortality.	*c.*500BCE Herodotus recounts the story of Scyllias diving to cut ships' anchor lines on the seabed.	*c.*332BCE Alexander the Great descends to the seabed inside a glass barrel during the siege of Tyre.

nearly all would have proved ineffective if put to use. Nonetheless, Spaniard Diego Ufano described the use of leather diving helmets during salvage work in his *Treatise on Artillery*, published in 1612.

Diving bell technology also improved during this period. In 1691, English astronomer Edmund Halley produced an advanced bell that was linked by a hose to weighted barrels of air, which were periodically replenished at the surface. Stale air was vented from the top of the bell. Halley and his bells were widely employed for commercial salvage work.

DIVING FOR PEARLS
The earliest divers relied only on breath-holding. Using this technique, female divers in Japan have been harvesting pearls for 4,000 years.

HALLEY'S BELL, 1691
A diver could swim out from under Halley's bell with an air line linked to a smaller bell over his head – a precursor of the modern diving helmet.

1500 Leonardo da Vinci designs equipment for underwater exploration, including snorkel tubes and bags intended to supply a diver with air.

1691 Edmund Halley develops a diving bell with a glass top to admit light, and an air replenishment system using barrels lowered from the surface. An umbilical tether supplies air to the bell's operator when venturing outside the bell.

| 1500 | 1600 | 1700 | 1800 |

1660 Robert Boyle identifies the relationship between water pressure and gas volumes, furthering the understanding of buoyancy.

1715 Inventor John Lethbridge uses a modified barrel as a diving vessel to recover salvage from the sea floor. The barrel has a glass viewing port and holes with watertight leather sleeves, through which the operator's arms protrude. The barrel reaches depths of 18m (6oft) in trials.

DEVELOPMENT OF THE DIVING SUIT

In 1715, Englishman John Lethbridge devised a pressure-proof wooden diving barrel. Reinforced and clad in leather, the barrel had a glass viewing-porthole and arm holes with watertight leather sleeves. Lowered from a ship to depths of 20m (66ft), the barrel enabled the diver inside to use his arms freely, pulling his way around a site and retrieving objects. Lethbridge was commissioned by the Dutch East India Company to recover treasure from wrecks around the world using these diving barrels.

The barrel was a forerunner of the armoured diving suit. Its usefulness, however, was limited by the inability to replenish the air in the barrel without hauling it back to the surface. Three other developments would be required before diving suits became a reality.

SALVAGE IN ARMOURED DIVING SUITS, 1932
Lethbridge's barrel was a precursor of armoured diving suits. Initially too clumsy, they now have a niche for specialized work at great depth.

The first of these occurred in 1779, when John Smeaton, another Englishman, used a steam-powered pump to supply air to a diving bell. Air-pumps allowed diving bells to stay down considerably longer than before, and would later supply the first diving suits. The next development, by the Scot Charles Mackintosh in 1818, was the production of a rubber-based coating for waterproofing canvas, providing an ideal material for a diving suit. The third innovation, in 1820, was the patenting by British salvage operators John and Charles Dean of a diving helmet – a modified fire-fighting helmet into which air could be pumped. The helmet rested on the

CAISSON DISEASE

Improved air-pump designs in the mid-19th century made it possible to build underwater chambers in which several men could work at depth. Called caissons, these chambers were ideal for tasks such as building bridge footings and excavating tunnels. Air-pumps delivered sufficient pressure to keep water entirely out of the chamber. However, workers often felt ill at the end of a shift. This was decompression sickness (DCS), or "the bends".

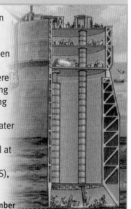

An illustration of a caisson chamber

KEY DATES

1779 Englishman John Smeaton pioneers the use of a pump system to replenish submerged diving bells with fresh air.

1818 Naptha, a coal-tar derivative, is discovered. When mixed with melted rubber it forms a waterproof coating, and is soon used in the manufacture of lightweight diving suits.

1839 British Army divers develop the practice of diving in pairs during salvage work on the warship *Royal George*.

1800

1825

1788 German diver Peter Kreeft successfully demonstrates the use of a leather diving helmet in the Baltic sea, witnessed by the King of Sweden.

1829 Brothers Charles and John Dean undertake wreck salvage work in Britain using a modified firefighting helmet to supply air during dives to the seabed.

diver's shoulders, held in place by its own weight, and air passed out from under the edge of the helmet. However, if the diver stumbled, it could easily fill with water.

In the 1840s, German-born inventor Augustus Siebe perfected a "closed dress" design, with the helmet sealed to a waterproof canvas diving suit. An exhaust valve was incorporated into the helmet, which was supplied with air by a pump at the surface. With a few modifications – such as neck and foot weights to help divers stay upright, and thick woollens under the suit to combat cold – Siebe's closed dress design remained standard for deep-sea divers for more than a century.

DEEP-SEA DIVING GEAR
The helmet and suit worn by this diver in 1954 are remarkably similar to those designed by Augustus Siebe in 1840.

DECOMPRESSION SICKNESS

In the mid-19th century, the consequences of breathing highly compressed air were being seen among divers and caisson workers, who suffered what we now know as decompression sickness (DCS). In 1878, French physiologist Paul Bert realized that these ill-effects were caused by nitrogen damaging the body during rapid decompression, and recommended that caisson workers and divers return to normal atmospheric conditions slowly.

Nearly 30 years later, Scottish physiologist J. S. Haldane devised the first decompression tables after researching the effects of gas poisoning and DCS. Haldane pushed diving to new limits, sending divers down to 65m (210ft) in 1906. The divers avoided DCS by performing decompression stops.

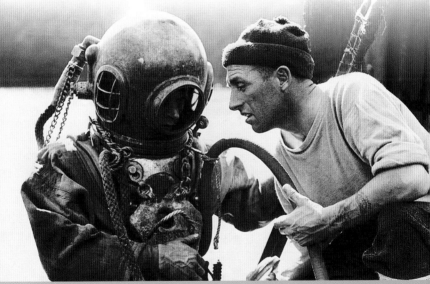

1869 Author Jules Verne popularizes diving with his novel *20,000 Leagues Under the Sea*, in which characters explore the seabed with compressed air breathing apparatus.

1878 French scientist Paul Bert publishes a paper explaining the causes of "Caisson Disease" (later known as Decompression Sickness), a condition associated with breathing pressurized air for long periods of time.

1850   1875   1900

1865 French inventors Benoit Rouquayrol and August Denayrouze invent compressed-air breathing apparatus that allows short periods of autonomy from surface air supply.

1878 English merchant seaman Henry Fleuss designs the first fully autonomous breathing apparatus. The device uses compressed oxygen as a breathing gas.

1893 The first underwater camera is designed by Frenchman Louis Boutan.

SCUBA DIVING IN THE 1960s
As other manufacturers introduced their own versions of Cousteau and Gagnan's scuba apparatus, the cost of equipment fell, and the 1960s became a boom-time for scuba.

AUTONOMOUS DIVING

In the 19th century, inventors strove to devise self-contained breathing systems that would allow autonomous diving – diving without an air line to the surface. In 1865, Frenchmen Benoit Rouquayrol and Auguste Denayrouze devised a compressed-air tank with a primitive regulator, which adjusted the air-flow to meet the diver's breathing requirements. In this "open-circuit" apparatus, air was inhaled from the tank and waste gases vented into the water. Although the diver was tethered to the surface by a hose that pumped air into the tank, he could disconnect the hose for a few minutes, and breathe from the tank alone.

In 1878, Englishman Henry Fleuss produced the first fully autonomous system, using a breathing bag fed by a copper tank of pressurized oxygen. This was a "closed-circuit" system, or "rebreather", in which the exhaled air is recirculated. Carbon dioxide was removed from the exhaled breath and oxygen injected to replace that consumed by the diver, enabling it to be breathed again.

In 1911, the German firm Draeger began producing oxygen rebreathers, soon developing these to use enriched air (compressed air with added oxygen). Rebreathers were used by naval divers during both World Wars, in preference to open-circuit systems, which emitted a tell-tale stream of bubbles.

SCUBA GEAR

The type of equipment used by divers today first began to take shape in the 1930s and '40s. American Guy Gilpatric created the first modern mask in the early 1930s, and the first diver's snorkel was

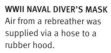

WWII NAVAL DIVER'S MASK
Air from a rebreather was supplied via a hose to a rubber hood.

KEY DATES

1908 John Scott Haldane, Arthur C Boycott, and Guybon Damant publish a landmark paper on "compressed air sickness". The first decompression tables are based on this research.

1917 The liner *Laurentic* sinks off the Irish coast after hitting a mine. Her cargo includes 35 tons of gold bullion. Royal Navy salvage divers succeed in recovering 3,189 ingots from the wreck over a period of seven years.

1910

1920

1917 The Draeger company of Germany manufactures an enriched air rebreather (a respirator that recycles exhaled air) that can be operated to a depth of 40m (130ft).

1925 French naval officer Yves Le Prieur develops an open-circuit (non-recycling) compressed-air respirator – a forerunner of modern scuba.

JACQUES COUSTEAU
From the 1950s to the 1970s, Cousteau's ground-breaking films and TV programmes revealed the wonders of the deep to a worldwide audience, and persuaded many to start diving.

developed by Englishman Steve Butler at about the same time. Fins were patented in France by Louis de Corlieu in 1933.

Open-circuit scuba (Self Contained Underwater Breathing Apparatus) as we know it today was pioneered by two Frenchmen, engineer Emile Gagnan and naval officer Jacques Cousteau. In 1943, they combined a two-stage regulator, from which the diver breathed, with a high-pressure air tank. The regulator supplied air to the diver on the slightest intake of breath. Other self-contained breathing apparatus used at the time either supplied air continuously or had to be manually turned on and off. (The primitive regulator design of Rouquayrol and Denayrouze had fallen out of use.) Efficient, reliable, and comparatively cheap to produce, Cousteau and Gagnan's "Aqua Lung", as it was known, went on sale in France in 1946. By the early 1950s, Aqua Lungs were available throughout the world.

The first commercially successful buoyancy compensator, which allowed divers to adjust their buoyancy in the water, was patented in 1961 by Frenchman Maurice Fenzy.

1930 American William Beebe descends to a depth of 435m (1,426ft) in a bathysphere – a tethered diving vessel launched from a ship.

1938 American Guy Gilpatric's book *The Complete Goggler* popularizes spear-fishing underwater.

1942 Jacques Cousteau and Emile Gagnan design and test the Aqua Lung compressed-air breathing apparatus. The design's ease of use helps to encourage recreational diving.

1930   **1940**   **1950**

1933 French inventor Louis de Corlieu patents rubber fins to aid underwater swimming.

1941 Italian navy divers use rebreathers to mount underwater attacks on moored Allied shipping during World War II.

1948 Aqua Lung first exported to the US.

DIVING TODAY

The Aqua Lung caused a revolution in diving, making it accessible to the public for the first time. In 1950, there were some 30,000 scuba divers globally; ten years later, there were in excess of one million. There are now estimated to be tens of millions of divers worldwide.

Modern diving equipment seems a world away from that used by Jacques Cousteau, yet the basics remain the same. Like Cousteau, we dive with a cylinder of compressed air, and use a mask, snorkel, and fins. Today, however, there is also a host of other kit items and gadgets to make diving even safer and more enjoyable. Mixed-gas diving (*see pp.194–95*), which allows deeper and longer dives, is becoming increasingly commonplace, and there are computers that give us data such as depth, water temperature, dive times, and breathing rate. Some dive computers even allow divers to play games during lengthy

DIVING FOR PLEASURE

Two divers prepare to explore beneath the surface of a tropical lagoon. The rebreather units on their backs allow very long dive times.

KEY DATES

1951 *Skin Diver* magazine goes on sale in the US, and plays a central role in popularizing diving.

1956 Jacques Cousteau's diving film *The Silent World* (based on his book of the same name) wins an Academy Award.

1961 Frenchman Maurice Fenzy patents an inflatable safety jacket for divers, which becomes the first commercially available buoyancy compensation device (BCD).

1950

1960

1953 Dr Hugh Bradner develops the first neoprene wetsuit for the US Navy.

1959 The first nationally organized scuba training programme is established in the United States by the YMCA organization.

1967 American Bob Croft is the first man to free dive (breath-hold dive) below 6om (200ft).

HUMAN TORPEDO
A diver clings to a battery-powered propulsion unit. These devices enable divers to explore large areas in a single dive.

decompression stops. Scooters eliminate the need to use our legs for propulsion, and waterproof MP3 players enable us to listen to music underwater. It may not be long before divers can take mobile phones underwater and send text messages and photographs from the bottom of the sea.

THE FUTURE OF DIVING

Many divers believe that the future of diving lies with using rebreathers (*see pp.82–83*). Once used only commercially, these devices are now available to leisure divers and are becoming increasingly commonplace. Rebreathers greatly extend the time divers can spend at the bottom, and reduce the need for multiple cylinders of breathing gas to be taken on a dive. Fifty years from now, it is possible that we may all be diving with sophisticated rebreathers.

There is also increasing interest in submersible vehicles for the private market. Billed as the ultimate rich-person's toy, such craft may well open up extended explorations of the seabed to their owners. Diving limits are also being extended every year. In the sport of free diving, where competitors use no scuba gear but simply hold their breath (*see pp.190–91*), records of more than 150m (500ft) have now been set. Scuba divers have reached similar depths breathing compressed air, and have decended to below 330m (1,100ft) using mixed gases. Will we one day be able to dive to the bottom of the Pacific Ocean – 11km (6.8 miles) underwater? Only time will tell, but it would be surprising if advances in technology and our understanding of the human body did not grant some extension of today's limits.

DIGITAL DIVE PLANNING
Sophisticated computers record and process vital dive information.

1968 Americans Neal Watson and John Gruener dive to 133m (437ft) breathing compressed air.

1979 Sylvia Earl walks untethered on the sea floor at a depth of 381m (1,250ft) in a special pressure suit.

1983 The first commercially available dive computer, the Orca Edge, goes on sale.

1999 Briton Mark Andrews dives to 152m (500ft) on air.

1970   **1980**   **1990**   **2000**

1971 Scubapro market a "stabilization jacket" for divers. Its waistcoat-style design sets the trend for modern BCDs.

1980 Divers Alert Network – a non-profit organization for promoting dive safety is founded.

1993 Italian free diver Umberto Pelizzari sets a depth record of 123m (403ft).

2003 Briton Mark Ellyat dives to 313m (1,024ft) on Trimix scuba.

Getting started

Introduction

Learning to dive is an adventure in itself. There are many different training agencies offering basic scuba qualifications, with branches in nearly all parts of the world. Though dive tuition makes demands on both your body and mind, it can be a very rewarding experience.

LEARNING TO DIVE

Diving is a safe sport provided that you have undergone formal training before taking to the water. It would be extremely foolhardy to proceed on your own, as there is no substitute for a proven programme of instruction. Moreover, no dive centre or charter boat will take you diving without recognized qualifications. Considerations of safety apart, you will feel more confident, relaxed, and prepared for the underwater experience if you are fully trained. Basic "open water" training qualifies you to go diving without supervision. It will not, however, teach you to dive under ice, in a cave, or beyond certain depth limits. For these activities you need to attain further qualifications and gain more experience.

WHO CAN BE A DIVER?

Practically anyone can learn to dive, but there are a few basic health requirements. For instance, if you suffer from asthma you will need to consult your doctor beforehand, although the condition need not be a barrier. Diving is not a strenuous sport, but you will encounter situations that require you to be reasonably fit:

EXPERT GUIDANCE
During basic training the instructor will tutor students in how scuba equipment works, as well as its use and assembly.

lifting yourself out of the water onto a boat, for example. Diving when pregnant is not advisable, but it is possible to pick up the theory and basic snorkelling skills during pregnancy, and continue with full training after your child is born.

There are special junior courses for those under 14 who wish to learn to dive, and advancing years are not necessarily a barrier to learning either, given a fair level of fitness and approval from a doctor. Many disabled people also enjoy the sport of diving, and dive training programmes have been adapted to embrace a wide range of disabilities.

FITNESS FOR DIVING
While it is not necessary to be an athlete to go diving, a basic level of fitness is required (*see p.150*) for both your safety and enjoyment.

HOW MUCH WILL IT COST?

Taking up a new hobby always involves a degree of investment and diving is no exception. New diving equipment can be expensive but second-hand kit is widely available, though it should be serviced before use. Equipment is almost always available to hire from dive centres and shops and it is advisable to try out a few different pieces of kit before investing in your own.

Dive training is fairly expensive, but learning with a club can make it cheaper, and most training organizations offer trial lessons to help you decide if you enjoy diving before paying for a full course of instruction.

NOVICE IN SHALLOW WATER
An instructor guides a student through his first dive, maintaining contact the whole time to ensure a safe learning experience.

Where to learn

There are a number of different diving organizations around the world with whom you can train. Other divers may recommend the one they learned with – which is not a bad start – but investigate all the training agencies, as each offers a different approach to tuition.

TAKING THE PLUNGE

The first question that you should consider is whether to learn to dive with a school or with a club. A diving school (confusingly, also called a diving club in mainland Europe) is a commercial venture – you pay to learn to dive. A diving club is a non-profit venture where members donate their time training up other members. You might think that a school sounds like a more professional option, but in truth, instructors in clubs are equally highly trained and the fact that they are giving their time free of

LEARNING THE BASICS
Be aware that courses abroad may have an instructor whose first language is not yours.

charge says much about their love for diving and desire to pass on their knowledge to others. Clubs also add a social dimension to learning, organize talks and trips both at home and abroad, and may offer a longer-term framework for gaining diving experience. However, clubs tend to run training sessions on just one day of the week and it can take a few months to become qualified.

By contrast, diving schools offer greater flexibility, and offer you the chance to learn the basics at home,

possibly over a couple of weekends, and then complete the rest of your course in warmer waters on holiday. Alternatively, they allow you to complete your training beforehand (and to your own timetable), then depart for your trip abroad as a fully qualified diver.

TRAINING ORGANIZATIONS

The world's largest training organization is PADI (Professional Association of Diving Instructors). They operate all over the world and most dive sites you visit around the globe will be affiliated to PADI. Several other training organizations are prominent in the US, including NAUI (National Association of Underwater Instructors) and SSI (Scuba Schools International).

In the UK, most diving clubs are affiliated to BSAC (British Sub-Aqua Club), and their training is tailored to the waters around the UK. You may also come across the SAA (Sub-Aqua Association) and the SSAC (Scottish Sub-Aqua Club); the CFT/IUC (Irish Underwater Council) in Ireland; and CMAS (Confédération Mondiale des

CLUB BOAT WITH DIVERS
Diving clubs usually pool resources to organize group trips that can cement long-lasting and rewarding dive buddy relationships.

Activités Subaquatiques) in Europe. There are other organizations for more advanced diving (*see pp.328–29*).

THE CHOICE IS YOURS

For the beginner, the various training agencies offer broadly similar courses in terms of content and standard. The best course of action is to take advice from experienced divers and do what suits you. Always ask to see a trainer's qualifications before starting a course, and try to get a recommendation for a diving school or club before enrolling.

RESORT INSTRUCTOR WITH TRAINEES
Many people choose to learn diving on holiday, and there are thousands of diving schools around the world that offer training to all levels of ability.

Basic training

Learning to dive involves gaining some knowledge of essential theory as well as training in practical skills. Sometimes these skills are practised in a pool before getting into open water but, depending on where you learn, they can be taught in a lagoon or in the shallows.

CRACKING THE THEORY

Your dive training will always start with theory. You will be taught about basic diving equipment, the principles involved in breathing gas at depth and under pressure, safety skills, communication, navigation, and much, much more. You will learn to carry out simple calculations relating to the physics of diving. Don't worry – none of the theory is difficult, but it does demand a few hours of study.

Dive agencies run this part of the training in different ways – some rely on traditional classroom teaching, others present materials on DVD or online – so choose the way that suits you best. In all cases, you will be provided with a reference manual containing all the material you need to know.

GOING DEEPER INTO DIVING
Learning to dive involves understanding some of the theory that underpins the sport. This training is given either in classes or one-to-one tutorials.

GETTING WET

Basic practical skills are taught in "confined water" – usually a swimming pool or shallow water just off a beach. You will be expected to pass a simple swimming test to show your instructor

TAKING THE PLUNGE
A trainee learns the basics in safe, shallow waters, under the guidance of an instructor.

that you are safe and comfortable in the water before they begin to teach the fundamental skills (*see below*). After this initial stage, you will progress into open water where you will undertake a few introductory dives in order to get used to diving in deeper water and build your confidence to swim in the open sea.

KITTING UP
Trainees are not expected to buy a full set of equipment. Kit can normally be hired from most diving schools.

dedicated to their job, but there will always be a few "bad pennies" in any profession, so take advice from friends, diving clubs, and specialist magazines and websites before you enrol. Do not be afraid to ask questions during your training, simple as they may seem; you can even request a different instructor if you do not feel comfortable.

KEEPING SAFE

Recreational diving is an extremely safe activity as long as you receive the correct training and keep your skills up to date. Choosing the right training agency, course, and instructor is therefore vital. Most instructors are highly trained and

Many people take up diving as a holiday activity, so only get a chance to practise once or twice a year. If you have not dived for a while, it is a good idea to take a refresher course, and carry out a trial dive (with your buddy) to check all your kit and your skills before venturing into deeper water.

BUILDING CONFIDENCE

Fundamental skills and safety procedures are taught in the security of confined water before you can venture into the open sea. The abilities you need to master include buoyancy control and finning techniques, out of air procedures, removing, recovering, and replacing your regulator, and clearing your ears and your mask underwater (*right*) – a common source of apprehension among novice divers.

1 **Water can accumulate** in your mask during diving, usually in small amounts. With practice, even a fully flooded mask can be cleared without difficulty.

2 **Blow clear** by tilting your head back and pressing in the mask's upper edge. Exhale through your nose. The water should be forced out, escaping under the mask's lower skirt.

3 **Check your mask** is free of water. If there is any remaining, repeat the process. This simple operation is quite normal during diving, and will quickly become second nature.

Specialized training

Diving is an inclusive, accessible sport and there are many training options for children and the disabled. If you are already qualified but wish to undertake further training, there are numerous courses of advanced tuition to make you a better and more confident diver.

TAILORED COURSES

Though standard open water diving qualifications have a minimum age requirement (usually 14), children are now well catered for in diving. This means it can be a family sport – not one that is just for adults. For younger children, introductory courses are available, such as PADI's Bubble Maker programme, or diving clubs for children, such as the Scuba Ranger organization. These

LIBERATING EXPERIENCE
A disabled diver undergoes training in a pool, with guidance from specially trained instructors.

programmes are designed to teach basic skills that lead to full open water diving qualifications. Junior diving permits, available for children aged between 10 and 14 years, are similar to basic open water qualifications, but place special restrictions on the maximum depth to which the holder can dive.

Advances in training techniques mean that more disabled people are able to take up diving than ever before.

BUBBLE-MAKER TRAINING
Special courses for children are taught by most schools. Clubs also offer training for budding junior divers.

Diving makes you effectively weightless, and the freedom of movement this offers makes the sport especially beneficial for those with limited mobility. The only condition that is an automatic bar to becoming a diver is epilepsy, due to the risk of seizures while submerged. However, blindness, paraplegia, cerebral

BECOMING INDEPENDENT
Your experience and judgement will build as qualifications are gained. Comprehensive training makes for a confident, safe diver.

palsy, and many other conditions have all been accommodated by adaptive training programmes. The general rule is that if you have been cleared to dive by a doctor specializing in dive medicine, then training can commence.

DEEPER INTO DIVING

All the major training organizations offer courses that aim to take you a step onwards from the basic open water qualification. Such courses serve to refine your basic skills and introduce you to new challenges, such as deep diving, or diving in conditions of low visibility. They will also cover rescue and survival skills, and can also be the first step on the path towards becoming a diving instructor. In addition to these skills development courses, there are also numerous specialist courses, which teach the technique and theory of activities such as cave diving, wreck diving, and mixed-gas diving. Such courses include dives to put new skills into practice, and help to improve your general diving experience. For more details visit the websites of the various training organizations (*see pp.329–30*), or ask at your local diving centre.

CAVERN DIVING
Specialized and difficult types of diving, such as cavern diving, ice diving, and other skilled activities, can be enjoyed after proper training.

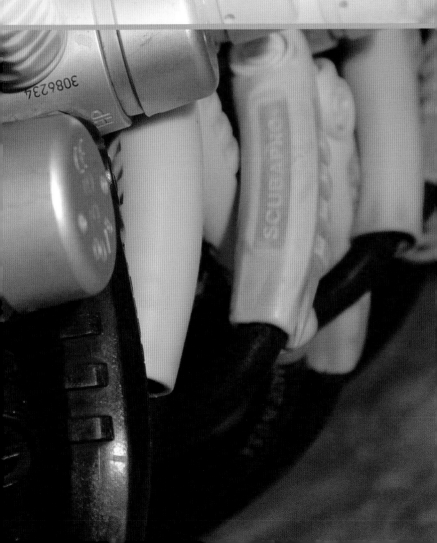

Equipment

Introduction

The wide array of equipment on offer is often bewildering to a novice diver. Some items are essential in all circumstances, while others are used only in specific diving environments. The more research you do and advice you seek, the more likely you will be to buy safe, suitable kit.

BUYING AND HIRING KIT

You could begin dive training with as little as a swimming costume, but it may be advisable to at least obtain a good quality mask, snorkel, and fins. This means that you always have three key pieces of kit that fit perfectly, and with which you are comfortable.

Many divers own no more than this basic kit, preferring to hire the rest. There are pros and cons to this approach: it frees you from carrying heavy gear around, but it can also mean using ill-fitting equipment that has been worn by many people, and which may not have been well looked-after. The alternative is to buy and transport all your own kit. This is recommended if

you are likely to be diving regularly in your local area (although a local club or shop may have kit you can hire). It is not so practical if you plan to dive any further afield – taking your own kit overseas can be expensive, although most dive tour operators are fairly generous with their excess baggage allowances. You can hire a cylinder and weights from any dive centre, so you need never travel abroad with these items.

The best places to buy equipment and obtain advice are dive shows or local dive shops. Second-hand kit is worth investigating, but inspect it for signs of wear and corrosion before making a purchase, and make sure that it is serviced before use.

DIVERS TOURING A REEF
Knowledge and care of kit is vital, since your equipment is your life-support system for exploring the underwater world.

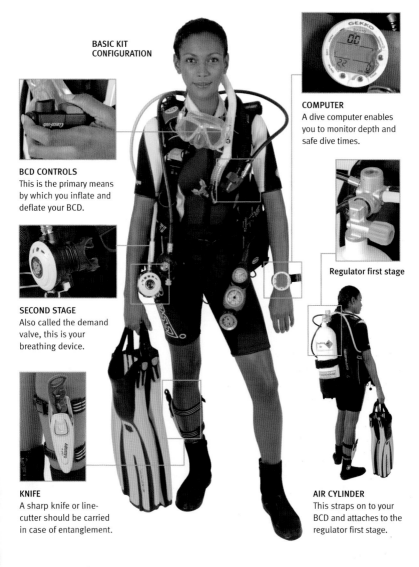

BASIC KIT CONFIGURATION

COMPUTER
A dive computer enables you to monitor depth and safe dive times.

BCD CONTROLS
This is the primary means by which you inflate and deflate your BCD.

Regulator first stage

SECOND STAGE
Also called the demand valve, this is your breathing device.

KNIFE
A sharp knife or line-cutter should be carried in case of entanglement.

AIR CYLINDER
This straps on to your BCD and attaches to the regulator first stage.

CORE EQUIPMENT

There are several items of kit that are essential, in addition to your mask, fins, and snorkel. A buoyancy compensation device (BCD) is an inflatable jacket that keeps you afloat at the surface, helps you adjust your buoyancy underwater, and supports other vital pieces of equipment. Weights, and a belt to mount them on, are another necessity, although weights can also be carried on some BCDs

(*see p.59*). You will also need some kind of dive suit (*see pp.50–55*) depending on the water temperature – and bootees. A regulator (the device that supplies air to the diver) is also necessary, preferably one that incorporates an alternative air source (an octopus) and an instrument console with a compass. Dive computers are a useful aid to safe diving, and you should also carry a knife to cut yourself free if you become snagged underwater.

DIVING ACCESSORIES

There is a range of equipment and accessory items designed for specialized diving. Try to borrow or hire specialist kit that you may only use infrequently.

Slates are useful accessories, since they allow you to write messages to your buddy, or to make notes from your dive – for example on species that you do not recognize, or to sketch a site. Torches are essential for diving at night, in murky water, and in low-light environments, such as caverns and wrecks.

If you will be doing a lot of open-water diving, especially in currents, you should purchase a marker buoy, either a surface marker buoy (SMB) or a delayed surface marker buoy (DSMB). These indicate your position to observers on the surface, and also aid your ascent.

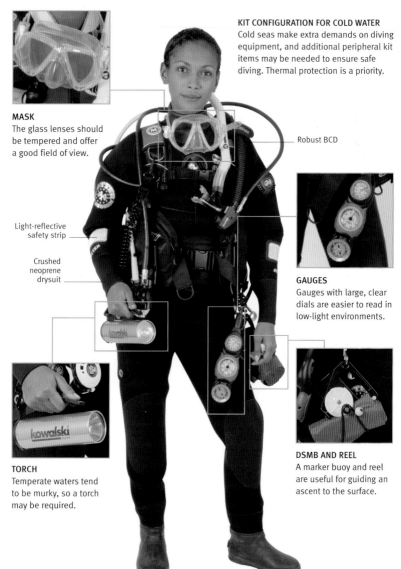

MASK
The glass lenses should be tempered and offer a good field of view.

Light-reflective safety strip

Crushed neoprene drysuit

TORCH
Temperate waters tend to be murky, so a torch may be required.

KIT CONFIGURATION FOR COLD WATER
Cold seas make extra demands on diving equipment, and additional peripheral kit items may be needed to ensure safe diving. Thermal protection is a priority.

Robust BCD

GAUGES
Gauges with large, clear dials are easier to read in low-light environments.

DSMB AND REEL
A marker buoy and reel are useful for guiding an ascent to the surface.

Lastly, you may wish to record your dive experiences with a camera. Digital cameras in housings are now small enough to fit into pockets in your kit.

DEMANDING ENVIRONMENT
Diving in cold water requires extra equipment, and appropriate training in how to use it. Safety devices are especially important in such waters.

DIVING IN COLD WATER

If you plan to dive frequently in cold water then you might want to invest in a drysuit (*see pp.54–55*). A good thermal underlayer is essential with a drysuit, since loss of body heat can result in poor decisions and lead to exhaustion, speeding

the onset of hypothermia. Dive clothing manufacturers make special thermal undersuits with wicking properties to draw moisture away from the skin. If you are planning on doing any extreme cold water diving or ice diving (*see pp.188–89*) you will need to use an environmentally sealed regulator, because these are more resistant to freezing.

Also necessary in cold water are a hood and gloves, the thickness of which will depend on the water temperature. The thicker the neoprene, the more insulation it offers, but the more it will restrict movement. Thick gloves or mittens reduce dexterity considerably, which is worth bearing in mind if you intend to use smaller items of kit.

MAKING THE RIGHT CHOICE

Don't rush into buying the first bit of new kit you see – always look at a range of products and compare prices. Take advice from fellow divers and shop staff, but remember that everyone has their favourite brands. Reviews in magazines and on the internet can give you more information, so that you can weigh up the options before you buy.

Masks

A well-fitting mask is arguably your most important piece of diving kit, so take time to choose one that is right for you. There are many styles and designs to choose from, but above all you need one that fits correctly, and suits your personal diving requirements.

SEEING UNDERWATER

Human eyes cannot focus in water, which is why you have to wear a mask when diving. The way masks work is to trap a pocket of air in front of the eyes allowing them to focus normally. A standard mask consists of a single or double panel of tempered glass inside a frame, with a silicone skirt forming an air-tight seal against the face. A strap and buckles hold it all in place.

If you look after your mask and keep it in a sturdy case to avoid damage, it should last for many years. The lenses of new masks have a protective coating from the manufacturers that should be removed before use. This can be wiped off using a non-abrasive cloth and non-gel toothpaste (or a fine abrasive cleaner) to clean the coating off without scratching the glass. If in doubt, consult the manufacturer's instructions. Make sure you rinse your mask in fresh water after use and store it away from direct sunlight in a dry place.

TESTING FOR FIT

There are lots of shapes and sizes of mask, so take time to find one you like that fits. A simple test is to offer it up to your face and inhale gently through your nose. If you then lean forward, it should remain in place.

1 **Hold the mask** in front of your face with the strap hanging loose.

2 **Place it on** your face. Inhale through your nose – the mask should stay on without support.

MASK DESIGNS

CLASSIC This is a slightly old-fashioned design but is still popular with photographers, because it gives a clear view of the diver's face. It offers a good field of view but its high internal volume of air makes clearing the mask a little harder.

Single tempered glass lens

Oval metal outer frame

EXTENDED VISION Many new designs of mask are constructed to give the diver an extended field of view, especially downwards. This model is a multi-lens design, which also allows corrective lenses of different strengths to be fitted.

Removable lenses

Lower lenses enhance downward view

MATT FINISH Some divers prefer to use a mask with a black silicone skirt to avoid confusing reflections on the inner surface of the glass. This is especially useful to marine photographers. However, this feature does reduce peripheral vision.

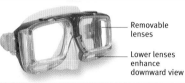

Opaque silicon skirt

Single-lens design

SIDE VIEW Some designs offer improved peripheral vision through glass panels either side of the main lens, but are still low-volume, so are easy to clear. When choosing, make sure that additional lenses do not distort perspective.

Side lenses widen view

Clear, light-permeable skirt

FULL FACE Mostly used in commercial diving, full-face masks are advantageous in very cold or polluted water. Some recreational models have intercom radio units so divers can communicate.

Quick-release faceplate

Primary lens

Radio intercom system

EYE TO EYE
Evolution has equipped fish with eyes that focus underwater, but divers must rely on masks for clear vision.

CORRECTIVE LENSES

Some masks can be fitted with prescription lenses, so if you wear glasses you will still be able to see underwater. Contact-lens wearers can use normal masks as they provide an adequate degree of protection from water, unless accidentally removed.

Lightweight plastic frame

Corrective lens

Outer lens bracket

Inner lens gasket

Snorkels and fins

Along with a mask, a snorkel and a pair of fins are probably the first pieces of kit you will buy. Snorkels vary very little, but there are plenty of styles of fins to choose from, depending on your budget. As always, look for a good fit and features that suit your diving needs.

CHOOSING A SNORKEL

A snorkel is simply a tube that allows you to breathe easily at the surface without needing to raise your head from the water. When diving, you do not need a snorkel underwater, however you may use one before and after submerging. A good snorkel should be easy to breathe through, and should not be too long – ideally no more than 43cm (17in) – so that it is easy to clear. Attach your snorkel to the left-hand side of your mask, leaving the right-hand side free for your regulator hose (*see pp.60–61*). Always rinse your snorkel after use and store out of direct sunlight.

DESIGN FEATURES

Basic snorkels are little more than a curved tube, but some models have a splash-guard at the top of the tube to prevent ingress of water, and a drainage valve at the lower end. Collapsible types are easy to stow away when not in use.

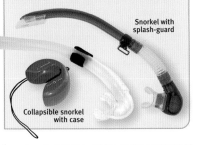

Snorkel with splash-guard

Collapsible snorkel with case

FITTING FINS

Sometimes incorrectly referred to as flippers, fins are used to aid propulsion when diving. A standard fin consists of a shoe made of rubber and a blade made of a stiffer material, often with ridges and vents to enhance performance. The shoe can either fit the whole foot like a slipper or leave the heel exposed. The latter is held on with a strap, and is designed to be worn over neoprene bootees. When buying fins of this type, it is advisable to take your bootees along with you, as their thickness will need to be taken into account when testing for fit.

SELECTING THE RIGHT PAIR

Advances in fin technology mean that there is a wide range for the diver to choose from, depending on their specific preferences. For example, split fins offer a high degree

of agility underwater, but many divers believe traditional models deliver more outright thrust. Before deciding which pair to choose, consider the sort of diving you will be doing, and seek advice from shop staff or other divers.

FIN POWER

A diver employing the "frog kick" with conventional fins.

TYPES OF FIN

CONVENTIONAL A basic fin with a single, fairly rigid blade, the conventional design is a good starter fin, but you may want to try other types to see if they offer features that suit you better.

Ridges to reinforce blade

Flexible plastic blade

FORCE FINS Made exclusively by a Californian manufacturer, this range of fins is designed to minimize the water turbulence produced, and reduce the diver's kicking effort.

Open-toed foot pocket

Blade curves upwards

Polyurethane blade

PIVOTING This fin features a flex-point in its structure, which is designed to present the blade at the most efficient angle for generating thrust at all points in the kicking stroke.

Hinged area to allow flexing

Softer plastic to scoop water

SPLIT A popular style, split fins offer better agility than standard fins. However, some divers believe they are less effective than conventional fins in strong currents.

Soft, flexible construction

Split blades

SNORKELLING Fins designed for snorkelling are lighter than scuba fins, and of a foot-pocket design, so they can be used with bare feet. Some also have shortened blades.

Foot pocket

Lightweight build

Short blades

Foot-pocket fin   Heel-strap fin

FIT AND FASTENING
Fins are held on the foot in two basic ways: in a form-fitting foot pocket, or by a strap over the heel.

Diving suits

In all but the very warmest waters, you will need some kind of thermal protection during your dive. Good diving suits (which are technically known as "exposure suits") are available in every price band, but always look for comfort, fit, and quality of construction.

BEATING THE CHILL

Water conducts heat away from the body much more efficiently than air. Unless the water you are in is the same temperature as the surface of your skin – about 32°C (90°F), which is hotter than most corals can withstand – your body will lose heat, and you will get cold. This means that in almost all diving environments, thermal protection is required. If you are diving in warm waters, a normal wetsuit will be sufficient. Only in the warmest waters should you consider a non-insulating or "skin" suit. Never be tempted to dive in just a swimming suit; even if you don't need insulation, a thin layer will prevent stings and abrasions. If you are diving in cooler waters then you should consider the heavyweight options: a semi-dry suit or a drysuit.

SECOND SKIN
Modern wetsuits are made of materials that offer highly efficient heat insulation.

WHICH SUIT?

Personal warmth requirements vary. If possible, take various suit options – you can layer these to give you the best protection. It is rare to be too hot underwater, but in tropical climates you may overheat in your suit before you enter the water. This can be prevented by wetting the suit before putting it on.

Buying a suit for every temperature range is too expensive for most divers, but most suits will suffice for a variety of waters. Although in the tropics you would be too warm in a drysuit, you could opt for a full-length wetsuit, as its extra warmth would be welcome in the cooler depths.

In addition to a suit, you may need accessories such as gloves, booties, a hood, and talcum powder, which is useful to ease entry into suits.

EXPOSURE PROTECTION

There are guidelines for the type and thickness of suit needed in different conditions. For the tropics, where the waters rarely drop below 20°C (68°F), a 2–3mm wetsuit is fine. In the Mediterranean in summer, a 5–6mm full wetsuit is more appropriate, rising to 7–8mm during winter months. A semi-dry suit of 10–15mm thickness, with a hood and thick gloves, will cope with most conditions in colder temperate waters, but in waters below 10°C (50°F), a drysuit is necessary.

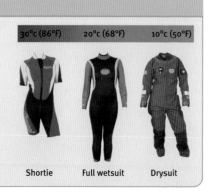

30°C (86°F)   20°C (68°F)   10°C (50°F)

Shortie   Full wetsuit   Drysuit

SUIT LAYERS

Wetsuits and drysuits keep the diver warm in different ways. In wetsuits, a thin film of water is trapped next to the diver's skin, which acts as an insulator. Drysuits seal a layer of air inside the suit, and this permits the use of thermal undergarments for extra insulation.

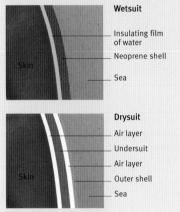

Wetsuit
Insulating film of water
Neoprene shell
Skin
Sea

Drysuit
Air layer
Undersuit
Air layer
Outer shell
Skin
Sea

SKINSUITS AND SHORTIES

In warm, tropical waters, you will probably not require any thermal insulation, but a thin layer over your body will prevent your equipment from rubbing on your skin, as well as giving protection from the Sun before and after dives and providing a barrier to stings and scrapes.

The thinnest skinsuits are made of Lycra, but some manufacturers offer suits made from 0.5mm neoprene. Lycra suits can also be

used as a base layer under a heavier suit, so they are a good add-on option if you are not sure how warm or cold your destination will be.

So-called "shortie" wetsuits offer slightly more thermal protection than skinsuits, typically being constructed of 3mm neoprene. However, they do leave the arms and legs exposed and unprotected from stinging plankton and jellyfish or abrasions on rocks or coral.

SHORTIE WETSUIT
This type of wetsuit is a good choice in warm waters, and does not cost as much as a full suit.

Non-chafing collar

Tough plastic zip

Thin neoprene

Leather palms

Light material

Light gloves

Skinsuit vest

TROPICAL DESCENT
Even in warm waters, a full-length wetsuit may prove invaluable, because water temperatures drop as the diver ventures deeper.

FULL-LENGTH WETSUIT
Scuba wetsuits are available in a range of styles, categorized by the thickness of neoprene they are made from.

Torso area has extra insulation

Side panels for better flexibility

Thin neoprene

Gloves

Zip for easy access

Bootees

FULL-LENGTH WETSUITS

The next level of thermal protection after shorties and skinsuits is a full-length wetsuit. These offer increased thermal protection for the arms and legs, and are typically made from 2–8 mm neoprene. But thickness is not the only factor in thermal efficiency – a close-fitting suit provides better insulation. A correctly fitting wetsuit should not only be easy to put on, but should follow the contours of your body as closely as possible. Wetsuits rely on trapping a thin film of water next to the body, which gradually becomes warm. If the suit fits badly, water flows more freely between the body and the suit, and chills – rather than insulates – the diver.

CARING FOR YOUR WETSUIT

A simple maintenance regime is vital to prolong the life of your wetsuit. After every dive, wash your suit to remove salt and debris, which can cause it to rot. It is best to use special wetsuit shampoo, as this helps to maintain the suppleness of the neoprene and prevent mildew. Once the suit is fully dry, place it on a hanger and store it in a cool, dry place.

SEMI-DRY SUITS

Though intended for colder temperate waters, where they are worn with a hood and gloves, semi-dry suits are a versatile style that can be used even in warm Mediterranean seas. Like standard wetsuits, semi-dry suits are made of neoprene and work by trapping an insulating layer of water between the body and the suit. However, they have more efficient seals at the wrists and ankles and around the neck or hood, which prevents water flushing through the suit and allows the trapped water to warm up. They also tend to be made of thicker neoprene and are often designed to be used in layers (with a jacket fitting over a dungaree-style base layer).

The thickness of the neoprene in some semi-dry suits has a tendency to restrict movement on land (although not in water). However, suits made of super-flexible material are available that offer an equivalent degree of thermal protection, but are much easier to put on and move around in. Although a semi-dry suit offers similar protection to a drysuit (*see p.54*), some divers prefer a drysuit, because a damp body can be uncomfortable after the dive, especially in cold weather.

Efficient neck seal

SEMI-DRY SUIT WITH EQUIPMENT
Good-quality semi-dry suits are suitable for a range of dive environments and conditions, and allow you to withstand the chill of greater depths.

DIVE COMPUTER
Often no bulkier than a wrist watch, a dive computer may need a strap extension when worn with thicker suits such as a semi-dry suit.

TORCH
In the colder and deeper waters accessible with a semi-dry suit, visibility can be impaired, so a torch should always be carried.

DIVING IN DRYSUITS

Drysuits are the most expensive type of diving suit but offer excellent thermal protection. They use trapped air, not water, as an insulating barrier. Drysuits are available off the peg, but it is worth spending a little extra to get a made-to-measure garment, because a well-fitting suit will be more comfortable and more likely to avoid buoyancy problems caused by unequal air distribution.

Drysuits are made from a variety of materials, including crushed neoprene and membrane materials. Crushed neoprene suits are tough and offer a good degree of thermal insulation. Membrane drysuits are made from strong, thin, waterproof fabrics, which offer less inherent thermal insulation than crushed neoprene, and are designed to be used with a thermal undersuit. They are more supple than neoprene types, and so easier to move around in. However, they can be looser-fitting, and allow excess air to move around inside, which can shift buoyancy to the legs, and tip the diver upside down.

KEEPING WARM
Even in conditions as extreme as those encountered diving under ice, drysuits provide good thermal protection, ensuring the diver stays comfortable.

INFLATOR VALVE
This is connected to the regulator first stage (*see p.61*) and allows air to be introduced into the suit.

CRUSHED NEOPRENE SUIT
The inherent buoyancy of a suit made of neoprene that has been "crushed" – treated with heat and pressure to flatten its internal air cells – remains the same at any depth.

Air-tight design

Dry gloves

Fabric resists abrasion

Integral boots

USING A DRYSUIT

More challenging to use than wetsuits, drysuits have variable buoyancy, due to their air-inflation mechanism. If you plan to use one for the first time, take an orientation course in a pool before diving in open water. Drysuits should be serviced once a year (or after long periods of storage) by an approved repair technician.

FASTENINGS AND SEALS

Drysuits are generally fitted with an "across the shoulder" zip to allow entry. You will need help from your buddy to do this up. These zips need regular coating with wax or "zip slip" to keep them lubricated and protected from corrosion.

To prevent water entering the suit, drysuits have watertight seals – made of thin neoprene or latex – at the wrist and neck. Latex seals are generally less likely to leak than neoprene versions, but do not offer any insulation and are more fragile, so there is the risk that they may tear. Neoprene seals, by contrast, are tough, easy to repair, and warm, but it can be difficult to get a good fit.

INFLATING WITH AIR

Drysuits have an inflator valve on the chest that injects air to reduce the "shrink wrap" sensation caused by water pressure squeezing the suit against the body. This air expands on ascent and must be dumped via a valve, normally located on the shoulder, which can be manual or automatic. Cuff dumps are also available that work by raising your arm to release excess air.

TOP COVER
A neoprene hood is necessary in cold waters to insulate the head.

THERMAL UNDERSUIT
Specialist garments, undersuits can be worn under drysuits for extra insulation and comfort.

Latex neck seal

Shoulder dump lets excess air escape

Knee pads

Thick neoprene

Heavy wetsuit gloves

Hi-tech fibres trap heat inside

MEMBRANE SUIT
The tough, lightweight fabric of a membrane suit is more flexible than neoprene and so allows greater ease of movement.

Buoyancy compensators

Unlike fish, humans have no natural way to adjust their buoyancy, or floating ability, when underwater. Divers wear a buoyancy compensation device (BCD) – a jacket that can be filled and emptied of air – to control their buoyancy underwater and at the surface.

HOW A BCD WORKS

The BCD (also known as BC, or buoyancy compensator) offers flotation at the water's surface and fine adjustment of buoyancy underwater, and acts as a harness for equipment items. At the surface, a fully inflated jacket will keep your head well out of the water. Underwater, buoyancy can be increased by inflating the BCD with small amounts of air.

All BCDs are connected via an air hose to the regulator first stage (*see p.61*), which supplies pressurized air from the cylinder for inflating the jacket. BCDs can also be inflated orally, via

STOWING KIT
Buoyancy compensators (*right*) are fitted with handy stowage points for peripheral kit.

a corrugated hose that hangs down over the left shoulder. Controls for automatic inflation and deflation are usually located at the end of this hose.

Of course, BCDs must be able to reduce buoyancy as well as increase it. This is achieved by venting air from the jacket via dump valves located at various points. Air can be released through the oral inflation hose by depressing a button, and can also be vented by using a pull-cord dump valve, which acts more quickly. These are often located on the opposite shoulder to the oral inflation hose, and at the bottom edge of the jacket. They should be used cautiously, as they alter buoyancy rapidly. Many BCDs will also vent air when the oral inflation hose is tugged sharply.

SURFACING IN SAFETY
When fully inflated, BCDs allow the diver to float effortlessly at the surface. Here, two divers signal OK after a dive.

FIXINGS AND FASTENINGS

The cylinder (*see p.68*) is also attached to the BCD. A strap attached to a rigid back-plate wraps around the cylinder and holds it in place with a cam-action buckle. It is important that your cylinder is fastened securely and does not move during the dive. A well-designed BCD will have various adjustable straps around the waist and at the shoulders, to ensure that it fits snugly. These can be easily re-adjusted underwater. Steel or plastic D-rings (*see below*) can be used to attach smaller items of kit.

FRONT VIEW OF BCD JACKET

Pillar valve of air cylinder

D-RING
Used for clipping on items of peripheral equipment, like a dive torch or reel.

WHISTLE
A safety feature for attracting attention. Here, it is tied to the oral inflation hose.

Air bladder

Corrugated hose

HARNESS RELEASE CLIPS
For quick release from the harness, and easy donning of the jacket.

Waist belt

Lumbar support pad

BUOYANCY CONTROL
The inflation and deflation controls and oral inflator are at the end of the hose.

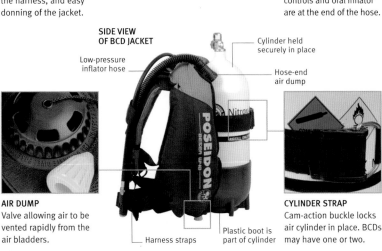

SIDE VIEW OF BCD JACKET

Low-pressure inflator hose

Cylinder held securely in place

Hose-end air dump

AIR DUMP
Valve allowing air to be vented rapidly from the air bladders.

Harness straps

Plastic boot is part of cylinder

CYLINDER STRAP
Cam-action buckle locks air cylinder in place. BCDs may have one or two.

CHOOSING A JACKET

A basic BCD is like a padded waistcoat, and these are often only adjustable at the waist. More advanced models have adjustable straps to make sure the jacket fits as snugly as possible underwater. Ideally, you should buy one that fits like a glove and does not roll around with a cylinder attached. You should also find it easy to take on and off. If possible, you should try it on with your wetsuit (or drysuit) to check the fit, and to ensure that there is room for more adjustment on every strap in case of changes in your suit or your body shape. Beyond the basic models of BCD there

SPECIALIST JACKETS
High-volume "wing" style BCDs (*top*) are used in advanced diving (*left*). The large air capacity of these jackets provides extra lift for heavily laden divers.

are the more specialized features available on some jackets, such as weight integration, or a "wing" style design (*see opposite page*). Whatever the features of the jacket you decide to buy, make sure they suit the type of diving you will be doing the most. Try out several different jackets before deciding.

CARING FOR YOUR BCD

As with all items of kit, your BCD should be rinsed with fresh water after every dive. The inside should also be rinsed by flooding it through the corrugated hose. The jacket should then be emptied again by turning it upside-down and draining it through the same hose. After this, you should re-inflate it to help locate and remove any remaining water, which will rattle around inside when the BCD is shaken. The jacket should be stored in a cool, dry place in a partially-inflated state.

SERVICING YOUR BCD

Careful maintenance of your BCD will keep it in good working order for many years. It should be serviced at least once a year, or after it has been stored unused for more than six months. Take it to a recommended dive shop. Only service it yourself if you have been trained to do so. Do not take risks by diving with old or unserviced kit.

BUOYANCY COMPENSATOR DESIGNS

INTEGRATED WEIGHT BCD
Some BCDs feature integral weight systems. Many people find these quick-release weight pockets more comfortable to use than a traditional weight belt. The weights should be removed before putting the BCD on and taking it off.

Inflator mechanism incorporates a back-up regulator

High-lift air bladder

Tough plastic back-plate

Quick-release weight pouches

INTEGRATED BREATHING BCD
The Mares HUB (Human Underwater Breathing) system was the first to integrate the regulator into the design of the BCD. A great advantage of this top-of-the-range product is its simplified profile, which reduces drag in the water.

Regulator integrated with jacket design

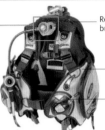

Regulator built into BCD

Reflective shell for visibility

Ergonomic inflator controls

WING / SEMI-WING BCD
Favoured by technical divers (see p.194), these offer high lift capacity. The air bladder is rear-mounted: this aids horizontal posture under the water, but can push the diver face-forwards at the surface. A semi-wing offers better surface support.

Semi-wing

Rear-mounted air bladder

Steel D-rings for fastening kit

Padded waist belt for comfort

Wing

WOMEN'S BCD Women divers are increasingly well catered for with special jacket designs to give a comfortable fit without the usual tension points across the chest. Such jackets offer other convenient options like weight integration.

Specially shaped harness

Tough nylon-weave fabric

Padded backplate

Quick-release weight pouches

TRAVEL BCD If you travel often, it is a good idea to consider a lightweight BCD without a rigid back, which can be rolled up. These designs have a lower lift capacity as they are mostly used in warm water sites, where minimal weight is carried by the diver.

Toggle for jettisoning weight pouches

Lightweight, foldable form

Inflator controls

Regulators

One of the most important items of your diving kit is a regulator. This two-stage gas-supply system provides you with air from your cylinder at the correct pressure for you to breathe underwater. As it is a key life-support device, most divers buy their own regulator.

BREATHING UNDERWATER

Your cylinder can store large amounts of air in a small space because the air it contains has been highly compressed (*see pp.68–69*). Before you can breathe this stored air, it must be reduced to a safe pressure, which varies according to how deep you are underwater. The deeper you go, the greater the weight of water pressing on your chest cavity from outside (*see pp.94–95*). This is called ambient pressure. Air for breathing must be supplied at an

STORING REGULATORS
Regulators are tough, but they should be carefully looked after. Hang them up in a cool, dry place away from sunlight.

equivalent pressure, otherwise your lungs will not be able to inflate properly.

HOW REGULATORS WORK

Supplying air at the right pressure is the job of the regulator, which is made up of the first stage (which fits on to the cylinder) and the second stage (the piece you put in your mouth), which is also known as the demand valve. The first stage reduces the air passing out of the cylinder to a lower pressure of around 8–10 bar (116–145psi) above ambient. A valve in the first stage allows some of this low-pressure air to pass into a hose, and then closes again. When the air in the hose has been inhaled by

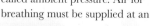

UNDERSEA EXPLORER
The regulator reduces the pressure of the highly compressed air in the cylinder to a level that is safe to breathe.

the diver, the first stage detects a decrease in pressure in the hose, and allows more air to flow in, to replace that which was used. It automatically alters air-pressure in the hose when depth changes occur. The first stage also supplies air for BCD and drysuit inflation (via separate hoses).

The second stage reduces the low-pressure air in the hose to the same pressure as the water you are swimming through, allowing normal breathing. The second stage houses a diaphragm that is subject to equal forces of water pressure on one side, and air pressure from your breathing passages on the other. When you inhale, the diaphragm flexes inward, causing an inlet valve to open, and air flows into your mouth. Exhaling causes the diaphragm to flex outwards and triggers an exhaust valve to open, allowing used air to be expelled. The unit can be cleared of water by using the purge button, which is located on its front surface.

A-CLAMP FIRST STAGE
A common and convenient clamp-style first stage, suitable for most recreational diving requirements. Less secure than DIN.

DIN-TYPE FIRST STAGE
A screw-in first stage that can handle high cylinder pressures of more than 200 bar (3,000psi). Highly secure.

SECOND STAGE
Designed to supply air safely at all depths, your second stage should fit comfortably in your mouth.

INSTRUMENT CONSOLE
A high-pressure hose from the first stage feeds directly into a pressure gauge, indicating remaining air supplies.

OCTOPUS SECOND STAGE
The octopus is for use in the event that your main second stage fails, or for donation to other divers.

BCD JACKET
A low-pressure hose from the first stage supplies air to your BCD to inflate the jacket underwater.

THE OCTOPUS SECOND STAGE

Most recreational regulators are set up in an "octopus" configuration (so called because of the multiple hoses emerging from the first stage). This incorporates a back-up second stage, which is intended for use if your main one fails, or if your buddy needs a donated air supply. Over time, this back-up air source has become known as the octopus second stage, or simply the octopus.

The octopus and the hose to which it is attached are usually finished in a bright yellow colour for easy location in an emergency, and to distinguish them from your main second stage (which ordinarily has a black hose). The octopus hangs unused from your BCD most of the time, and for this reason it is often de-tuned (adjusted) to prevent "free-flow" – an accidental discharge of air that occurs more easily when the mouthpiece of the regulator is left continually flooded. Some types of octopus are attached to the hose via a swivelling joint, so that they can be easily and safely donated to your buddy regardless of whether they are beside you, or face-to-face.

The hose supplying an octopus should be longer than the one feeding the main second stage. This will allow it to be offered to a buddy easily and for the buddy pair to remain face-to-face during a shared-air ascent (*see p.140*). Practise air-sharing procedures regularly.

STOWING THE OCTOPUS

Consider where to stow your octopus so that it can be easily located in an emergency by either you or your buddy. You can buy specialized clips of various designs to attach the octopus to your BCD, which allow it to be freed easily

SAFE STOWAGE
Attach your octopus to your BCD at a point where you can easily access it, and where it will be clearly visible at all times.

when required, and replaced again afterwards. Many divers hang their octopus near their midriff, but others mount it higher up on the chest, so it remains constantly within sight and close to hand. You can also buy regulator retainers made from rings of surgical tubing. These go round your neck, meaning the octopus is always right under your chin, though some find this arrangement constricting.

EMERGENCY ACCESS
Special quick-release clips are available for fastening your octopus to your kit.

TYPES OF REGULATOR

BASIC REGULATOR Simple, inexpensive regulators at the budget end of the market can be very reliable and durable. However, some may deliver air a little less smoothly than high-performance models.

Plastic construction

OCTOPUS SECOND STAGE Octopus second stages are often just standard second stages with high-visibility colour schemes. However, some dedicated designs can be swivelled to any angle for easy access.

High-visibility covering

HIGH-PERFORMANCE REGULATOR At the top end of the market are regulators that combine high build quality with low inhalation effort and toughness. Many are environmentally sealed for cold-water use.

Tough metal construction

Purge button

OXYGEN-COMPATIBLE REGULATOR Divers who wish to use Nitrox mixes (*see pp.194–95*) that are very rich in oxygen will need a regulator designed to handle high oxygen concentrations without risk of combustion.

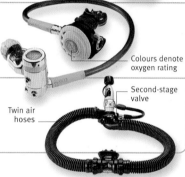

Colours denote oxygen rating

VINTAGE-STYLE REGULATOR In twin-hose regulators, the valve of the second stage is separated from its mouthpiece, and sits behind the diver's head, where it releases bubbles out of the diver's field of vision.

Second-stage valve

Twin air hoses

CHOOSING A REGULATOR

As with all items of dive equipment, prices vary enormously, but the regulator is one piece of kit worth investing decent money in. Basic regulators use a piston valve in the first stage and can be very reliable but often feature rather chunky second stages. The more expensive models use a diaphragm in the first stage and tend to have more streamlined second stages. Top-of-the-range models may be designed specifically for cold water diving, or be optimized for efficient air delivery on deep dives. They may also have dials to adjust the

inhalation effort required to open the valve and deliver air. These can be used either to tune the unit to free-flow less easily, or maximize air delivery during a normal dive. Always rinse your regulator in fresh water after use, and have it serviced annually by a qualified dive-equipment technician.

DEEP BREATH
Regulators are designed to stringent standards, and are very reliable if well-maintained.

Gauges and consoles

To stay within safe time and depth limits and avoid running out of air, you must carry instruments that monitor your air consumption, time underwater, and depth. There are various devices on the market to help with this, from simple gauges to complex digital consoles.

BASIC INSTRUMENTS

You should never dive without some means to measure the time you spend underwater, the amount of air you have left in your cylinder, and your depth. A waterproof watch with a bezel – a rotatable outer ring – allows you to mark significant times, and so keep track of how much time has elapsed. It also serves as a back up in case of failure of digital equipment used to monitor time, such as a dive computer.

Depth gauges allow you to monitor your depth even if you cannot see the water's surface. They are usually analogue (needle-and-dial) devices, although digital versions are also available. Both work in the same way: they measure the pressure of the water around you, and convert this into an accurate reading of your depth. Make sure you buy one that records the

INDICATING REMAINING AIR SUPPLY
The air-pressure gauge allows you to keep track of the amount of air in your cylinder; let your buddy know (see p.145) when your supply is running low.

maximum depth of your dive, and remember to reset it after every dive. Equally important is an air-pressure gauge, also known as a submersible pressure gauge (SPG) or contents gauge. This is connected to your regulator first stage via a high-pressure hose and measures the pressure of the air in the cylinder. You should check your air-pressure gauge every few minutes during the dive to carefully monitor your air consumption.

GAUGE CONSOLES

Depth and air-pressure gauges are often combined in a single integrated console that attaches to your regulator first stage and hangs by your side during a dive. Mounted together like this, the gauges are easy to locate and can be read

CHOOSING A CONSOLE

Your console is your dive information centre, so you must be happy with the way it handles. Different consoles need to be held at different angles to read the dials; experiment before you buy to find out which is easiest for you to use. Choose one with large, easy-to-read numbers. Some are fitted with other instruments, such as a compass – these can be either on top of the console or on the back.

Back   Front

Compass

Pressure gauge

Depth gauge

Shockproof casing

High-visibility luminous dial

TYPES OF GAUGE AND CONSOLE

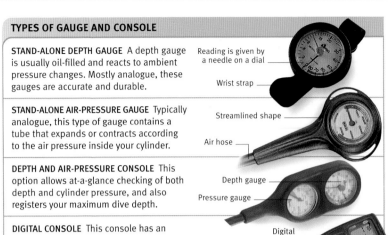

STAND-ALONE DEPTH GAUGE A depth gauge is usually oil-filled and reacts to ambient pressure changes. Mostly analogue, these gauges are accurate and durable.

Reading is given by a needle on a dial

Wrist strap

STAND-ALONE AIR-PRESSURE GAUGE Typically analogue, this type of gauge contains a tube that expands or contracts according to the air pressure inside your cylinder.

Streamlined shape

Air hose

DEPTH AND AIR-PRESSURE CONSOLE This option allows at-a-glance checking of both depth and cylinder pressure, and also registers your maximum dive depth.

Depth gauge

Pressure gauge

DIGITAL CONSOLE This console has an integrated computer and displays a range of information, such as air consumption, temperature, depth, time, and ascent rate.

Back-lit screens for night diving

Digital read-out

simultaneously – like a "diver's dashboard". They can sometimes also include other instruments, such as a compass or a thermometer.

Consoles should be rinsed with fresh water after use and stored away from direct sunlight, and kept in a padded or protective case to avoid damage.

ADVANCED CONSOLES

Some manufacturers offer instrument consoles with digital rather than analogue gauges. Consoles are also available that perform the same advanced functions as a dive computer (see pp.66–67). As well as indicating dive time, depth, and decompression schedules like a normal computer, these also incorporate a digital air-pressure gauge. For divers that use a wrist-mounted computer to monitor dive information, console instruments can provide an essential back up.

ANALOGUE VERSUS DIGITAL
Although less easy to read, analogue gauges sometimes give slightly more accurate readings than digital ones, particularly at shallow depths.

Dive computers

To avoid decompression sickness, it is critical to monitor your depth and time underwater on every dive. In the past, this would have been done using a watch and a depth gauge, but these functions and many others can now be performed by a dive computer.

USING A DIVE COMPUTER

The main functions of a dive computer are to monitor your dive time and depth and calculate safe dive schedules. A basic model uses this data to assess the level of nitrogen absorption in your body while you are under the water, and also displays information about your ascent rate, including any stops you may need to make during an ascent to avoid decompression sickness (*see pp.100–01*). More advanced models also inform you about the temperature of the water and your air consumption (if linked via a transmitter to your regulator first stage), both for normal air and technical gas mixes (*see pp.194–95*).

Computers are more flexible than dive tables (*see pp.100–01*). Dive tables show how long you can spend at different depths before needing decompression stops. Most tables assume that you spend your entire dive at the greatest depth; computers can make more complicated calculations, including the time spent at all the different depths reached on a dive. Some computers will also schedule deep decompression stops. These reduce the risk of nitrogen micro-bubbles forming in your body, meaning that less time is spent decompressing in shallow water. When making repeat dives, especially in places where you are not limited by times of tides and slack water, using dive

TYPES OF DIVE COMPUTER

MULTI-GAS This type of computer can calculate dive schedules for several different mixtures of breathing gas, from normal air to various oxygen-enriched blends of Nitrox.

Computer can be linked to rebreather

Detailed display, which uses icons as well as numbers

CONSOLE-INTEGRATED This computer is built into the diver's instrument console (*see p.65*), which is attached to the high-pressure hose from the regulator. As such, it also displays remaining air supplies.

Integrated compass

Hand-held device with finger-tip controls

WRIST-MOUNTED This machine is typical of a basic level, watch-style dive computer. It provides data on depth, dive time, ascent rate, and safe dive schedules, and is for use with normal breathing air.

Data displayed in basic form

Push-button controls alter information displayed

RADIO-UPDATED This wrist-mounted computer also displays how much air remains in the diver's tank by means of radio updates from a module screwed into the regulator's first stage (*see pp.60–61*).

Wrist strap

Radio module

Connection to PC

Wrist-mounted
dive computer

DIGITAL INTERFACE
Peripheral devices are available that link dive
computers to PCs, enabling you to download
dive profiles and create dive logs.

tables instead of a computer may not
give you the maximum number of dives
you can safely make each day.

Computers are also able to monitor
your ascent rate accurately. In your dive
training, you will be taught to ascend no
faster than the smallest exhaled bubble,
but it is more accurate to follow a digital
read-out that tells you the safe ascent rate.

BUYING A DIVE COMPUTER
A key consideration when buying a
computer is the readability of the display.
Too many figures on a small screen are
difficult to read – the simplest models are
often the best. Choose one with digits that

SAFETY CHECKS
As you ascend, keep a close watch on your dive
computer to make sure that you are not exceeding
the maximum ascent rate it recommends.

are large enough to read with ease,
without any non-essential data on the
primary screen. It is also advisable to opt
for a brand with a proven track record.

Computers are the most precise way
of monitoring your dive, but they are not
a fail-safe means of avoiding DCS. It is
impossible for data from a computer to
exactly reflect your body's requirements.
All models have in-built safety margins,
but to be sure of avoiding problems you
should always dive conservatively, and not
push your depths and times to the limit.

MALFUNCTION PRECAUTIONS

Never rely solely on a computer. As
a precaution against malfunction, it is
always worth practising how to calculate
dive times using tables. Although your
computer will give early warning of a low
battery, make sure you carry back-up
devices – either a watch and depth
gauge, or a second computer, which
can be mounted on your console.

Cylinders

Also referred to as "tanks" and "bottles", cylinders contain pressurized air for breathing underwater and have a valve that delivers this air to the regulator. Requiring regular testing and inspection, they can almost always be hired from dive centres.

SIZE AND MATERIALS

Different sizes of cylinder are available, but most commonly they have a volume, or capacity, of 7, 10, 12, or 15 litres. The maximum pressure to which these can be filled varies – it can be as much as 300 bar (4,350psi), but is usually 232 bar (3,365psi). These figures are stamped on the neck of the cylinder, along with the dates of manufacture and most recent testing. Visual inspection at a certified dive shop must be carried out annually, and hydrostatic testing (for metal fatigue) is required at different

SECURED AGAINST MOVEMENT
Cylinders stored upright must be secured. Always store them out of direct sunlight.

intervals (from one to five years) in different countries. Your test stamps must be in date for your cylinder to be filled by any reputable supplier.

Most divers use a 10- or 12-litre cylinder, but if you find you usually run low on air before your buddies do, you should consider using a larger size. On deeper, or more lengthy dives, two cylinders (a "twin-set") may be needed. Compact "pony cylinders" are often used as a backup air source; mounted next to the main cylinder, these are fitted with an independent regulator.

TYPES OF CYLINDER

Cylinders may be made of aluminium or steel. Steel is heavy and corrodes in salt water, but if well maintained it is durable and long-lasting. Aluminium is a lighter metal, but because cylinder walls must therefore be thicker this adds bulk, and largely negates any weight advantage; they are also more prone to damage.

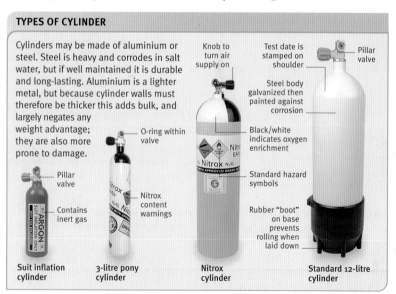

Knob to turn air supply on

O-ring within valve

Pillar valve

Contains inert gas

Nitrox content warnings

Test date is stamped on shoulder

Steel body galvanized then painted against corrosion

Black/white indicates oxygen enrichment

Standard hazard symbols

Rubber "boot" on base prevents rolling when laid down

Pillar valve

Suit inflation cylinder

3-litre pony cylinder

Nitrox cylinder

Standard 12-litre cylinder

Cylinders are most commonly filled with compressed air. For technical diving (*see pp.194–95*), however, they can be filled with special gas mixes, such as Nitrox and Trimix. Drysuit inflation cylinders, used mainly by technical divers, are filled with the inert gas argon, which, being denser than air, retains body heat for longer.

Because the air inside the cylinder is used up during the course of a dive, it gradually becomes lighter. Most people forget that air weighs a certain amount too, and compression packs a great deal of it into one cylinder. Aluminium tanks may even become positively buoyant as air is used up.

THE CYLINDER VALVE

A valve screwed into the neck of the cylinder provides an attachment for the regulator first stage, either for an A-clamp or DIN (*see pp.60–63*), and a means of turning the gas supply on and off. Always check that there is a sound O-ring in the valve before fitting your regulator. Without one, or with a damaged one, the fitting won't seal.

MAINTENANCE AND STORAGE

Fill your cylinder at reputable dive shops or centres and ensure it is "in date" and regularly serviced. If you are storing your cylinder on a boat, do not leave it standing up (especially if kit is attached) unless secured in a rack. Take care to lay it down and secure it so that it does not roll around. Cylinders are heavy, so handle with care. Store cylinders out of direct sunlight, especially when full, as this can cause a pressure buildup inside. If you have not used your cylinder for more than six months, the air may have gone stale, so have it refilled.

DOUBLE CAPACITY
A twin-set is ideal for deep dives that require long, scheduled decompression stops.

Weight systems

When diving, your suit, BCD, and even your own body all add to your buoyancy. There are many systems for carrying the lead ballast used to offset this, and they can be tailored to the environment you will be exploring. Comfort and ease of use should be a consideration.

STAYING DOWN

When wearing a drysuit or thick wetsuit (*see pp.50–55*), you will need to wear a considerable amount of weight to counteract the buoyancy of the suit. The most inexpensive way of wearing ballast is on a belt carrying hard lead tablets. Other systems use lead shot as the ballast, which is more comfortable to wear around your waist, as it moulds to your contours. This is of most relevance to women, who often find that a standard weight belt is uncomfortable on the hips.

PASSING A WEIGHT BELT
When handing over a belt, always hold it with the buckle lowest, so that the weights cannot slide off.

Many BCDs now feature integrated weight pockets, offering a more adjustable approach to weight distribution and trim. The lead carried by such BCDs is mostly stored in quick-release pockets, but there are usually secondary stowage areas that are inaccessible during a dive. It is important to make sure the amount of releasable lead in the BCD will give you sufficient positive buoyancy to guarantee an unassisted return to the surface if you have to jettison it.

WEIGHT SYSTEMS

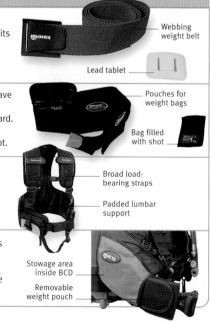

STANDARD WEIGHT BELT A basic nylon belt carries lead tablets that have two slits through which the belt is threaded. The entire belt is dumped in an emergency, via a rapid-release cam buckle.

Webbing weight belt

Lead tablet

POUCH-STYLE WEIGHT BELT Some belts have pouches that hold bags filled with lead shot, which are easy to pull out and discard. A variation on this is a belt with a single compartment to which you add loose shot.

Pouches for weight bags

Bag filled with shot

WEIGHT HARNESS Taking weight off your waist and suspending it from both shoulders makes carrying the load more comfortable. Quick-release catches allow dumping in an emergency.

Broad load-bearing straps

Padded lumbar support

WEIGHT-INTEGRATED BCD This is perhaps the most comfortable way of carrying weight. The weight can be distributed around your body, aiding correct posture in the water (*see also BCDs, pp.56–59*).

Stowage area inside BCD

Removable weight pouch

SECURING WEIGHTS TO A BASIC BELT

To prevent the lead tablets from sliding along your belt and altering your stability during a dive, you can secure them in place with plastic keepers. Alternatively, you can twist the belt to hold them in place. Insert the belt through the first slit in the weight, make a half turn, and then run the belt through the second slit.

Securing weights by twisting the belt

1 **To use a keeper** on a basic weight belt, thread the belt through the weight tablet, and locate in the desired position.

2 **Take the belt** up through the keeper, bend and thread back through the keeper, then through the weight.

3 **Pull the belt** taut on each side of the weight. Be careful to avoid kinking the webbing as you do so. Repeat as necessary.

REFINING YOUR WEIGHT SYSTEM

Weights are something you will not want to travel far with – and you do not need to, because they can be hired at dive centres. You will find that when you dive in different environments and in different suits, your weight requirements change. Record the configurations that work best for you somewhere handy, such as at the back of your log book. Whichever way you decide to wear your weights, it is vital that you can release them quickly and safely in an emergency.

LEAVING GRAVITY BEHIND
Heavy weights, though awkward on land, will not be a burden underwater.

ANKLE WEIGHTS

When a diver wears a drysuit (*see pp.54–55*), the air within the suit can become trapped around the legs and feet, inverting the diver. Ankle weights will help to counteract this undesirable effect.

Weights mounted in ankle strap

Dive torches

A torch is an essential element of dive kit. Although primarily used when diving at night and in conditions of reduced visibility, such as in caves or in murky water, torches also have other useful roles, including illuminating subjects for underwater photography.

LIGHTING UNDERWATER

Torches vary enormously in design and cost, but the basic function is to provide reliable illumination when submerged. There are good designs in nearly every price band, but since torches, especially hand-held models, are easy to lose and damage it is worth weighing up carefully how much you want to spend. It is also wise to obtain an equally reliable back-up torch, such as a smaller pencil-style model, to stow in a pocket, for use if your primary lamp fails during a dive.

BURN TIME AND BATTERIES

One of the most important factors to consider when buying a torch is burn time, as you do not want your torch to run out of battery charge halfway through a dive, which could compromise safety.

USING A DIVE TORCH

Torches are easy to lose, especially during dives in strong currents. Wrist lanyards offer a degree of security, but it is safer to clip them on with a flexible leash. Stow them close to your body to minimize the risk of being hit on rocks. Also, try not to switch the torch on and off too often during the dive, because this may cause the bulb to fail.

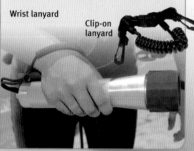

Wrist lanyard

Clip-on lanyard

LIGHT IN THE DARKNESS
A cavern diver surveys the inside of a sea-cave. Torches are an essential piece of diving safety equipment.

TYPES OF TORCH

HIGH-INTENSITY DISCHARGE This type of lamp burns brighter than a halogen bulb and, because it requires less power, has a long burn time. Such lamps can be heavy and expensive, however.

Long casing for batteries

Powerful, intense beam

BACK-UP A range of torches have evolved that are intended for use if the diver's primary lamp fails. As such, they are small and lightweight, but only generate enough light for emergency use.

Holster can be clipped onto mask strap

Plastic casing

Twisting collar activates light

PISTOL-GRIP This is probably the most widely used style of lamp among recreational divers. They are fairly inexpensive and usually use conventional non-halogen filament torch bulbs.

Pistol grip for ease of use

Wide reflector for broad beam

UMBILICAL An umbilical torch has the battery housed in a separate case. This model uses high-intensity light-emitting diodes (LEDs) to generate a beam. Umbilicals have long burn times.

Battery pack worn by diver

Six LEDs for efficient burn

HI-TECH RECHARGEABLE This model can be charged via a special "wet" contact that means the case does not have to be opened, minimizing the risk of accidental flooding through careless reassembly.

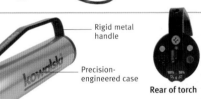

Rigid metal handle

Precision-engineered case

Rear of torch

There is usually a trade-off between output and burn time. Some lamps are very bright and offer the diver an excellent field of illumination for a short duration. But many lower-output models can outlast much brighter competitors, so consider carefully which would be more useful for you before making a purchase.

Rechargeable torches are more cost-effective than those requiring battery replacements, and tend to offer the greatest light output but the shortest burn time. Also consider the recharge time, especially if you are diving from a liveaboard boat and the vessel's generator is run only for short periods of time.

BUOYANCY AND BEAM

Another factor to consider is buoyancy. Some torches are positively buoyant, because they have a large airspace within the reflector. This makes them unbalanced in the water and difficult to handle. A positively buoyant lamp cannot be laid down, for example, if you need to light a subject for photography.

Lamps also vary in the size of the hotspot (central area of beam) and peripheral halo. The halo can be useful because it lights up a wider area than just the main hotspot. The hotspot is the brightest part of the beam, and is best for highlighting specific objects or for illuminating murky surroundings.

Surface marker buoys

Marker buoys may be used either during a whole dive or just before you ascend, to let those at the surface or on the shore know where you are, and also to aid your ascent. These devices offer a sense of security for both diver and surface cover, and aid safe recovery.

SMB OR DSMB?

A surface marker buoy (SMB) is an inflatable float linked to the diver by a line. It allows an observer at the surface to monitor the diver's position underwater. SMBs should be in a high-visibility colour – most are orange.

The line to which the float or buoy is attached is usually stowed on a purpose-built reel. The reel should be held in one hand, with not too much slack on the line. You should use an SMB when your boat cover needs to be aware of your position at all times, such as during drift dives (where undersea currents propel the diver along), or where there is a likelihood of heavy boat traffic overhead.

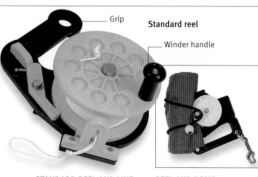

Grip — Standard reel — Winder handle

STANDARD REEL AND LINE
Reels are available for both right- and left-handers for ease of winding.

REEL AND DSMB
Line and buoy can be wound and clipped together for compact storage.

Another type of buoy is deployed only at the end of a dive, or in an emergency. The delayed SMB (DSMB) is carried deflated during the dive then inflated underwater (*see pp.130–31*) before ascent, carrying a line from the reel up with it to the surface. When it pops up, it

DIVER WITH DSMB INFLATED
By the time you surface, your boat cover should be en route to pick you up.

DIVER WITH SURFACE MARKER BUOY
Only one SMB, inflated before the dive, is needed per buddy pair provided that you remain together during the dive.

indicates where you are about to surface. Its line also acts as a guide for making a slow, safe ascent and for decompression stops (*see p.101*) along the way. Ensure you are some distance from other divers using buoys before deploying a DSMB, or you risk fouling each other's lines.

USING A REEL

Both SMB and DSMB lines should be tied with a bowline knot to the reel. Reels should be compact enough to fit into a pocket or clip on to your BCD, but not so small that they are difficult to operate, especially if gloves are worn. Some reels have a ratchet action to stop the line unwinding on its own, and this helps to avoid tangles. The length of line you use should correspond to the depth you are expecting to dive to; this may be 40m (130ft) or even more. If the line is too short, then when it runs out, the DSMB will yank you upwards at a dangerously fast rate until the buoy reaches the surface. This can also happen if the reel jams, which is why you must never deploy a DSMB while the reel is still clipped to your BCD: you must hold the reel in your hand so that in an emergency you can simply let it go.

TYPES OF DSMB

The cheapest lifting bags have an open base from which air can escape after inflation. Self-sealing types are more reliable.

Lifting bag

Self-sealing

Self-inflating

Tough nylon fabric

Small air cylinder for auto-inflation

Webbing straps

Dump valve for venting air

Internal baffle stops air escaping

Safety and signalling devices

It is rare to be lost at the surface, but you must be equipped for such an eventuality. To guide rescuers to your position, you should carry high-visibility surface location aids. The boat crew must know what colour equipment you are wearing, and which aids you are likely to be using.

SIGNALLING OPTIONS

Even on a relatively straightforward dive, the current can take you a long way away from your boat cover, and heavy swell can make you difficult to locate. If this happens, stay close to your buddy, and, if possible, secure yourself to them. Signalling to the boat will speed up recovery, and there are various gadgets available for this. The devices that are most commonly used are delayed surface marker buoys (DSMBs; *see pp.74–75*). It

DELAYED SURFACE MARKER BUOY (DSMB)
This tall, inflatable signal is easily seen by boats or aircraft. It is inflated using compressed air from your cylinder.

is best to use a long, sausage-shaped version that stands up in the water, and remains inflated once deployed, rather than an open-ended one. If you opt for the latter, make sure you also carry an alternative device, such as a collapsible flag. Surface horns and power whistles are also used. They are of limited range,

SIGNALLING DEVICES

FLAG Collapsible plastic flags in high-visibility or fluorescent colours are excellent for signalling at the surface, especially in a swell. They can be rolled and stowed alongside your cylinder.

- Folding or telescopic handle for easy storage
- Fluorescent for maximum visibility

STROBE LIGHT Strobes are particularly effective when attached to the top of a folding flag. If attached to your BCD, the flash may only be intermittently visible as waves lap over and around it.

- Strobe gives up to 8 hours constant use
- Battery housed in waterproof casing

DISTRESS FLARES Aerial flares do not pinpoint your position, so they are best used in conjunction with other devices. They can be difficult to operate when wearing gloves, or with cold hands.

- Unbreakable plastic box
- Box houses firing mechanism

PERSONAL LOCATOR BEACON (PLB) Devices that broadcast radio distress signals can be used to alert surface and air searchers to your presence. Some are also fitted with bright lights for close-range visual detection.

- PLB antenna flashes to aid location
- Signal from beacon has range of at least 55km (35 miles)

but can help to attract attention if the boat is not too far away. You should always carry a torch, as the beam can be easily spotted at night, especially when moved slowly in a scanning motion, both vertically and horizontally (*see pp.184–85*). Make sure you also carry a back-up torch. Strobe lights are even more effective, since their flashing light travels in all directions, eliminating the need for scanning. Torches and strobes must be robust and reliable; regular inspection and maintenance is vital, ensuring that you pay special attention to sealing surfaces and O-rings.

Reflective signals are useful in bright weather. It is worth carrying an old CD or mirror to use as a reflective device to attract attention. Reflective patches on your hood and upper body may be visible to aircraft searching overhead. Dye markers stain the water and can help a search from the air, but should only be used once the aircraft is overhead, since the dye rapidly dissipates.

If you find yourself on the surface with no signalling devices whatsoever, waving your arms or even your fins and shouting may help to alert attention if your boat cover is nearby. Keep calm and persist with signalling.

INTEGRATED SAFETY DEVICES

Some safety devices can be integrated into existing kit. Air-horns, for example, can attach to the low-pressure hose on your BCD. These are far louder than conventional whistles, and useful if you are out of breath or under stress. Some SMBs can also be inflated by your BCD.

Standard BCD

Air horn attachments

RESCUE FLAGS
A brightly coloured flag is a cheap, simple to carry, easy to deploy, and highly visible location device.

Knives

A dive knife is essential for freeing yourself if you get snagged by fishing lines and other obstacles. The simplest dive knife – little more than a basic blade in a plastic mount – will get you out of most tangles, but a good one will prove an invaluable multi-purpose tool.

SELECTING A KNIFE

Knives must be rustproof, but the better the rust-proofing of stainless steel, the harder it is to maintain a sharp edge. Titanium knives, while expensive, are light, rust-resistant, and stay sharp. Knives come in various sizes. Small ones can be mounted on your BCD or belt, where they are easy to reach and out of the way.

Line-cutter notch

Scabbard with locking system

Ventilated light-weight handle

TITANIUM KNIFE
This state-of-the-art blade has a tough sheath and an integral line cutter.

SHEARS AND MULTI-TOOLS

Multi-tools incorporate both types of knife blade, for slicing and sawing – useful for rope and monofilament line. Underwater secateurs and shears are only really needed if diving in very hazardous conditions or for use as tools in salvage.

Underwater shears

KNIFE SIZE
Large knives are popular, but a smaller blade can be just as useful on a dive.

Standard knives with 11.5cm (4½in) blades are most popular. Blades may be serrated for sawing rope or smooth for slicing monofilament line, and may have a line-cutter notch. Blunt-ended blades are ideal for tasks that need leverage, such as prying open containers. It is worth choosing a knife with a metal pommel on the end, which can be used as a hammer.

POSEIDON *master* *diving knife*

Bags

Whenever you move to and from a dive location, you will need a bag to carry all your kit. Ideally, your chosen dive bag should be capacious and light, but must also be durable enough to survive the rigours of transporting heavy equipment.

BUYING A BAG

When choosing a bag, check that it has strong seams, sturdy handles, and no parts that are liable to rust. Also consider security, especially when travel will involve you being separated from your baggage. Thin bags can be cut open, so a padlock will not guarantee that the contents stay safe. You may want to invest in a rigid or semi-rigid bag (*see p.238*).

Many divers use a large carryall for travel, and a smaller day bag (or even two) for dive days. Carryalls range in size from 100 to 180 litres (6,000 to 10,000 cu in), while day bags can be anything from 30 to 80 litres (1,800 to 5,000 cu in). There are countless "extra" bags, such

FLIGHTS TO FAR-AWAY LOCATIONS
Dive baggage has to be hard-wearing and tough, especially as several transfers are often needed to reach a dive location.

as fin bags, mask bags, tool pouches, and pony-cylinder pouches. While useful, most of these are not essential if you pack your kit carefully into one large carryall.

BAGS FOR DIVERS

MESH BAG Perforated bags can be used to rinse all your gear at once in fresh water, or to carry small items of kit aboard a boat without fear of water ruining the bag.

Water-permeable mesh fabric

CARRYALL These can accommodate most of your kit, and also have various compartments where you can stow small items, such as slates and karabiners.

Rustproof plastic zips

REGULATOR BAG Your regulator is valuable, and needs its own padded bag. It can be put in your main kit bag, but when flying, most divers stow it safely in hand luggage.

Protective padded sides

DRY BAG When you reach the dive site, a watertight bag or case is essential to protect clothing and electrical equipment, such as cameras, from moisture and salt.

Aperture can be sealed

TRAVEL CASE A secure, rigid-sided case gives extra protection to your kit while in transit. Wheels and a telescopic handle make transportation easier.

Outer pockets for non-valuable items

Gadgets and accessories

There are a host of diving gadgets on the market, including fun items such as underwater MP3 players. Other accessories, however, have more practical uses. Clips and lanyards are very useful for securing equipment, and may save you the loss of a camera or torch.

DIVER PROPULSION DEVICES

Underwater scooters, usually referred to as DPVs (Diver Propulsion Vehicles), make great toys, but they can be practical and useful too – for example, when exploring a large wreck site. There are two basic types: those that you sit astride, and those you hold on to, which tow you along. It is safest to use DPVs only to travel on a horizontal plane. Descending or ascending under power can be very dangerous, due to rapid pressure changes. DPVs are not cheap, but there are less expensive models suitable for general recreational use –

that is, where failure of the device would hardly constitute an emergency. The more expensive but tougher, more reliable machines are generally aimed not at the leisure diver but for expeditions, such as cave explorations, where failure of the unit mid-dive would be a more serious development.

Jetboots, made by a Californian diving company, also propel the diver along effortlessly: they comprise a pair of propellers that attach to your legs, controlled by a switch at your waist. Jetboots can propel you as fast as some DPVs, and leave your hands free.

DIVER USING SCOOTER
A Diver Propulsion Vehicle, or DPV, takes the effort out of exploring large dive sites.

BANDS, CLIPS, AND FASTENINGS

Cambands – webbing straps that hold your cylinder to your BC – are available with a number of different buckle mechanisms that ensure the tank is secure and held close to your body. Retractor lanyards are very useful for attaching items, such as a torch or slate, to your BCD because they pull the item close to your body when not in use. Karabiners and boltsnap clips (as used on dog leads) are useful for attaching equipment securely to your BCD during the course of a dive.

Retractor lanyard

Spring-loaded snap clips

SAFE STOWAGE
When you have your hands full, retractor lanyards retain loose items, such as torches.

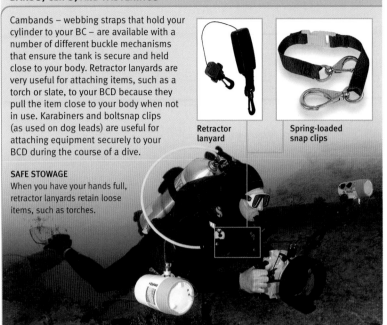

ATTRACTING ATTENTION
There is a range of gadgets that you can use to attract your buddy's attention underwater. Some BCDs have a buzzer that uses a small amount of compressed air to generate a sound. Slightly more low-tech are tank pingers – a piece of elastic with a hard plastic ball attached. This is slipped around the cylinder and can be stretched and released to "ping" against it, creating a metallic sound that travels well underwater. Shakers are tubes filled with metal balls. When agitated these create a clearly audible rattle.

WRITING UNDERWATER
Slates are handy for mapping dive sites or making notes on any unusual species encountered on your dive. They are made of white plastic, with a matt

surface that can be written on with a pencil. Flat slates can be attached to a BCD or slipped into a pocket; wrist-mounted slates are contoured to fit around your arm. The latter are especially useful when making technical dives with various decompression stops: you can read your computer and the list of stops from the same arm. A compass can be mounted on a flat slate, enabling you to look at navigational notes while checking your bearings.

AIR-LOCK CYLINDER CAMBAND
Some dive gadgets are labour-saving devices. Cylinder band buckles that can be tightened using compressed air are a useful example.

New technology

In the 1950s, development of the scuba unit revolutionized diving, and its technology continues to develop apace. Modern equipment is sleek, lightweight, and colourful, and advances in the efficiency of rebreather systems are transforming diving once again.

MASKS AND VEHICLES

One of the most notable recent advances in modern dive equipment is the use of head-up displays in masks, which are similar to those used by military pilots. Essential dive information is sent via radio frequency from the tank to the mask, where it is presented on an LCD. Masks with an integral radio communication system, which allows divers to talk directly to one another, are also available.

Advanced synthetic materials have made dive equipment stronger and lighter, and have been used in the development of Diver Propulsion Vehicles (DPVs; *see p.80*) that are smaller and easier to handle.

MASK TECHNOLOGY
New mask developments include head-up displays of critical information (*top*) and masks that correct optical distortion underwater (*left*).

FROM SCUBA TO REBREATHER

In the last decade, rebreather technology has become available to the recreational diver, representing the most dramatic leap forward in diving equipment since the development of scuba itself.

In contrast to scuba – an "open circuit" system that discharges most of a diver's air supply into the water with the exhaled breath – rebreathers recycle the diver's exhaled breath, using chemicals to remove waste (mainly carbon dioxide) and allowing the diver to inhale the gas again. Each breath uses about 4 per cent of the oxygen in the inhaled gas mix, so one of the main tasks of a rebreather is to maintain oxygen levels in the breathing loop, generally by adding extra oxygen.

UNDERWATER SCOOTER DPV
The Breathing Observation Bubble (BOB) is powered by an electric motor and has a top speed of 2.5 knots.

Rebreathers using pure oxygen were used by frogmen in World War II, for whom the absence of bubbles was vital to hide their presence. Dive depths were limited to 6m (20ft), at which point pure oxygen becomes toxic. A revolution in rebreather technology occurred in the mid-1980s, allowing the use of nitrogen–oxygen gas mixes rather than pure oxygen. Modern rebreathers electronically monitor the concentration of oxygen in the mix and adjust it to safe levels for a given depth.

Rebreathers offer longer dive times and fewer decompression stops. They remain costly, and need careful maintenance and specialized training.

REBREATHER TECHNOLOGY

Modern rebreathers are divided into two categories – semi-closed rebreathers (SCRs) and closed-circuit rebreathers (CCRs). SCRs expel a small quantity of exhaled gas into the water, whereas CCRs only dump gas into the water on ascent. Both types clean exhaled gas in a scrubbing unit, which removes CO_2. They also ensure that the oxygen content of the inhaled gas is at a suitable level for the diver, and monitor toxicity, which the diver can check manually on a gauge, or on a computer display. Computer control has dramatically increased the efficiency and safety of rebreathing devices.

Data cable

Mouthpiece

HOW A REBREATHER WORKS
A chemical in the scrubbing unit absorbs carbon dioxide from exhaled gas, while pure oxygen is introduced to the breathing loop to replace that consumed by the diver.

Exhaled gas from mouthpiece flows into scrubbing canister

Pure oxygen cylinder replaces O_2 used by diver

Absorbent chemical in scrubbing unit removes CO_2

Air from cylinder maintains volume of gas in breathing loop

Oxygen flow
Inhaled gas flow
Exhaled gas flow

Computer display

REBREATHER BENEFITS
Because gas is recycled in a rebreather, you use it up at a slower rate than with scuba gear, and so can spend longer underwater. The consistently high levels of O_2 help reduce post-dive fatigue.

Kit assembly

The kit assembly process is a key part of any dive. During your training, you will be taught the basics of assembling dive kit. With experience and a few simple tips you can perfect this process, and make it efficient, rapid, and – most importantly – consistently safe.

THE IMPORTANCE OF PREPARATION

With clear, blue water at hand, the Sun shining, and the dive site awaiting you, you may find that there is a great temptation to rush the kit assembly process. However, the equipment used for diving is nothing less than life support gear, and should be treated with a corresponding level of respect. It is reasonable to say that putting dive kit together safely before jumping into the sea is as important as packing a parachute correctly before jumping out of a plane.

CHECKING FOR DAMAGE

The first stage in assembling your kit is to carry out a visual inspection. This is particularly important if the equipment is unfamiliar or rented. It is essential to examine the test dates (*see p.68*) for the

1 **Lay out equipment** on a mat or other clean, grit-free surface where you can assemble the kit easily.

2 **Wet the cylinder** band on your BCD, if possible, as this helps improve its grip on the cylinder's metal surface.

3 **Position the cylinder** with the pillar valve O-ring facing the backplate of the BCD, then fasten the band around it.

4 **Attach the regulator** first stage to the cylinder. Do not overtighten the clamp (or screw thread, on a DIN fitting).

INFLATOR VALVE
The spring-loaded collar on the end of the hose fits on to the inflator valve.

5 **Pass the inflator hose** from your regulator's first stage (*see pp.60–61*) through the jacket's guides and straps before connecting it to the BCD's inflator valve. Make sure the valve has engaged securely with the hose fitting.

KIT ASSEMBLY

cylinder and also the integrity of the O-ring (*see p.88*). Any nicks or cuts in the O-ring may lead to serious problems during the dive, yet replacing a damaged O-ring before the dive takes only seconds. Also look for wear and tear on the regulator hoses, particularly where they join the ports of the first stage. This is a common point of strain for regulator hoses, resulting in cracks and splits in the hose with sustained use. If the integrity of a hose has degraded it may rupture when the air supply is turned on.

Check for signs of damage to the BCD. With regular diving, there will be inevitable signs of wear and tear, but be sure to check the integrity of the buckles and load-bearing straps. These must be completely sound.

ASSEMBLING YOUR KIT

When you are satisfied that your equipment is in good order, follow the steps below to make it ready. Take particular care to ensure the band securing the cylinder to the BCD is neither too high (resulting in the cylinder possibly coming free), or too low (resulting in the pillar valve restricting movement of your head during the dive, or actually striking it on entry).

6 Turn on the air supply, opening the cylinder's pillar valve all the way. Then turn the knob a quarter-turn back.

7 Test air supply by breathing from both your primary and secondary air sources. Check air quality and delivery.

8 Secure the kit, if you are not diving immediately, by tucking any loose parts inside the BCD for protection. Most breakages occur in transit.

Disassembly

The end of a dive is an exciting time, and neglecting your dive gear at this stage is an easy trap to fall into. Take a little time, however, to clean and store your equipment properly: not only will it last much longer, but everything will be in order at the start of your next dive.

DEVELOPING A ROUTINE

As with so many things in diving, routine is the key. Many experienced divers attend to their kit the moment the dive is finished, and regard the dismantling, rinsing, and storage of their gear as an integral part of the dive itself. This is particularly true for diving from a boat, where a shortage of space frequently leads to cluttered decks and broken dive kit.

Diving equipment can cost a considerable amount of money – so it is worth taking a few moments to make sure it is properly dismantled and safely stowed.

The first stage of disassembly is to turn the cylinder off, and purge any remaining air from the hoses using the purge button on the second stage (*see also pp.60–63*). The regulator first stage may then be removed from the pillar

1 Shut off the gas supply, turning the knob on the cylinder's pillar valve all the way off before disassembly.

2 Purge gas from the system using the purge button on the regulator to vent any air remaining in the hoses.

3 Disconnect the inflator hose from your BCD's inflator valve, and the hose from the drysuit inflator, if worn.

4 Disengage the regulator first stage from the pillar valve of the cylinder, and free the hoses from the BCD by undoing all the clips and straps.

A-CLAMP FIRST STAGE
Remove this type of first stage by loosening the clamp first.

DIN-TYPE FIRST STAGE
Turn the knurled collar to unscrew the regulator first stage from the pillar valve.

valve of the cylinder. It should take no more than finger pressure to turn the clamp or collar; any more resistance indicates that compressed air remains in the system. You will need to check that the cylinder is completely turned off, then purge the hoses again.

After removing the regulator first stage from the cylinder, use a blast of air from the cylinder to dry the dust cap and filter. Fit the dust cap securely, then rinse the regulator thoroughly in fresh water. Never forget to put the dust cap on, otherwise water will enter the delicate mechanism of the first stage: this is to be avoided at all costs. Hang the regulator up to dry, ensuring that the hanging method does not put strain on the hoses

at any of the points of attachment to the first stage. You can then detach your BCD from the cylinder and drain it of any salt water. Rinse the BCD inside and out with fresh water, and inflate it orally to allow quick drying and prevent the formation of salt crystals inside.

Dive gear must be dried thoroughly between dives, ideally by hanging it up out of direct sunlight. Do not store it where it is compressed or where moisture may accumulate, for example in a boat deck locker or a diving bag.

5 **Remove the BCD** from the cylinder by undoing the cam buckle on the strap, and then sliding the BCD upwards until it is clear.

6 **Drain the BCD** of salt water by depressing the deflator button at the end of the corrugated hose. This allows the water to escape through the oral inflation point.

Kit maintenance

Diving equipment is your life-support system underwater, yet many divers take a worryingly relaxed approach to maintaining their gear. A few simple steps will increase the lifespan of your dive kit, avoid the expense of constant replacements, and increase your safety.

TOOL KITS

Most divers carry a set of Allen keys, screwdrivers, or adjustable spanners. Scuba multi-tools are all-in-one alternatives that incorporate virtually every basic tool that a diver might need on a dive boat or at a dive site. These include a range of hexagonal Allen keys designed to fit dive equipment and standard spanners for regulator adjustment, as well as screwdrivers and a marlinspike.

Diving shops also sell "save-a-dive" kits, which consist of a set of lubricants, parts, and tools that can be used in the majority of equipment-related incidents on site. O-ring replacement and

SCUBA MULTI-TOOL
A useful gift for any diver, this contains tools for most small maintenance jobs.

adjustments to hose configuration, for example, are simple, commonly required tasks that can be undertaken by anyone with such a kit.

Experienced divers also carry spare parts with them. This is sensible diving practice, and while the range of items differs from diver to diver, it usually includes items such as spare O-rings, silicone grease, tape, adhesive, an O-ring extractor, spare plugs for the regulator first stage, and any spare buckles or straps that might be necessary.

O-RING MAINTENANCE

The most disappointing reason for having to cancel a dive is the lack of a spare O-ring for a cylinder. O-ring malfunction may be indicated by air escaping once the regulator is fitted, but even in the absence of this you should make regular inspections to check that

the O-ring has not degraded. In many cases, simply cleaning the O-ring and the valve groove with a lint-free towel will solve the problem. Pull the O-ring through your fingers, and if you can feel cracks it should be replaced. When removing an O-ring, never use a sharp tool, as this is likely to damage the ring.

1 **To remove the O-ring** from a cylinder's pillar valve (see pp.68–69), use a specially designed extractor tool. Alternatively, use the rounded end of a tie-wrap or even a credit card.

2 **Inspect the O-ring closely** and replace it if any cracks or tears are visible. Clean the valve groove with a lint-free towel, then press the new O-ring in carefully with your fingertips.

ADDING A REGULATOR HOSE

To add a hose to your regulator or change an existing hose is a simple process. You must avoid attaching a low-pressure hose to the high-pressure port, as this will rupture the hose. Most regulators now make this impossible by having differently sized ports, although older models may not have this feature. The high-pressure port is for the pressure gauge, while other ports are for a second stage or the inflator hoses. It is worth taking time to ensure that the hose configuration is practical and comfortable, to avoid strain on the base of the hoses and reduce drag.

1 **When adding a hose,** be careful to select the correct port (high/low pressure). If the ports are not clearly differentiated, or if you are in any doubt, consult the manufacturer's manual.

2 **Remove the plug** from the regulator port using the correctly sized Allen key. Some regulators still have raised bolts – these can be loosened with a spanner.

3 **Attach the hose** by simply screwing it into place. Tighten the nut with a spanner of the appropriate size – hose nuts are soft and can easily be damaged by pliers.

4 **Exactly the same** procedure can be used to attach further hoses to the other ports, and to replace damaged hoses. Always check hoses for cracks, fraying, and abrasion.

KIT MAINTENANCE

Post-dive, wash all of your kit in clean, fresh water, and check out any problems you may have noticed.

The diving environment

Introduction

When you go diving, you are introducing your body to an alien environment. Evolution has not equipped our bodies for the underwater world, and you will encounter unusual sensory phenomena when you descend into the depths for the first time.

LIGHT AND VISION

Our eyes are designed to focus in air; underwater, our vision blurs unless we wear a mask, which puts an air space in front of our eyes. However, light travels more slowly in water than it does in air, and as it passes through the mask from water to air it bends, causing refraction – an optical effect which makes objects appear bigger and closer than they are.

Colours also look different to us as depth increases (*see p.183*). Objects near the surface look as colourful as they would above water, but as you go deeper, first reds disappear, then oranges, yellows, greens, and blues until all light is lost. Colours can be revived by illuminating a submerged object with a torch.

SOUND AND HEARING

Above the surface, sound travels at approx 350m (1,150ft) per second, but underwater it travels four times faster.

This makes it hard to identify the direction of a sound source: if your buddy signals to you by tapping his cylinder, you will hear the sound easily but may not be able to pinpoint where it is coming from. The range of audible sounds is also reduced, but the underwater environment is not as quiet as is popularly supposed: you can hear the scratching and snapping sounds made by fish and crustaceans, along with the sound of your breathing and any

Direction of sounds harder to discern

Objects appear closer to the observer

Verbal communication impractical

ANATOMY OF A DIVER
The land-based development of the human frame means that your body is not adapted to many aspects of the underwater environment.

Exposed skin radiates heat more quickly into water, which is an efficient conductor

Internal cavities, such as the gut, are subjected to external water pressure as depth increases

Lungs must adapt to a longer, slower breathing cycle underwater

boat noise close by. However, you will find it difficult to communicate verbally underwater, even if you remove your regulator and shout, which is why divers use hand signals (*see pp.144–45*).

Sounds made above water do not easily penetrate below the surface, so any noises made to alert divers must be made underwater. A typical recall signal from a dive boat is to bang on the metal ladder on the craft's stern, which, as its lower part is in the water, transmits sound to divers beneath.

SEA CHANGE
Divers patrol a reef wall in the Red Sea. As depth increases, physiological effects become more profound, and numerous.

HEAT AND PRESSURE

Water conducts heat 25 times more efficiently than air, so the human body loses heat quickly underwater. In extreme cases, a diver may lose heat faster than it can be generated by their body, leading to hypothermia. When diving, it is important to always wear thermal protection appropriate to the conditions.

The airspaces in the body – not just the lungs, but the inner ear, sinuses, and gut – will be increasingly affected by pressure as you make your descent. This can lead to uncomfortable sensations (*see pp.98–99*) that must be relieved by equalizing internal and external pressure manually using the Valsalva manoeuvre.

Depth and pressure

To understand the principles of diving, it helps to have a grasp of basic physical laws. When you dive, water exerts pressure on your body, and this pressure increases with depth. This simple fact influences all aspects of diving, from buoyancy control to safety considerations.

UNDERSTANDING PRESSURE

On land, your body is constantly subjected to external pressure generated by the weight of all the gases in the atmosphere. This is called atmospheric pressure, and it is measured in bar or pounds per square inch (psi). Atmospheric pressure at sea level is 1 bar (14.7psi). This is the equivalent of 1kg pressing on every square centimetre of your body's surface. This pressure is not fixed; it varies slightly with weather conditions and decreases with altitude. At the summit of Mount Everest (8,848m; 29,028ft), atmospheric pressure is only 0.31 bar (4.5psi).

When you dive underwater, pressure is also exerted on your body by the weight of the water above and around you. Because water is denser than air, the pressure generated by just 10m (33ft)

of seawater is equal to that generated by all the gases in the atmosphere above sea level. Seawater is denser than freshwater, because it contains dissolved salts and minerals. This increased density means that pressure increases slightly faster with depth in seawater than in freshwater.

When you dive you are subject to the cumulative weight of both atmospheric pressure and water pressure. The combined total is known as absolute pressure. Your depth gauge translates pressure into an accurate depth reading, but it is calibrated to ignore atmospheric pressure, so it indicates zero depth when you are at the surface. This is known as gauge pressure. Always use absolute pressure to calculate the total pressure at a given depth.

HOW PRESSURE RELATES TO DEPTH

Because water is much denser than air, pressure increases quickly with depth underwater. Water cannot be compressed and transmits pressure freely, so pressure increases cumulatively, and at a constant rate, as you dive deeper. At a depth of 10m (33ft) of seawater, absolute pressure is 2 bar (29.4psi). This represents the combined pressure generated by the atmosphere (1 bar) and 10m of water (1 bar). At 20m (66ft) absolute pressure is 3 bar (44.1psi), and at 30m (98ft) it is 4 bar (58.8psi).

If diving at a high altitude site, like a mountain lake, remember that atmospheric pressure is reduced; consequently, absolute pressure is lower, too. You must use special dive tables to dive safely at such sites.

PRESSURE GRADIENTS
Normal recreational dives take place within a 30m (100ft) depth range from the surface.

Surface	1 bar (14.7psi) air pressure
10m (33ft)	2 bar (29.4psi) absolute pressure
20m (66ft)	3 bar (44.1psi) absolute pressure
30m (98ft)	4 bar (58.8psi) absolute pressure

HOW PRESSURE AFFECTS GASES

In the 17th century, scientist Robert Boyle made an important discovery. He found that at a constant temperature, the volume of a gas is inversely proportional to the pressure exerted on it – meaning that as pressure increases, the volume that a gas occupies decreases. This relationship is known as Boyle's Law.

Boyle's discovery has important implications for divers. Buoyancy devices such as BCDs contain bladders filled with air. These provide upward lift to help you float weightlessly underwater. As you descend, however, increasing water pressure compresses the air inside the BCD. This means it displaces a smaller volume of water, and so generates less buoyancy (see p.97), causing you to sink. You must then inject more air into the BCD to boost volume to its former level. On ascent, this must be released again, because as pressure decreases, the extra air inside the BCD expands, causing you to become very buoyant and rise too quickly. For the same reason, you should never hold your breath underwater. Compressed air inhaled at depth expands as you ascend and if it is not exhaled, it can burst delicate vessels in your lungs.

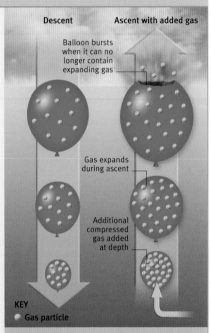

Descent

Ascent with added gas

Balloon bursts when it can no longer contain expanding gas

Gas expands during ascent

Additional compressed gas added at depth

KEY

● Gas particle

If you took a volume of gas, like that contained within a balloon, and submerged it, the space the gas occupied would get smaller with increasing depth.

If you added extra gas to the same balloon at depth, it would expand slightly. During ascent, the gas inside would expand to more than the balloon's original volume.

IN DEEP
Diving exposes you to pressure effects not encountered on land.

Breathing compressed gas

On land, we seldom need to worry about the availability of air, its composition, or the pressure it is supplied at. But when you venture underwater, things are very different. Being aware of how the diving environment affects your respiration cycle is of prime importance.

BREATHING UNDERWATER

Scuba divers draw breath from a cylinder of highly pressurized air, via a regulator. The regulator (*see pp.60–61*) reduces the pressure of the air in the cylinder to that of the water around you (ambient pressure), allowing it to be inhaled safely. As depth increases, so does ambient pressure, meaning the regulator must adjust the pressure of the air it delivers to match.

Air, like any gas, is compressible, and becomes denser when pressurized. This means that at depth you will be inhaling more air per breath than you would at the surface (because the gas molecules are packed in more tightly). Because air is mainly composed of oxygen and nitrogen, this means you will be breathing higher concentrations of both gases than you would be at the surface, though the percentage of each in the mixture does not change. Both of these gases can have toxic effects on the body when pressurized. Nitrogen enters your body's tissues, and can have a narcotic effect (*see pp.100–01*). Oxygen is vital for supporting life, but becomes toxic if inhaled in sufficient concentrations. As the pressure of the air you are breathing rises, there are more and more molecules of oxygen packed into each breath you take. Beyond a depth of 60m (200ft), there is a risk that the concentration of oxygen in pressurized air could have a

Oxygen 20.9%

Misc. gases 1.1%

Nitrogen 78%

WHAT AIR IS MADE OF
Air is mainly composed of nitrogen, with oxygen forming nearly 21 per cent. Inert gases like argon and freon form the remainder.

CALCULATING AIR CONSUMPTION

At the surface, most people use around 25 litres of air per minute. This rate increases with depth. The rate for a given depth can be calculated with a simple equation:

Rate of consumption at surface x absolute pressure (in bar) = rate of consumption (at depth)

So, at 20m, where the pressure is 3 bar, 25 litres per minute x 3 bar = 75 litres per minute. If you want to calculate air consumption for a dive you are planning to do, calculate as if you were at the dive's planned maximum depth throughout.

To work out how much air your cylinder can hold, you need to know its size, and the pressure to which it will be charged to. A typical example would be a 10 litre cylinder charged to 200 bar. Thus: 10 litres x 200 bar = 2,000 litres of air.

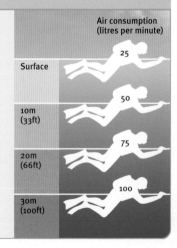

Air consumption (litres per minute)

Surface — 25

10m (33ft) — 50

20m (66ft) — 75

30m (100ft) — 100

toxic effect on the body, leading to convulsions, loss of consciousness, and even death, in extreme cases.

To get around these problems, "technical" divers going beyond the limits of normal recreational diving (*see pp.194–95*) use special gas mixes. These contain altered percentages of oxygen and nitrogen, and also include helium. These mixes are used during dives in excess of 50m (164ft).

WASTE GASES

One by-product of the respiration cycle is carbon dioxide. The more you exert yourself, the more carbon dioxide is produced. Since your body's breathing reflex is triggered by a build-up of carbon dioxide in the blood, not by falling oxygen levels, over-exertion underwater will make you feel short of breath. On the surface, your body would respond to this by breathing faster, thus flushing out carbon dioxide. Your regulator, while efficient, cannot process the same volume of air as you can breathe on land. Always rest for a moment if you begin to feel breathless.

BREATHING AND BUOYANCY

An object immersed in water is subject to an upward thrust equal to the weight of the water it has displaced. You will only float, therefore, if your weight is less than that of the water you displace. If it is greater, you will sink; if the two are equal, you will do neither – you will have neutral buoyancy. The compressed gas you breathe underwater alters your buoyancy. When you inhale, the volume of your chest gets larger – you displace more water without becoming any heavier, and so become more buoyant.

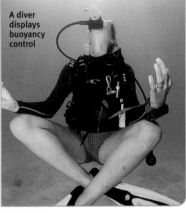

A diver displays buoyancy control

DEEP BREATH
Slow, even breathing patterns promote low air consumption and help prevent hyperventilation.

Pressure and the body

When you dive, your body is subjected to pressure generated by the weight of the water around you. As you descend, you will feel the increase in pressure in some of your body's internal air spaces, chiefly your ears. If you do not act to correct this, you may sustain injury.

EQUALIZING PRESSURE

The body contains four major air spaces that are affected by pressure underwater: the ears, the sinuses, the airways and lungs, and the stomach and gut. Air spaces in our respiratory and digestive systems are compressible, in that they are contained by soft tissue that can expand or contract to accommodate pressure changes. However, your regulator (*see pp.60–63*) ensures that the air pressure in your lungs and airway is always in equilibrium with external water pressure, so pressure effects are never felt here. You should barely notice any effect on your stomach and gut, although you may break wind, especially on ascent.

The air spaces in your head, however, such as the ears and sinuses, are rigid and cannot be compressed. When the pressure outside them is

ROUTINE MANOEUVRE
Equalize pressure in your ears and sinuses every metre (3ft) or so, during your descent to the bottom. Don't wait until your ears begin to hurt.

greater than that within, a "squeeze" is created, which can cause pain and damage, especially to the eardrum. You must equalize the pressure in these cavities with the ambient pressure of the water around you as you descend. Equalizing is simple, using a procedure that clears the ears called the "Valsalva

THE IMPORTANCE OF EQUALIZATION

The ear is divided into the outer, middle, and inner ear. The eardrum separates the middle and inner ear from the outside world, and it is this membrane that is most vulnerable to pressure changes. If you do not equalize as you descend to raise the pressure behind your eardrum – by sending air to the ear from your throat via your Eustachian tubes – then the eardrum will eventually rupture and let water into your middle ear, leading to possible infection and deafness. Your sinuses are pairs of cavities within the bones of your face. Under normal circumstances they are open, via your nasal passages, but if you have a cold, or congestion caused by allergies, they fill with mucus and become blocked. Failure to equalize will cause blood vessels in the lining of the sinuses to rupture and bleed into the sinuses, which can be quite painful.

Air spaces involved in equalization

- Frontal sinus
- Middle ear
- Eustachian tube
- Auxiliary sinus
- Nasal passage

manoeuvre". You just have to hold your nose and breathe out against your nostrils. This will send air from your throat through the Eustachian tubes into the middle ear so that the pressure there becomes equal to that of the water outside, thus easing the discomfort. This manoeuvre should also equalize the pressure in your sinuses, and in addition resolve any problems of dizziness or vertigo you may be experiencing (as balance is also controlled within your ears). Some people get the same result by simply swallowing repeatedly.

You need to equalize regularly on descent, but on ascent equalization should occur automatically. If you have problems equalizing on the way down, ascend a little to reduce the pressure slightly, and try again. This equalization process is vital for comfort when diving;

never dive with ear plugs or with anything tight over your ears. Check that your hood does not fit too tightly, as this can hinder efficient equalization. If you have any problems with your sinuses or ears, do not attempt to dive as this may make them worse. A cold, or any nasal congestion, may cause blockages in your airways and you will not be able to clear your ears and sinuses. If you notice a slight nosebleed after a dive, this is a common sign that you have a mild sinus blockage and you should not dive again until it has cleared up. Decongestants will not necessarily help once you are at depth, and you should not dive while you are taking them.

SAFE DESCENT
To adapt safely to the underwater world, you must understand how depth affects the human frame, especially internal cavities.

Nitrogen and decompression

When you dive using scuba gear, nitrogen gradually accumulates in your body, and is released when you ascend. In order for this to happen safely, you must plan your dive carefully and employ diving procedures that minimize the risk of decompression sickness (DCS).

GAS ABSORPTION

Gases are soluble in liquids, and dissolve more easily when they are pressurized. When you breathe compressed air underwater, the two main gases it is composed of (nitrogen and oxygen) enter and dissolve in your bloodstream. This "gas exchange" takes place in the lungs, via tiny sac-like vessels called alveoli.

Nitrogen is particularly easily absorbed into the blood and body tissues. Your regulator supplies denser and denser air as depth increases (*see also*

BOTTOM TIME
The longer you spend at depth, the more nitrogen builds up in your body.

p.60), which means that every breath you take is loaded with more nitrogen molecules than an equivalent breath at the surface. This surplus of nitrogen rapidly accumulates in the tissues of your body. If you ascend too quickly from depth, the nitrogen in your tissues can re-enter the blood in the form of harmful bubbles. It is therefore very important for you to manage your dive time and

NITROGEN AND BODY TISSUES

When you breathe compressed air underwater, its nitrogen content enters the blood and begins to penetrate the body's tissues. When you ascend, ambient pressure drops and nitrogen starts to come out of the tissues again. If your ascent is slow and controlled, the nitrogen re-enters the blood and exits the body harmlessly,

via your lungs. If your ascent is too fast, the escaping nitrogen can form harmful bubbles, leading to decompression sickness (DCS; *see pp.142–43*). DCS can cause minor discomfort if the bubbles are lodged under the skin or in the joints, but if they are in the brain or nervous system, it can lead to paralysis or even death.

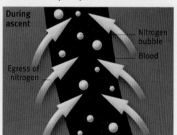

During descent

Ingress of nitrogen

Blood

Tissue

During ascent

Nitrogen bubble

Blood

Egress of nitrogen

NITROGEN ENTERS BODY TISSUES
Pressurized air dissolves in blood and its nitrogen content enters tissues, especially fatty areas, where it is temporarily stored.

FORMATION OF NITROGEN BUBBLES
If pressure drops too quickly during ascent, nitrogen forms bubbles in the bloodstream, which can lead to decompression sickness.

PERFECT PERCH
Dive boats sometimes lower a "trapeze" for divers to hold on to while making decompression stops, with a spare cylinder attached for safety.

depth, using either dive tables or a dive computer, to ensure that nitrogen does not build up to levels that cannot be safely dissipated during ascent.

Dive tables help you to calculate how long you can safely dive at a given depth, and what the safe limits are for any following dives that day (excess nitrogen takes 24 hours to fully leave the body). The tables will also tell you if you need to perform a decompression stop. This is a scheduled pause in your ascent that allows nitrogen to dissipate safely.

It is a good idea to halt at 5m (16ft) for three minutes during ascent, even if your dive tables do not require it, just as a precautionary measure. This is called a "safety stop". Dive computers can also generate safe diving schedules, by making continuous calculations during the dive (*see pp.66–67*).

NITROGEN NARCOSIS
The nitrogen in compressed air can also have a narcotic effect at depth, ranging from a feeling of euphoria to anxiety. Nitrogen narcosis rarely causes death directly but at depths below 30m (100ft) it causes divers to make increasingly bad judgments. If you feel the effects of narcosis during a dive, ascend to a shallower depth and the narcosis should rapidly disappear. Keep an eye on your buddy for symptoms of narcosis, such as sluggish responses and irrational behaviour.

USING DIVE TABLES
An understanding of the use of dive tables is a key element in all dive training programmes.

Tides and currents

The tides have a huge impact on the marine life and conditions of many dive sites, and localized currents can create unseen offshore hazards. Knowing how tides and currents work and how they impact on diving procedures is essential for safe diving at any location.

TIDAL MOVEMENT

Water levels at the shoreline can vary considerably over the tidal cycle, in extreme cases by as much as 15m (50ft). The region between the highest and lowest tide marks is called the intertidal zone.

Make a thorough check of local tidal conditions and coastal topography when planning a dive, otherwise you may encounter unexpected hazards, like areas of strong tidal flow. Water clarity varies

INTERTIDAL ZONE
Sometimes submerged and sometimes exposed, this is a harsh habitat for marine life.

from site to site, but it is often best at high tide, while incoming tides tend to bring marine species closer in to shore with them. The most important tidal event for divers is "slack water", a short interval when tidal flow halts at the changeover of every tide. Tidal currents mean that some sites are only safe for diving during the slack water period.

HOW TIDES ARE FORMED

The Earth's seas are subject to the gravitational pull of both the Sun and the Moon. Although the Moon is smaller than the Sun, it is much closer to the Earth, so its influence is stronger. The gravitational pull of the Moon draws water into a bulge on the side of the planet closest to it. A counter-bulge forms on the opposite side of the Earth because the water there is pulled less toward the Moon than the planet is itself. As the Earth rotates, the two opposing bulges of water move across the face of the planet, creating two high tides and two low tides in just over 24 hours.

NEAP TIDES: FIRST AND THIRD QUARTER MOONS
With the Sun and Moon at right angles, high tides are at their lowest, as they are subject to the gravitational pull of the Moon alone, but low tides are at their highest, pulled by the Sun.

SPRING TIDES: NEW AND FULL MOONS
Twice a month, the Sun and Moon are in line with the Earth. Their combined gravitational pull creates the highest high tides, and low tides are at their lowest.

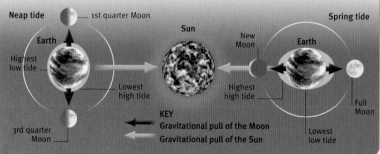

Neap tide   1st quarter Moon   Sun   New Moon   Spring tide

Earth   Earth

Highest low tide   Highest high tide

Lowest high tide   Full Moon

3rd quarter Moon   Lowest low tide

KEY
← Gravitational pull of the Moon
← Gravitational pull of the Sun

TYPES OF CURRENT

Currents are created by winds, tides, the rotation of the Earth, and the confluence of bodies of water of differing salinity and temperature. Tidal currents occur when local topography, such as a narrow channel, creates an area of unusually strong flow when the tide is coming in (flooding) or going out (ebbing). These currents can be powerful enough to carry away even strong swimmers.

DIVERS EXITING SEA
Plan your entrance and exit so that you avoid swimming against the tide. The best time to dive is usually at "slack tide" – at high or low tide, when the tidal pull is weakest.

Standing currents are permanent currents independent of tides. Longshore currents, which flow in one direction along the coast, are localized standing currents. There are also standing currents in the open ocean, such as the Gulf Stream, which flows upwards from the Gulf of Mexico, driven by the prevailing southwest winds, to the mid-North Atlantic, where it divides into two lesser currents.

WAVE SURGE
Underwater topography and weather conditions can combine to create dangerously strong water movement where surf breaks on the shore.

Rip currents occur when incoming waves force the backwash from previous waves sideways. The backwash streams along the shore until it finds a route back to the open sea, such as a gap in a sandbar, and surges out in a strong, narrow current, perpendicular to the shore.

To escape a rip current, swim across the current, parallel to the shore. You may find that trying to swim out of a rip current leads you into a longshore current, which pushes you back into the rip current. If this happens, swim out of the rip current in the opposite direction.

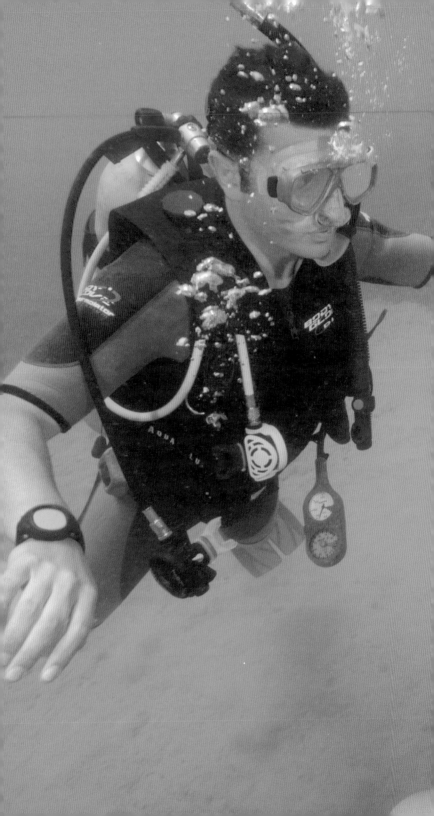

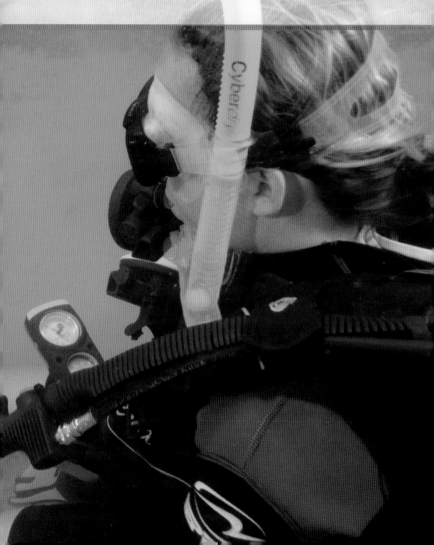

Diving skills

Introduction

Good basic skills are key to being a competent diver. Some techniques, such as buoyancy control, may seem difficult to master at first, but with practise they will become second nature, allowing you to relax and enjoy your dives. Skilled divers are also safer divers.

SUPPLEMENTING YOUR TRAINING

This chapter of the book discusses diving skills, but is not intended to be, or in any way replace, a training manual. While it covers the skills and techniques that are taught in the basic dive training offered by approved agencies, it must not be used in place of any element of that training. There is no substitute for comprehensive dive training with a certified instructor.

In this chapter, therefore, we outline the skills you need in order to be a safe and competent diver. Many people only dive once a year on holiday, or even less frequently, so it is very important to keep up to date with your diving skills. If you have been away from diving for any length of time, carry out a refresher course or an easy trial dive. You will find

STEPPING OUT
Knowing how to enter the water properly will help you get your dive off to a good start.

USING A COMPASS
Don't forget to practise navigation skills regularly. Getting lost can spoil a dive, and may hinder your return to a safe exit point.

that most of your basic skills are still familiar to you after a break, or will come back in due course. However, if you are put in a stressful situation, you may not be able to react quickly and effectively if your skills are rusty. Even experienced divers can benefit from regular practice of basic skills, and you should always be thinking about how to improve your kit configuration and technique.

KEEPING SKILLS CURRENT

A great way of keeping your skills up to date is to practise in a pool (*see pp.146–49*). This might not be as much fun as getting out into the open water but it will certainly provide you with a safe environment in which to perfect key skills such as buoyancy. Regular training in a pool or sheltered water can help you to meet the challenges of open water diving more confidently. If your local waters are cold and stormy in winter, use the off-season to brush up drills and procedures. Joining a diving club may give you access to a nearby pool.

DEPLOYING A BUOY
Diving requires the use of many items of specialist equipment that you must learn how to use safely.

Pre-dive skills

Good organizational skills will help ensure a trouble-free diving trip. A successful dive begins before you even leave your home, with checks on weather conditions and equipment. Even if someone else is organizing the dive, make sure you are well prepared and informed.

GETTING OFF TO A GOOD START

On the morning of the dive, get a detailed, up-to-date weather forecast specific to the site you are diving, and double-check tide times if appropriate. If you don't feel well for any reason, make an honest assessment of whether you are fit to dive that day. It is better to sit out a dive than to feel unwell underwater and have to abort. Illnesses affecting lung or circulatory efficiency also increase the risk of decompression sickness (*see p.142*) – a very good reason for giving the dive a miss.

BRIEFING FROM DIVE LEADER TO GROUP
While a group leader will take overall charge of the dive plan, you must take responsibility for your own fitness and kit-readiness.

Always check your kit before you set off on a diving trip. Before you leave home you must be sure that you have everything you need. It is good practice to make a checklist of all the items you will need, and keep this in your kit bag. When you arrive, be sure to transfer all your kit from the initial mustering point to the actual dive site, or onto the boat you are diving from. All too often, divers leave a vital piece of

DIVING WITH A NEW BUDDY

Diving abroad often means that you will dive with strangers. Make sure you give the dive organizer an honest assessment of your level of ability and interests, so they can pair you with a suitable buddy. Even if you don't know your buddy, give them all the respect and assistance you would offer a familiar dive partner.

kit on the quayside, such as a weight belt or mask, and only realize their mistake when the dive boat reaches its destination – by which time it is too late.

DIVING FROM A BOAT

The boat should have been booked in advance, but even so, it is polite to call the skipper again before you arrive. He or she will be able to confirm that weather and conditions are favourable for diving. When you board, check that the boat has adequate first aid and safety signalling devices on board, and appears to be in a seaworthy condition. Before you leave shore, notify the coastguard or relevant authority – and do not forget to inform them of your safe return when you

GETTING READY TO DIVE
If you have organized your day efficiently, you will be able to relax and concentrate on getting yourself ready to dive.

COMFORT AFLOAT
Remember to bring seasickness tablets with you on boat trips. Test them 24 hours beforehand to make sure they have no adverse effect on you.

get back. Ensure that the skipper reviews safety procedures, including the location of lifejackets, flares, and life-rafts, and demonstrates the underwater recall signal.

DIVING FROM THE SHORE

If you are diving from the shore, always check for the easiest possible access to your dive site on arrival (or before) to avoid long walks down to the beach with heavy gear. You may need permission to drive to the water's edge to unload kit.

WATCHING THE WEATHER

Obtain a forecast that includes the wind speed and direction, sea state, and visibility (fog, mist, etc). Do not take any risks about diving in bad weather – it is better to miss the dive than dive in surging seas or in visibility so poor your boat cover will not be able to locate you. You should also check tide tables to establish the timings of slack water. This is critical when diving areas affected by strong tidal currents.

Rough seas

Final checks

Diving with a partner (or buddy) means that there is someone to help if you encounter problems underwater. For the system to work properly, however, you and your buddy need to conduct your own briefing before a dive and check that all equipment is functioning properly.

MAKING BUDDY CHECKS

Just before the start of the dive, get together with your buddy and assemble your kit (*see pp.84–85*) and put it on. There is no particular order in which to do this, but most divers find that to avoid anything being overlooked, it is useful to develop a routine. When you are both kitted up and before either of you enter the water, you should carry out a buddy check – sit or stand next to your buddy and carefully check each other's kit, following the sequence shown below. Do not be tempted to rush these vital checks – you may regret it later. They ensure that you know how each other's kit is assembled, how it works, and that it is functioning. They also serve as a double-check that neither of you has overlooked anything before you dive.

1 **Check BCDs** so that you and your buddy know where each other's inflation and deflation points are, and ensure that they are working. Do the same for drysuits, if worn.

2 **Check that weights** are present and securely fastened. You and your buddy must be especially aware of how each other's weights are released, in case either diver is incapacitated.

3 **Check harness is secure** and note where, on your buddy's kit, key fastening points and harness release clips are located, and how they are operated.

4 **Check air contents** gauges and breathe from your regulators to check they are working. Test each other's octopus second stage.

BUDDY BRIEFING

Kitting-up provides a good opportunity to talk over a dive plan with your buddy. Ensure first that you are both agreed, as a pair, on the aim and course of the dive, your entry and exit points, and your predicted maximum depth and time for the dive. Check that you both have the required amount of air for your plan (including a reserve for emergencies). Agree on who will lead the dive and on whether you will dive to the left or right of your buddy. Decide on all communication signals, including how and when you will signal for the end of the dive, and on what you will do if you become separated. Once you have agreed a plan, stick to it unless it becomes impossible to do so. If circumstances change during the dive, use hand signals to discuss how, as a pair, you are going to modify the dive.

5 **Ready to dive?** Give each other a last once-over to establish who is carrying any miscellaneous pieces of kit, such as reels and slates, and where they are fastened. When you are ready to dive, make a final OK signal.

PREVENTING FOGGING

Mask fogging is a very common inconvenience, and is caused by oils on the mask's lens allowing moisture to bead. The traditional way to prevent fogging is to rub saliva onto the inside of the lens glass, then lightly rinse clear, before putting on the mask for a dive. Anti-fogging sprays are also available.

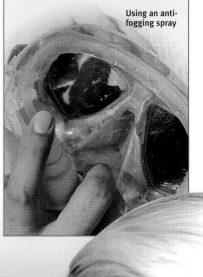

Using an anti-fogging spray

Entry

Every site will require a different method of entry, and the easiest method possible at each site is the best one to use. In all cases, it is safer to enter without large, heavy equipment, such as cameras, so if conditions allow, have them passed to you once you are in the water.

SHORE ENTRY

When entering the water from a beach, ensure your kit is assembled and on your back, then carry your mask and fins to the water's edge. There, fit your fins and mask with your buddy's help and walk backwards into the water (walking forwards with your fins on is difficult). As soon as you are deep enough, lower your centre of gravity by bending down, then start to swim, or "fin", out into open water. If there is surf, ensure your BCD is partially inflated and wait until a big wave approaches; lean into it, and let the return surge take you away from shore.

ENTERING FROM THE SHORE
If entering through surf, be careful not to lose your fins as you put them on. Breathe from your regulator throughout entry.

CONTROLLED SEATED ENTRY

This is the easiest method of entry into a pool or from a platform just above water level, and an especially useful method if you have difficulty with mobility on land or with keeping your balance when standing on a floating platform. It also enables you to put on your kit while seated.

2 **Pivot your body around,** using your hands to support you, so that you turn to face the side while easing yourself into the water.

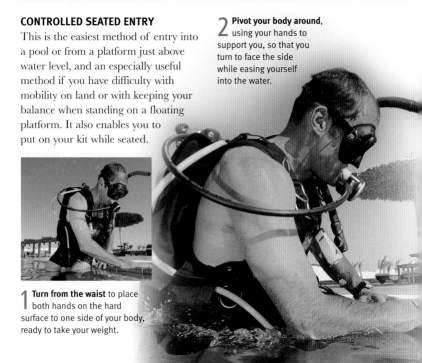

1 **Turn from the waist** to place both hands on the hard surface to one side of your body, ready to take your weight.

GIANT STRIDE ENTRY

Stepping into the water is a good entry method to use from a large diving boat or off a jetty or platform, provided there is sufficient depth of water. Partially inflate your BCD, place your regulator in your mouth and hold it and your mask in place with one hand, and take a large stride out into the water.

Hold on to any kit, such as a torch or camera, that could rise up on impact and hit your face

1 Take a giant stride, holding your mask and regulator in place. Keep looking forward, not down.

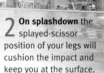

2 On splashdown the splayed-scissor position of your legs will cushion the impact and keep you at the surface.

BACKWARD ROLL

Use this entry from small boats with a low freeboard (distance from deck to waterline). With your regulator in place, check that your fins are free from obstruction, and that the water behind you is clear. Ease yourself over the edge and roll over backwards, aiming to hit the water first with your upper back.

ENTRY POSITION

Hold your mask and regulator in place with one hand and ease yourself backwards until your cylinder is hanging over the water.

BUDDY PROCEDURE AND SIGNALS

After entering the water, meet on the surface and make an OK signal (hand on head or fingertips together) to shore or boat cover. One exception to this is when making a negatively buoyant entry through strong surface currents. In this case, descend as quickly as possible, and rejoin your buddy on the seabed.

Standard "OK" signals

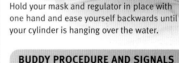

Descent

Descending to the seabed is always an exciting experience, but while you may want to get there quickly, you must always descend in a controlled manner. The method you use will depend partly on the site and prevailing conditions, and partly on your own preferences.

MAKING YOUR DESCENT

Having met up with your dive buddy in the water, follow the preparatory steps below. If you find that you do not sink, check that no air remains in your BCD (and drysuit, if applicable). If the problem persists, you probably do not have sufficient weight on your belt (*see pp.70–71*), and should return to the boat or the shore to collect some more. It is a good idea to note how much weight you need each time you try a different kit configuration – record the details in your log book for reference on later dives.

At a depth of 3m (10ft) you should carry out a bubble check. This involves briefly stopping so that you and your buddy can check each other's equipment for signs of air leaks, for example, from an incorrectly fitted hose. This will allow you to return to the surface to resolve the issue before you resume the dive. By sorting out minor problems now, you may avoid bigger problems during the dive that could lead to an emergency.

As you descend, you will feel pressure in your ears. Release this regularly by swallowing or holding your nose and

1 **Meet up with your buddy** on the surface, well clear of any boat cover. If using a snorkel, remove it, and switch to breathing from primary regulators.

2 **Give an OK signal** to each other when ready to begin the dive. If using a "buddy line" to link yourselves together (useful when one buddy is a novice), ensure now that you are both attached.

3 **The "down" signal** confirms your intention to descend immediately. If your buddy is a novice or nervous, reassure them by holding their hand and helping them to descend.

4 **Both you and your buddy** should deflate your BCDs and exhale together, so that you become negatively buoyant and start to sink simultaneously. If you have a problem sinking, address it now.

blowing against the closed nostrils – a process called "equalization" or "ear-clearing" (*see also pp.98–99*). If you feel you are descending too fast, allow a little air into your BCD. Your mask will also start to press on your face; relieve this by exhaling gently through your nose. If you are wearing a drysuit, you will feel the water pressing it against your body. Ease this by letting air into the suit, but not so much that it alters your buoyancy too greatly – and remember to release it again on ascent.

EQUALIZATION
Pinch your nose and blow at intervals to equalize pressure in the skull with that of the water.

BUBBLE CHECK
Buddy pairs check each other's kit for tell-tale air leaks before descending further.

an SMB (*see pp.74–75*), ensure before descent that the buoy is fully inflated and the line is free. Your buddy should stay on the same side throughout the descent to avoid confusion and tangling in the line.

On group dives there may already be a weighted line – known as a shotline – in place, attached to a buoy and leading to a wreck or fixed point on the seabed, which will give you and your buddy a handy point of reference. Do not use the line to pull yourself down, as it may not be anchored securely at the base.

DESCENT OPTIONS

Many divers prefer to descend feet-first so that they can remain face to face with their buddy and maintain eye contact. This is good practice, unless you need to descend quickly through a current and therefore have to use your fins.

A free descent is where no line is used and you descend freely (head- or feet-first) to the seabed. If you are using

FINAL CHECK
A group of divers meeting at the bottom of a shotline give a last "OK" signal to each other before exploring the dive area.

Breathing underwater

Swimming freely underwater for the very first time can be exhilarating, but also potentially unnerving and even frightening. Learning and perfecting good breathing techniques allows the novice diver to become calm and relaxed in this new environment.

LEARNING TO RELAX

The sheer thrill of your very first dive will cause your heart-rate to increase and make you breathe faster than normal. You may be alarmed at how quickly your air supply runs out, but after a few dives, you will learn to be calmer and more relaxed, and your air consumption will decrease. When you feel comfortable underwater, take a few moments to concentrate on your breathing and remind yourself of the dos and don'ts of underwater breathing.

CONSERVING AIR
The more relaxed you are, the less air you will use and the longer your dive will last.

Firstly, and most importantly, never hold your breath underwater, because you will run the risk of bursting a lung. Inhale and exhale more deeply than you would normally do on land. Try to maintain neutral buoyancy (*see pp.118–21*), as this will decrease your need for leg and arm movements to maintain a constant position, and thus reduce air consumption. Furthermore, avoid

BREATHING OUT
If you remove your regulator, exhale slowly to minimize the risk of lung expansion injury.

CLEARING THE REGULATOR
A regulator can be cleared of water by simply exhaling, or by pressing the button on the front to purge the water.

swimming unnecessarily against currents – it is better to go with the flow than to waste your air by overexertion.

Always be aware of where your buddy is and what he or she is doing; many novice divers lose sight of their buddy and rapidly become anxious. If there is a problem, stop, breathe, and think before taking action. Acting too quickly and without thought could lead to panic and further problems.

Make sure that you are familiar with your equipment and fully understand how it works. You must know exactly where each item is stored to avoid panic if things go wrong during a dive – for example, if you lose your regulator or your mask begins to fill up. Regularly practise emergency procedure drills (*see pp.136–43*), either in the pool or in open water, to ensure confidence in a real crisis.

PLANNING YOUR AIR CONSUMPTION

On an open-water, fairly shallow dive, the rule of air consumption is to plan your dive so that you can carry out your descent, exploration, and ascent, and still surface with a reserve of 50 bar (725psi). If you have to come back to a given point to exit, such as a shotline or anchor line, start

FREQUENT CHECKS
Buddies should regularly check each other's air reserves, to maintain a good awareness of the remaining levels of both members of the team.

your return when you have 100 bar (1,500psi) left. If there is a current, swim out against it and swim back with it, so that the return is never longer than the outward trip. It is also wise to swim back to your point of entry or shotline at a shallower depth than on the outward journey, as this reduces air consumption. In more difficult environments, follow the "Rule of Thirds" (*below*).

THE RULE OF THIRDS

When planning a dive in an environment that is covered overhead – such as a wreck, cave, or under ice – or when making deeper dives, always apply the Rule of Thirds. The rule states that you should use a third of your air for descent and exploration, and a third returning to your guideline or point of entry and for ascent. The remaining third is an emergency reserve.

Descend and explore

Return and ascend

Emergency reserve

Buoyancy control

One of the most important skills for a diver to master is undoubtedly that of buoyancy control. Until you achieve this, you will be constantly expending effort in order to maintain your position in the water, wasting air resources and distracting you from your dive.

SUITS AND WEIGHTS

Wearing any type of exposure suit will make you more buoyant in the water, and thus make it more difficult to dive. Drysuits contain an airspace between the suit fabric and the diver's body. Wetsuits have air cells within their neoprene fabric, and so the thicker the neoprene, the more buoyant you will be. The function of weights is to counteract the buoyancy your suit gives you so that, with your lungs full of air but your BCD uninflated, you float at the correct level at the water's surface.

Correct assessment of how much weight you need to carry for a given dive is very important. Spend time conducting weight tests for different suit and kit combinations, and note your findings for future use. Remember – saltwater is denser than freshwater, so you will require more weight when you dive in the sea than in freshwater.

USING YOUR BCD

At the start of a dive, you will usually enter the water with your BCD inflated, as having positive buoyancy allows you

CONDUCTING A WEIGHT TEST
Empty your BCD, and take a deep breath and hold it. Float in an upright position. If you are wearing the right amount of weight, you will float at eye-level to the waterline. Add or discard weights as necessary until this is achieved.

Too high　　Too low

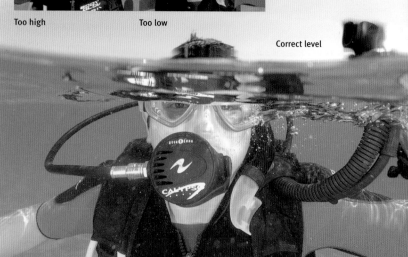

Correct level

to float at the surface effortlessly while you meet up with your buddy – the only exception to this is at sites where there are strong surface currents, when it is important to get to the bottom quickly.

In order to descend you must be negatively buoyant, which you achieve by deflating your BCD and exhaling (*see pp.114–15*). However, as you sink, you will find that your descent rate accelerates as your suit – and the remaining air in your BCD – becomes compressed. To counteract this, you must add air to your BCD. If this halts you before you have reached the desired level, let air out. Repeat the process, letting small amounts of air in and out of your BCD until you become stationary at the desired depth.

When this happens, you will have achieved neutral buoyancy underwater – a state in which you neither float nor sink. Achieving this perfect equilibrium

PRACTISING BUOYANCY SKILLS
An instructor looks on as a student diver practises fin pivots (*see pp.146–49*), an exercise designed to improve basic buoyancy control.

of weight ballast and lifting forces means you do not waste effort and air using your fins to maintain a certain depth.

When you want to ascend, the same control principles apply, but in reverse. As you go up, the air in your suit and BCD expands as external water pressure decreases, making you increasingly buoyant, and causing you to rise rapidly. As it is important to ascend at a slow,

HOVERING OVER A REEF
Buoyancy control is critical when diving over delicate coral that can be damaged by physical contact.

steady rate (*see pp.128–31*), you'll need to vent air accordingly as you rise. To descend and ascend as smoothly as possible, you must become familiar with how your BCD responds to inputs of air, and how quickly it vents air.

Drysuits have independent inflation and deflation controls (*see pp.54–55*). If you are diving in a drysuit, the air space between your suit and your body will become compressed, and you will need to inject a little air into the suit to avoid discomfort from being "shrink wrapped" by external water pressure. This will make you more buoyant, so you will need to vent air from your BCD to counteract it. On ascent, you will need to dump the excess air from your drysuit.

FINE CONTROL OF BUOYANCY

Small movements up and down – to look at different parts of a reef, for example – are best achieved through breath control, rather than letting air in and out of your BCD. Good buoyancy control only comes

JETTISONING YOUR WEIGHTS

In extreme circumstances, such as being caught in a powerful downcurrent, it may be necessary – as a last resort only – to dump your weight belt. You will instantly start to rise up rapidly through the water, so be ready to vent air from your BCD to slow your ascent. Breathe out on the way up, to minimize the risk of lung expansion injury (*see p.95*).

with practice and is worth perfecting. Take time at the start of each dive to practise fine control of buoyancy before you set off exploring. From a neutrally buoyant position on the seabed, slowly inhale – you should rise up and hover just above the seabed. Breathe out a little – you should sink. Practise breathing in and out and become familiar with how it influences your gentle rise and fall. You should be able to hover over the seabed and control your buoyancy by breathing alone, without constantly filling and

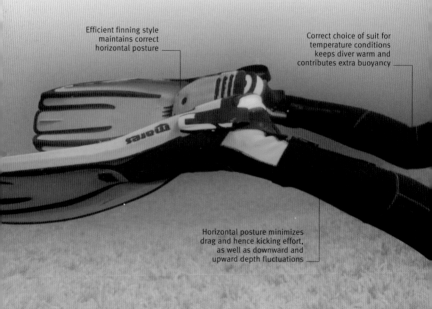

Efficient finning style maintains correct horizontal posture

Correct choice of suit for temperature conditions keeps diver warm and contributes extra buoyancy

Horizontal posture minimizes drag and hence kicking effort, as well as downward and upward depth fluctuations

emptying your BCD. Once you have mastered this, you will be able to float at any depth without effort.

TRIM AND WEIGHT DISTRIBUTION

The position of your weights and equipment has an important part to play in maintaining good "trim" (correct posture and balance) underwater. Distribution of weight is key in achieving a good horizontal attitude, which makes buoyancy control easier and helps you to propel yourself along with the minimum of drag. A streamlined profile also helps

posture and ease of movement, which helps to reduce air consumption. Experiment with different weight systems and stowage points until you find a comfortable combination that helps you achieve the best position in the water. Some designs of BCD allow you to stow weight at different points, not just on a belt. For example, some have special quick-release pouches which are designed to take moderate weight loads (*see p.59*). Always check that you are able to jettison the bulk of your weight load in case of emergency.

ACHIEVING PERFECT BUOYANCY
Thinking about buoyancy as a system of influences to be harmonized, rather than just weights and BCD, will help you perfect the art of moving underwater.

BCD filled with correct amount of air for depth and weight load

Additional weight to fine-tune weight distribution

Relaxed mental attitude helps maintain buoyancy; tense divers make too many corrective movements and find it hard to adopt a horizontal posture

Weights evenly spaced and held in place with retaining buckles

Console and octopus second stage clipped close to body to minimize drag and avoid damage or entanglement

Moving underwater

The duration of your dive is limited by your rate of air consumption, which in turn depends on how much energy you expend. Good finning technique, buoyancy control, and a streamlined profile will all make your movement underwater more energy-efficient.

EFFICIENT PROPULSION

Your movement through the water should be driven and controlled by your legs. If you watch experienced divers, you will notice that they use their arms very little, and move effortlessly through the water, saving energy, minimizing air consumption, and avoiding damage to reefs and the marine environment.

Swimming with fins should be an extremely efficient way of propelling yourself through the water, but many

MINIMIZING ARM USE
To practise with your legs only, cross your arms in front of you or let them hang by your side.

divers are let down by a poor finning technique. There are several different strokes you can use, but all should be carried out with strong, rhythmic movements, fully extending the leg (or legs) with each kick. Uncontrolled thrashing and incomplete kicks will simply waste energy. It is worth asking your buddy to give you feedback on your technique – even to photograph or film you. You may be surprised at the results.

Scuba diving is not a race, and the faster you go, the less you see. Learning to pace yourself and move at a leisurely speed will help you to relax, and a relaxed diver is an aware, efficient, and safe one.

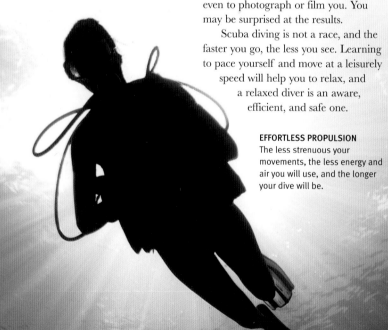

EFFORTLESS PROPULSION
The less strenuous your movements, the less energy and air you will use, and the longer your dive will be.

PROFILE AND BUOYANCY

To achieve the most streamlined (and therefore most energy-efficient) swimming position, you should be almost horizontal in the water. Your hips will be slightly lower than your upper body due to that area being weighted. During a dive you should look forwards and downwards most of the time – raising your head too much will lift your upper body and make your profile less streamlined.

POOR PROFILE
Swimming with the wrong profile may mean that your fins kick up silt, impairing visibility.

Carrying the correct amount of weight is important. Being over-weighted will drag your hips and lower body downwards. Swimming will then require greater effort due to your unnatural angle in the water, which will produce increased drag. You can improve your profile by repositioning the weights in your BCD, or refining your weight requirements (*see pp.118–21*).

Achieving neutral buoyancy (*see pp.118–21*) is the key to maintaining a good dive profile with ease, and also increases your efficiency. If you are positively buoyant, you will be constantly swimming downwards; if negatively buoyant, you will have to swim upwards all the time or crawl along the bottom – all of which require more effort than horizontal, neutrally buoyant, swimming.

TYPES OF KICKING STROKE

With the flutter kick (*below*), all fin movement takes place above the body's centreline, reducing the amount of water directed downwards. This can be useful when you wish to avoid stirring up sediment on the seafloor. The frog kick is also ideal for use where fine silt can ruin visibility if disturbed, because it directs thrust horizontally behind you. The swimmer kick is good for power, but uses up energy quickly. Most divers tend to drift slightly when using the flutter kick or the swimmer's kick, because one leg is slightly stronger than the other.

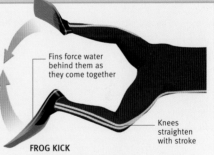

Fins force water behind them as they come together

Knees straighten with stroke

FROG KICK
Spread your legs and bring up your knees. Rotate your fins so that the bottoms of the blades face behind you. Bring the fins together in an arc, thrusting out behind.

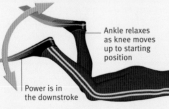

Ankle relaxes as knee moves up to starting position

Power is in the downstroke

FLUTTER KICK
Bend the knees slightly, shorten the stroke of the kick, and keep the hips fairly static. The stroke ends when the knee is straight.

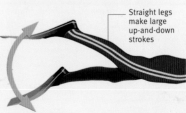

Straight legs make large up-and-down strokes

SWIMMER KICK
Lock your legs straight and kick from the hips with long strokes. This technique exploits the power in your thigh and hip muscles.

Exploring and navigating

Learning how to use instruments and natural features to find your way around underwater is important. Accurate navigation will help you to reach your planned exit point at the end of a dive, and will also help you find and explore features of interest, such as wrecks.

MAPPING THE SITE

It is easy to become disorientated in poor visibility, but good navigation skills will help you find your way, even when conditions are against you. Developing such skills will make you less dependent on other divers for your own safety –

if you always rely on your buddy to lead the way, you could find yourself in trouble if you become separated.

On first entering the water, make mental notes of the surrounding features, such as unusual rocks, coral, or your position on a wreck site. As you progress through the dive, try to build up a map of the site in your mind. At every turning point, note nearby features and which direction you turned in relation to them.

FOLLOWING A REEF WALL
In clear conditions, a reef wall makes an easy navigational reference point. Try to remember distinctive features as you go along.

Look at the seabed geology too: rocks often have features or show strata that make memorable visual markers. It may be helpful to jot notes down on a slate.

NATURAL NAVIGATION AIDS

A compass (*see pp.126–27*) gives the most accurate directional information, but there are also clues in nature. If the water is clear and shallow enough, or if there are any shadows cast by rocks, you can

MENTALLY MAPPING THE DIVE SITE
Reef, rock, and seabed features, sunlight, and even shoals of fish can all help you to orientate yourself at the dive site.

use the Sun as a directional reference. On a morning dive, for example, the Sun will be in the east. Take note of which way the current is running. (If you are diving close to slack water (*see pp.102–03*), at high or low tide, this may change by as much as 180° as the tide begins to turn.) Even if you cannot feel the current, you can find visual clues to its direction. Plankton, for example, drift along with the current, so shoals of fish station themselves facing into the current so that they can feed on them. Kelp fronds flow in the direction of the current. Exhaust bubbles will rise up towards the surface (unless you are in a down current).

READING SAND RIPPLES

Sand ripples run parallel to the shore, at 90 degrees to the path of incoming and outgoing tidal currents. Sand ripples get closer together nearer to shore, providing a useful reference point for underwater navigation. If the spacing of sand ripples underneath you appears to be getting narrower, you are swimming towards shallow water and a possible exit point.

Sand ripples on the seabed

FOLLOWING A REEF

On a basic reef dive, swim out with the reef wall on one side of your body and then return with the wall on your other side. When diving around a wreck, try to maintain either a clockwise or anti-clockwise motion, especially if the wreckage is fragmented. Keep the main part of the wreck to one side of your body during the dive, so that you return to your starting point after one circuit.

USING A HANDHELD COMPASS
In case you are separated for any reason, both you and your buddy should carry and be confident at using a magnetic compass.

USING A COMPASS

A compass has a circular body, often divided into 360 degree increments, and a needle that swivels to point to magnetic north. Many also have a "bezel" – an outer ring also marked with increments and the points of the compass, that can be rotated independently to the body. This can be used in conjunction with the "direction of travel" arrow (known as the "lubber line"), which is marked on the compass body, to establish the direction you want to travel in relation to magnetic north. Point the lubber line in the direction in which you wish to travel, then turn the bezel so that its "north" mark matches the direction in which the needle is pointing. If you ensure that the needle always points to the north mark, as you move in the direction indicated by the lubber line you will maintain your intended direction. Digital compasses work in the same way, but display the information on an LCD.

A compass is a fairly basic device, but it is easy to use it incorrectly. If it is a wrist-mounted model, ensure that your

MEASURING DISTANCE
When navigating underwater, you can judge relative distances by counting how many fin strokes you have made in a given direction, or by timing your progress along a course.

wrist is held square to the direction of travel, and not at an angle. It is simpler to use a compass mounted on a console or a retractable lanyard, which can be held out straight in front of you. Use both compass readings and environmental observations, so that you can correct any inaccuracies in either method. Mark readings down on a slate as you go, and try to integrate these into your mental map of the dive site. In slack water, timing how long it takes to get from one point to the next gives you an idea of your position if you return along the same compass course. Combining this information with depth readings taken along the way will help you navigate with more accuracy.

LAYING A DISTANCE LINE

In low visibility environments – such as murky temperate waters – it may be necessary to lay lines to aid navigation back to a convenient point. Lines can also be used to search an area: if you know the approximate position of a specific site, natural object, or artefact, you can use a line, in arcs of different lengths, to scan a large area of seabed efficiently.

1 **Find a solid anchor point** to attach the line to. Make a couple of turns around the object for extra security. Do not secure a line to jagged edges that will fray or cut through it.

2 **Secure the line** to the anchor point. If you have a reel and line you use regularly, fit a spring clip to the end of the line so that it can wrap around the anchor point and clip back on to itself.

3 **Unspool the line** as you explore, making sure that your buddy keeps clear to one side. The line should be tied off again wherever you change heading.

Ascent

All good things come to an end, and at some point your dive will be over. Ascending at the end of a dive should be carried out with great care. This is the part of the dive where decompression sickness (*see pp.142–43*) can develop, so your ascent must not be hurried.

WHEN TO ASCEND

Dives often end when you reach a pre-arranged time to surface, either to meet the boat cover or to account for changing tides. However, you may decide to ascend before this if the site proves uninteresting, or if you or your buddy are cold or tired. You may also be forced to ascend if you have only 50 bar (725psi) left in your cylinder, if you are making a decompression dive (*see pp.130–31*) and reach the scheduled minimum volume of air in your cylinder, or if problems cause you to abort the dive.

SIGNALLING TO ASCEND
To ask your buddy if they are ready to ascend, or to signal your intent, raise your thumb.

Before ascent, you and your buddy should signal the "thumbs up" to each other that you are both able and ready to ascend to the surface.

If possible, avoid making a "free ascent", with no visual reference to guide you. If you can follow a reef wall or a permanent mooring line, for example, this will give you a natural sense of your ascent rate, in addition to your computer readings, and can help avoid disorientation. Sometimes, though, it is not possible to ascend up a line or along a natural feature, and it can be helpful to deploy a delayed surface marker

MONITORING A DIVE COMPUTER
Dive computers (*see pp.66–67*) help the diver judge ascent rate. Some devices give audible warnings if safe limits are exceeded.

BUDDY PAIR ASCENDING A SHOTLINE
A buoyed line moored to a wreck or seabed feature offers one of the safest guides for an ascent, especially in a strong current.

and, in a current, can provide something to hold on to. If you do not manage to get back to the shotline, send up a DSMB.

MAKING YOUR ASCENT

To start your ascent, slowly breathe in or let a little air into your BCD – this should cause you to rise up. Rise up next to, and ideally face-to-face with, your buddy so that you can check each other's rate of ascent and condition. As ascent continues, carefully monitor the amount of air in your BCD (and drysuit if relevant) as the air will expand as the pressure decreases during your ascent, causing your rate of ascent to increase rapidly. Keep one hand on the BCD exhaust hose in order to vent air from it as you ascend. You may also need to

buoy, or DSMB (*see pp.130–31*) – this will give you a vertical reference and also signals your position at the surface. Ideally, both members of the buddy pair should carry a DSMB. If you are diving on a wreck or a site with a shotline, aim to get back to the line for your ascent – not only will boat cover know where to pick you up at the surface, but the line will assist you in making decompression stops

FOLLOWING A SLOPE
Ascending next to a natural feature, such as a reef, offers a reassuring reference point.

dump air from your drysuit. You can fin to assist your ascent, especially to gain momentum to begin with, but this will not be necessary if you are correctly weighted and positively buoyant. Keep breathing normally and do not hold your breath.

A conservative estimate of a safe rate of ascent is 15m (50ft) per minute (or slower) up to 5m (16ft) in depth. At this point many divers make a 3-minute safety

MAKING A SAFETY STOP
Divers make a precautionary safety stop at 5m (16ft) to allow nitrogen to exit the body's tissues at a safe rate.

stop as a precaution. Whether you do or not, the final 5m (16ft) to the surface should then take another full minute. If making a decompression dive, ensure you make all your scheduled safety stops and check with your buddy as you do so.

DEPLOYING A DSMB

Since ascent must be conducted in a controlled way, it is helpful to carry your own portable shotline – a delayed surface marker buoy (DSMB). These highly visible tubes are launched using

air from your second stage, and allow you to ascend up an attached line. Using them is a real skill, so seek training before your first attempt. Remember to reel the line in as you ascend, as slack line can easily get wrapped around your kit.

1 Unfurl the buoy, which should be attached to a reel. Unclip the reel from yourself, taking care not to drop it.

2 Partially inflate with a small burst of purged air from your octopus (*see p.61*) to stand the buoy upright.

3 Hold the reel in one hand, and with the other, hold your octopus valve under the buoy's inflation point.

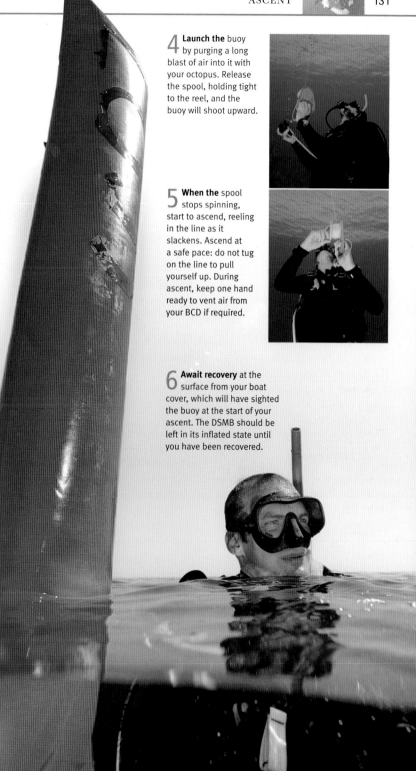

4 Launch the buoy by purging a long blast of air into it with your octopus. Release the spool, holding tight to the reel, and the buoy will shoot upward.

5 When the spool stops spinning, start to ascend, reeling in the line as it slackens. Ascend at a safe pace: do not tug on the line to pull yourself up. During ascent, keep one hand ready to vent air from your BCD if required.

6 Await recovery at the surface from your boat cover, which will have sighted the buoy at the start of your ascent. The DSMB should be left in its inflated state until you have been recovered.

Surface skills and recovery

Once you and your buddy have completed your dive and are at the surface, you need to head back to shore or wait to be picked up by your boat cover. Always remember that the dive isn't over until you and your buddy are back on dry land or on your dive vessel!

EXITING ON TO THE SHORE

If completing a shore dive, you and your buddy should swim to the shore and find a safe, appropriate method of getting back on to dry land. If you are diving from a sandy beach it is usually best to keep your fins on for as long as possible and walk backwards up the beach until you are well out of the way of any swell. Removing your fins too early can lead to problems if you are swept off your feet or back out to sea, as you will have no propulsion.

If diving from a rocky shore, try to find an easy route back on to the rocks. Again, aim to keep your fins on for as long as possible. As you take off your kit, place it clear of any swell that could carry it back into the water.

EXITING ON TO A BEACH
Only remove your fins and walk forwards when exiting the shallows of a calm sea, or once you are out of the way of any swell.

SIGNALLING TO A BOAT
Your dive plan should ensure that your boat cover knows roughly when you will surface. If you need help quickly, shout and wave a signalling flag.

SIGNALLING TO BOAT COVER

If you are diving from a boat, remain close to your buddy with your regulator in place and signal to your boat that you are OK and awaiting recovery. If there is a problem or emergency (*see p.141*) and you or your buddy require immediate recovery, wave to the boat, or draw extra attention to yourselves by blowing a whistle, shouting, or waving

a flag. As the boat approaches, move to it with caution, keeping your distance until you have a signal from the boat that it is in neutral and safe to approach.

EXITING ON TO A BOAT OR RIB

To get into a rigid inflatable boat (RIB), you should first get a hold on the boat, either by a rope or handle on the side. Make sure your BCD is inflated, hand your weight belt in first, and then slip out of your BCD by unclipping one of its shoulder straps. Keep hold of it until someone from the boat can pull it in, along with your cylinder. You should then be able to kick with your fins and pull yourself up on to the RIB.

If returning to a hard boat, head for the ladder and hold on to the bottom. Take

DIVER GIVES "OK" SIGNAL
A standard signal for "I'm OK" at the surface is to put your hand on top of your head, forming a closed arc.

BOARDING A BOAT
It is usually easiest to hand up any small items first, then hoist yourself up the ladder while still kitted up.

great care in a swell as the ladder will move in the water. The skipper or dive master will probably tell you whether to de-kit in the water or to enter the boat wearing your kit.

You may be able to hand in your weight belt, BCD, and cylinder, but often it is easy enough to remove just your fins at the base of the ladder, hand them up to someone in the boat or hold on to them, and simply climb the ladder fully kitted up. If you feel you are not strong enough to do this, let someone on board know (preferably before you dive).

Once on the boat, be aware that others may be waiting in the water to get on board. Stand back to let others on, stow your gear quickly and tidily, and then offer assistance if it is needed.

Post-dive and debriefing

Your dive is over and there is kit that needs to be cleaned and stowed, and records to write up while your dive is still fresh in your mind. Problems may have occurred during the dive and questions may have arisen that need to be addressed. Now is the best time to do this.

PRACTICAL MATTERS

The first post-dive task is to wash your kit. You need to ensure that it is clean and free from mud or sand. If you have been diving in saltwater, then this also needs to be thoroughly rinsed off before the salt starts to corrode metal parts. Large dive boats and liveaboards usually have one facility for washing electronic equipment, such as computers and cameras, and another for your BCD, regulator, and other kit items. Rinse all items thoroughly to remove excess salt

and sand, which can easily work itself into O-rings and regulators. There may also be facilities on board to dry your kit before stowing it away in a bag or box for your next dive. Make sure you follow instructions and do not leave kit lying around – this can lead to loss or damage, which may impede your next dive. If you are diving from a rigid inflatable boat (RIB) or small dive boat, you will need to find a water source back on land to rinse your kit, and then leave it to dry or stow it for transport.

ANALYSING THE DIVE

There will normally be some sort of debriefing with your dive leader after a dive. This gives you an opportunity to ask questions about the dive (for example, to identify fish and coral species that you did not recognize or discuss problems with kit, navigation, or currents). This is a time when you can learn about the site for a future dive and share with others ways to improve skills.

DIVER CLEANING KIT
Rinsing, drying, checking, and stowing your kit should become a post-dive routine.

You should always fill in a log book after every dive, recording the depth, time, and conditions (including visibility, water temperature, and currents), as well as key features of the dive – details of a wreck, species encountered, kit configuration, the type of suit you were wearing and the weights you used, and any problems you experienced. The log will be a valuable reference for future dives.

Finally, ensure that after every dive you are well rehydrated. You will have expended a high level of energy, so will have lost fluids. Choose non-fizzy soft drinks or, ideally, water, to ensure that you rehydrate your body properly. Keep your energy levels up, especially if you are diving again soon, by having a good meal or eating a snack with a high energy content. If you are cold after a dive, get warm and dry – have a hot drink and get out of your wetsuit, if possible.

REACHING THE SHORE
Eager as you may be to chat about what you have seen, attend to your kit first.

LOOKING FORWARD

If you are planning to make more than one dive in the same day, consider beforehand what your surface interval will be between dives. Aim to do your deepest dive first, and shallower dives subsequently. Make sure you are in good health to dive again – if you have become cold or fatigued on the first dive, it is better to spend time recovering than to dive again too soon.

DIVERS DEBRIEFING
Talking to other divers in the post-dive get-together will help broaden your knowledge of diving, and you may pick up some handy tips.

Problem solving

Diving is a safe sport if you follow the rules, avoid taking unnecessary risks, and always dive with a buddy. But that does not mean you will never encounter difficulties during a dive. Learning how to anticipate and solve problems is part of becoming an accomplished diver.

KNOW YOUR LIMITS

One of the most exciting things about diving is that no two dives are ever the same. Even consecutive dives on the same dive site, with the same buddy, will be different due to changes in currents, visibility, and your own attitude. Some days you will feel great, and everything will work out perfectly, and other days you might be tired, have a slight headache

REGULAR SIGNALLING
Remain in close communication with your buddy at all times, and signal to each other regularly that you are OK.

perhaps, and there may be minor problems underwater that you have to deal with. In this unpredictable sport, you must be mentally and physically prepared for every eventuality.

To minimize the likelihood of problems and incidents occurring during a dive, do not dive in conditions with which you are unfamiliar without preparation. For example, if you have never dived in a cave, wreck, or under ice, make sure that you undergo the relevant training before attempting to do so. Diving in conditions for which you are unprepared will lead to anxiety, and sometimes to panic – and that is when problems often arise.

The buddy system is important for your safety, but as a diver you must ultimately take responsibility for your own welfare. If you feel uneasy during a dive, tell your buddy, and either change or abort the dive. Never let peer pressure push you beyond your limits and training, even if this means that your buddy's dive may be unsatisfactory. Buddy compatibility is important, as accidents can occur when two egos clash.

LOOKING AFTER YOUR BUDDY

Your buddy is your underwater lifeguard, but it is a two-way relationship – you also have to support your buddy when problems arise.

MENTAL AND PHYSICAL FITNESS
Confidence, a positive mental attitude, good health, and good levels of fitness are essential ingredients for a safe, successful dive.

ANTICIPATING KIT PROBLEMS

It is rare that equipment fails during a dive, but you should nevertheless take great care when assembling, storing, and servicing your kit. After all, this is what keeps you alive underwater, so it is worth spending time and money on keeping it in perfect working order.

Consider "what if" situations ahead of a dive, and think through how you will deal with the failure of any element of your kit. Do you have a spare if your buddy is not close by? Your regulator should always have an octopus second stage (*see p.61*), to use as a back up in case your main second stage fails.

HANDLING INCIDENTS CALMLY

Many things can go wrong on a dive, but most are minor issues that can be solved without aborting the dive. Even serious problems can be dealt with if you remain focused and positive. Be persistent, and say "no" to failure. When you become

aware of a problem, stop, think, breathe, and then act. Whatever happens, do not panic – remember that your buddy is there to help. Make sure you are there for your buddy too, and be quick to reassure or assist them if they appear disorientated or anxious.

THE INCIDENT PIT

Minor problems can escalate into major ones if you do not stay calm and deal with them methodically. Imagine that you lose your regulator while trying to ease cramp in your foot, and then fumble as you try to retrieve it. If you panic, you may inhale water, choke, and become disorientated. This type of scenario is known as the "incident pit" – stay out of it by thinking clearly and acting methodically.

TROUBLE-SHOOTING

The equipment problems you will encounter most commonly will involve your regulator, mask, and inflator hose.

If your regulator comes away from your mouth and you cannot retrieve it, reach for your octopus second stage (*see p.61*) and breathe from it. If your octopus is not accessible for any reason, signal to your buddy, who should offer you their own octopus to use. Take a few breaths from this to calm down and, with your buddy's help, locate your main regulator and replace it.

Should air start to flow uncontrollably from your regulator, take the regulator out of your mouth and push the purge button, which should clear any grit that may be jamming the valve open. If this does not work, switch to your octopus second stage and signal to your buddy that your air supply is running down more quickly than normal. Monitor

RETRIEVING LOST REGULATOR
A lost regulator is usually easy to retrieve, but if your buddy is finding this difficult, go to their aid and, if necessary, offer them your octopus.

your air supply carefully, and ascend immediately with your buddy. Note that in very cold freshwater, freezing-up of the regulator will probably be the cause of any free-flow, in which case purging will not help. In this scenario, you may need to breathe from your buddy's octopus while performing a shared-air ascent together (*see p.140*).

CALMING YOUR BUDDY
Reassuring physical contact can help to calm a disorientated buddy and prevent panic from setting in.

SECURING A BUDDY'S LOOSE CYLINDER
Some problems are difficult to solve alone, and you should not hesitate to alert your buddy if you need assistance.

SOLVING MASK AND HOSE ISSUES

If your mask is dislodged or starts to fill with water, simply clear it in the normal way. Lean your head back, press in the upper edge of the mask, and breathe out through your nose. The air bubbles you exhale will clear any excess water in your mask. At depth, this can seem daunting, so be

REMOVING YOUR WEIGHT BELT
You must be competent in removing your weight belt underwater, in case you need to adjust your weights or if your belt becomes snagged.

prepared to practise this procedure until you are comfortable with it and can execute it confidently.

On occasion, you may find that the inflator hose for your BCD or drysuit fails to work. This is usually caused by grit becoming lodged in the valve. If necessary, BCDs can be inflated orally, both underwater or at the surface.

LOCATING A LOST BUDDY

During a dive, you may find you lose sight of your buddy, especially in low visibility conditions. The correct procedure is to look around for a minute or two, and then surface independently. If your buddy is using a surface marker buoy (*see p.74*), it will indicate their position. Having located it, you can then follow the line down to find your buddy again. If neither buddy nor buoy is visible, signal to any boat cover to recover you; alert the coastguard if your buddy has not appeared after a few minutes. In all probability, your buddy will surface shortly after you do. You can then decide whether or not to resume the dive.

FREE AND BUOYANT ASCENTS

If you run out of air, locate your buddy and follow the procedure below. If you cannot find your buddy, you will need to make a rapid "free ascent" by finning to the surface. This can be aided by ditching your weights, but be ready for a suddden increase in buoyancy. Breathe out slowly during ascent to prevent lung expansion injury. If, however, you have a little air left you can make a more controlled "buoyant ascent". Let some air into your BCD to kick-start your ascent, and tilt your head back to watch for the surface. Again, breathe out during the ascent. Control your ascent rate by venting air from the BCD, but not so much that you lose buoyancy. Do not rise any faster than

1 **Signal to your buddy** that you are out of air by making a chopping motion at your neck with the flat of your hand.

2 **Your buddy will offer** you their octopus second stage, or, if they have one, a separate regulator attached to a pony cylinder.

3 **When your buddy is** sure that you are OK and your breathing has settled, you should lock arms and ascend to the surface.

OUT-OF-AIR PROCEDURE WITH BUDDY

If you have not kept track of your air consumption and find that you are out of air, locate your buddy and ascend using their octopus or pony cylinder. If no alternate air source is available, then buddy breathe. This involves both divers using the same regulator, with each diver taking two breaths before passing it to their buddy. This is a complex procedure, however, that needs to be practised if it is to succeed in a real-life crisis.

4 **Hold on to one another** as you rise to the surface. Make any decompression stops as you would do during a normal ascent.

your exhaled bubbles. At the surface, signal to boat cover immediately. If there is no boat, swim to the shore. Your buddy will need to be found and, as you have ascended without safety stops, you will need to be monitored for DCS (*see p.142*).

MAKING EMERGENCY LIFTS

If your buddy is unconscious or injured, keep their regulator in their mouth and perform a buoyant lift to get them to the surface. This means holding on to your buddy's harness as you ascend, using their BCD to adjust buoyancy for both of you. Alert any boat cover once at the surface. If your buddy is not breathing, artificial ventilation (AV) may be needed until medical help arrives. If there is no cover, or if you are close to shore, you may decide to tow your buddy to safety. Both towing and AV require special training; if your dive training did not cover them, a lifesaving course is recommended.

OVERCOMING PANIC

If you feel panic coming on, alert your buddy, stop moving, and steady your breathing. If your buddy panics, reassure them with hand signals but observe them from a safe distance, since a flailing arm can knock your regulator from your mouth or injure you. When they have calmed down, hold their hand or arm, make sure their regulator stays in place, and remain close until normal breathing resumes.

SIGNALLING FOR HELP
Supporting your buddy at the surface, wave one arm in a wide arc and shout to alert boat cover.

Decompression sickness

If a diver ascends too quickly, the rapid pressure change causes bubbles of nitrogen to form in tissues and blood vessels *(see pp.100–01)*, resulting in decompression sickness (DCS). This condition must be watched closely and treated quickly, since in extreme cases it is fatal.

DCS SYMPTOMS

Severe DCS may cause impaired vision and balance, convulsions, and even unconsciousness. Nitrogen bubbles can form under the skin, or become trapped in capillaries and restrict the blood supply to the lungs, slowing breathing, lowering blood pressure, and causing shock. If a bubble enters the brain or spinal cord it can lead to paralysis or even death. Symptoms usually appear between one and six hours after surfacing, but occasionally do not manifest themselves until 24 hours later. They start with minor aches in joints, rashes, and itching. These will disappear

EMERGENCY OXYGEN
It is vital that the dive boats carry an oxygen administration kit in case of emergencies.

after a few hours in mild DCS, but with severe DCS they will be precursors of serious complications. At the first sign of symptoms, request emergency medical attention (from the coastguard, if you are at sea) and give basic first aid: supply the patient with 100 per cent oxygen; keep them warm and still (lying down if possible); provide non-alcoholic fluids (ideally sports or rehydrating drinks); and apply pressure to joints to alleviate pain. The patient should be referred for medical attention and may need to be treated in a recompression chamber.

If so, provide those in charge of the chamber with the diver's symptoms and details of the dive. In the chamber, the pressure is raised until it causes gas bubbles in the diver's tissues and blood to shrink. The diver is decompressed under controlled conditions, allowing any residual nitrogen to dissipate safely.

LOOKING FOR SYMPTOMS
Skin rashes and joint pains may be precursors of more serious problems.

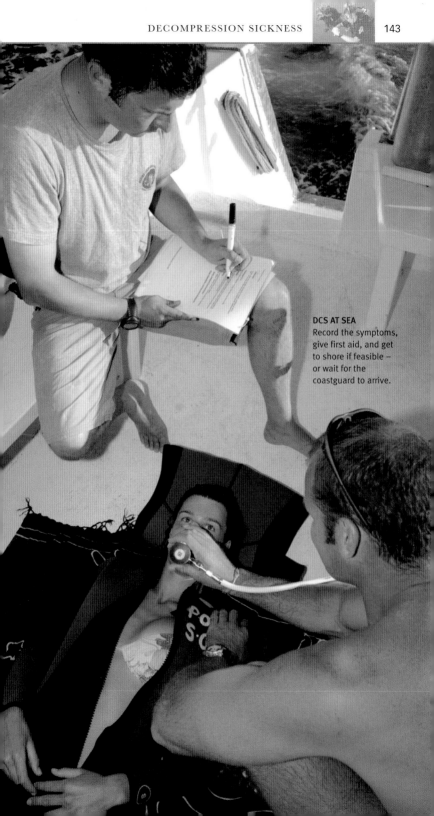

DCS AT SEA
Record the symptoms, give first aid, and get to shore if feasible – or wait for the coastguard to arrive.

Hand signals

Good communication with your dive buddy is important, not just in an emergency, but also to monitor each other's progress, share underwater experiences, and to agree when to end the dive. The most effective method of communication is to use hand signals.

USING HAND SIGNALS

Verbal communication is not an option underwater (see p.92) unless you are wearing a full-face mask, but most messages can be conveyed using a combination of hand signals and drawings on a slate. Using hand signals will allow you to exchange information with your dive buddy and even ask each other questions underwater. They can also be reassuring.

Signal to your buddy regularly during a dive, as this will ensure that you remain in close contact and can easily notify each other of any problems that may develop. Repeat any sign that is not clear to your buddy, and acknowledge every signal that he or she makes with an "OK" to show you understand. If your buddy is slow to respond to a

signal, check that they are OK. If you are diving at depth, sluggish responses may indicate the onset of nitrogen narcosis (see pp.100–01), which impairs reaction times and mental acuity.

Signals are not just limited to showing each other how much air you have left or highlighting problems. They can also be used to inform your buddy of interesting things you have seen, or to alert them to something you are both looking for, such as a particular marine organism. There are numerous signals for marine animals, and you can develop your own within your buddy pair. A common example is the use of a straight, upright hand (representing a fin) on top of your head, meaning "I have seen a shark". Signals for animals like turtles and rays can be readily improvised.

QUALIFYING THE SIGNAL
To make it clear that a signal refers specifically to yourself – for example, "watch me" – point to yourself first.

COMMON HAND SIGNALS

There are a number of standard hand signals that are essential to all divers, and you can also improvise new signals with friends. Always review signals at the start of a dive, especially if you are diving with a new buddy. Give signals to your buddy slowly and clearly, to ensure that they are understood. Use combinations of signals to convey messages more precisely (for example, something is wrong/I can't clear my ears). Below are some of the most important and common diving signals.

OK/Are you OK?
Form an O with thumb and forefinger. Point the other fingers up.

Something is wrong
Tilt the flat of your hand from side to side, palm down.

Up/Let's ascend
Point thumb straight upwards with fingers clenched in a fist.

Down/Let's go down
Point thumb downwards with fingers clenched in a fist.

100 bar (1,500psi) left
Form T-shape with hands to indicate 100 bar remaining.

50 bar (750psi) left
Make a fist, with palm outwards, to indicate 50 bar remaining.

I am out of air
Make a horizontal chopping motion across base of neck.

Stop
Present flat of hand, palm outwards, to halt buddy or other divers.

Slow down
Move palms slowly downwards together (pivoting at elbows).

Stay/Move together
Move forefingers together, until touching side by side.

Stay at this depth
Hold both hands horizontally and move one over the other.

Watch/Look
Point at your eyes, then at subject of interest, or self, or another diver.

I am cold
Hug yourself with both arms crossed to indicate chill.

I can't clear my ears
Point at ear to indicate you are having difficulty equalizing.

Feeling breathless

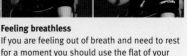
If you are feeling out of breath and need to rest for a moment you should use the flat of your hand to mimic your chest rising and falling.

Developing your skills

With any skilled pastime, it is important to keep your technique sharp. Many divers only dive once a year (or even less frequently) and it is easy to forget even basic skills during your time off from diving. Honing your skills in sheltered water is a good way to stay proficient.

PERFECTING BUOYANCY

Beginners, occasional divers, and even those who dive regularly will benefit from practising key skills in a pool or sheltered water. Buoyancy is the most fundamental diving skill of all, so is a good place to start when revising your technique. Re-familiarize yourself with buoyancy control with "fin pivots", using inhalations and exhalations to make the upper part of your body rise and fall. Keep your fins on the bottom and your legs apart. They will act as the "hinge" of your upward and downward movements. The value of this exercise is that it trains you to use breathing to adjust your buoyancy, rather than controlling it only with your BCD. Also, try swimming through a hoop with your arms folded – this will also test your buoyancy control and give you an idea of the space you can squeeze through with full kit on.

1 **To practise fin pivots,** breathe in gently and feel your upper body rise, keeping your fin tips on the floor. Stop at a 45° angle to the bottom.

2 **Slowly release the air** in your lungs until your body begins falling. Then, before you hit the bottom, begin inhaling again.

CONFIDENCE-BUILDING EXERCISES

Mask clearing is one of the most basic, yet important, skills in diving. Building co-ordination and confidence by removing and replacing your mask, and even performing tasks without it, will improve your diving. It will also prepare you for minor upsets like your mask being accidentally dislodged. Begin building up your confidence slowly by removing and replacing your mask in shallow water, before repeating the exercise in deeper water. Repeat whilst swimming and then try it with your regulator removed. You can also try swapping masks with your buddy. This is simply a variation on the solo exercises but also helps you to develop useful co-operative skills.

Giving yourself other kit handicaps can also help improve your confidence underwater. Try swimming with just one fin, for example. Losing a fin can happen on an open-water dive, but if you are already prepared, you will be able to cope with the situation calmly and effectively. Practise all of these exercises in a pool or sheltered water.

REDUCED VISIBILITY
Most divers feel uncomfortable swimming with their mask removed, but, with practice, you will become confident performing tasks without it.

1 **To exchange masks**, kneel on the bottom facing each other. Give each other the "OK" signal, then remove your masks, while continuing to breathe normally.

2 **Swap masks** with your partner. It is much easier to keep your eyes open throughout the exchange, but perfecting this by touch, with your eyes closed, is a very useful exercise.

3 **Don each other's masks**, and blow them clear (*see p.139*). Ignore any urge you feel to hurry when putting the mask on. In particular, make sure the strap is not twisted.

4 **Adjust the mask** for comfort, then open your eyes and signal OK to indicate a successful swap. The masks can then be swapped back again for further practice.

VARYING THE ROUTINE

Skills exercises don't have to be simple drills. Introducing an element of fun or setting an objective can motivate you to train for longer. Games for the pool or sheltered water include "hide the mask", which forces you to navigate and search without your mask; or, you can practise breath control by performing simple exercises without breathing apparatus, such as retrieving objects from the bottom, or swimming through a series of hoops, extending the course as your stamina improves.

1 **"Hide the mask"** begins with an "OK" signal from the seeker, once the diver who is going to hide the mask has removed it.

2 **The seeker closes his eyes** while the hider finds a corner of the pool to put the mask in, and returns to signal the seeker to start searching.

3 **The seeker opens his eyes** and starts to methodically search the pool bottom until the mask is found and replaced.

REMOVING AND REPLACING KIT

Familiarity with your basic kit is a vital skill. One exercise that helps to foster confidence in this area is to remove your scuba unit – that is, your BCD and breathing apparatus, all fully connected – and put it back on underwater, keeping your regulator in your mouth throughout. This exercise should be carried out at the bottom of a pool or in sheltered water, and if you are a beginner or haven't tried this before, it may be useful to have an instructor present who can guide you through the process. Start by undoing all fastening clips on the front of your BCD and pull your left arm out of it first (even if you are left-handed), using your right arm to pull it around to your right. The BCD jacket should now be in front of you, between you and the cylinder. Keep the hose for your regulator second stage between your arms (otherwise it may get caught under your shoulder strap when you re-don the unit). Then put the scuba unit back on by reversing the operation.

For an extra challenge, once you have removed your BCD, try removing your regulator from your mouth and swimming away to a distance of about 10m (33ft), before returning and putting your kit back on again.

Alternatively, try entering the water without your kit, then putting it on while treading water, keeping your head above the surface. This is a much more difficult exercise, and should only be carried out under the guidance of an instructor.

1 **To take off** your scuba unit underwater, undo all clips and take your left arm out of the BCD, gripping the jacket with your right hand. Breathe normally through your regulator.

2 **Pull the whole unit round** in front of you. Keep a firm grip on your BCD to avoid losing hold of the scuba unit.

3 **To re-don kit** reverse the operation, making sure all clips and fastenings are re-connected as before.

Dive fitness

As a diver, you are reliant on your body as well as your kit for a safe and enjoyable dive – so make sure both are well maintained. Diving regularly helps keep you in shape, but it is important to maintain your fitness levels if you go for long periods without diving.

HOW FITNESS AFFECTS DIVING

Staying fit reduces some of the risks associated with diving, and makes it more enjoyable. Having healthy lungs and an efficient circulatory system means you will use less air, so dives last longer. A good level of cardiovascular fitness will also help to prevent panic attacks, which can be triggered by a buildup of carbon dioxide in the blood. A fit body will expel this by-product of respiration more efficiently, reducing that risk. General strength is required for lifting equipment and other incidental tasks.

Maintaining a healthy weight for your size is also advisable. When you dive, nitrogen builds up in the tissues of your body with each intake of breath, and fat retains nitrogen longer than all other tissue types. Therefore, if you are overweight and breathe rapidly because you are out of shape, you expose yourself to an increased risk of DCS (*see pp.142–43*).

Weight loss and gain can also alter your buoyancy. Fat is inherently buoyant, so if you have put on or lost a lot of weight since your last dive, you must adjust how much lead weight you carry as ballast accordingly (*see pp.118–21*).

based on the exercises overleaf could start, for example, with ten repetitions of each, building up to 50, three times a week. You should also aim to undertake regular cardiovascular exercise (such as walking or cycling), for 30 minutes twice or three times a week to improve your general fitness and respiratory health.

Whatever exercise routine you decide to adopt, try to incorporate it into your normal daily routine wherever possible. A walk to work every day does more good than a monthly gym session. Never exercise after diving. This is a time when it is important not to do any strenuous activities as there is still residual nitrogen in your body, and this may form bubbles if you exercise too hard. Do some gentle stretches and take it easy for the rest of the day. Avoid hot baths or showers after diving as these can also raise your vulnerability to DCS.

TALKING THINGS THROUGH
If you have any injuries or physically weak areas, let those diving with you know before you dive. Don't be afraid to ask for assistance if this will help prevent injury.

DEVELOPING A FITNESS REGIME

There is no quick fix for getting and staying fit. Aim to exercise regularly, tailoring your routine to strengthen the muscles you use most during diving: those of your back, legs, shoulders, and arms. If you do not already exercise regularly, seek medical advice before embarking on a fitness routine. Start gently with easy exercises, and build up slowly. A routine

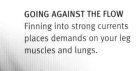

GOING AGAINST THE FLOW
Finning into strong currents places demands on your leg muscles and lungs.

PROTECT YOUR BACK

Be very careful when carrying and loading heavy kit. A poor lifting technique can result in pulled muscles, and possibly long-term back problems. A back injury can spoil a trip, but diving with a weak back can also be a safety risk: surface manoeuvres, climbing onto boats, and exiting surf, for example, are all compromised by weakness in this area. If your lower back is vulnerable, consider transferring your weights from a belt to a harness (*see p.70*).

Loading dive equipment

WARMING UP

Always warm up and stretch – especially your thighs, calves, and upper and lower back – before exercising, and spend a few minutes gently stretching and cooling down afterwards. Many sporting injuries are caused by failure to warm-up properly, so treat it as an important part of your fitness routine.

ARM AND LEG EXERCISES

Basic squats build up strength in your legs. Standing upright with your feet shoulder-width apart and your knees soft, place your hands on your hips and shift the weight back into your heels. Keeping your head and chest pointing forwards and your back straight, bend at the hip and knees, as if you were sitting down on to a chair. Keep your heels on the floor; you should be able to move your toes as all your weight is on your heels. Straighten and repeat.

Lunges are a more advanced exercise for legs. Stand upright with one foot a good stride in front of the other, with your

BASIC PRESS-UP
The press-up is a great all-round exercise for the upper body and arms. Beginners can start with their knees resting on the ground.

hips parallel and your toes forward. Your back heel should be off the ground and your front foot flat on the floor. Both knees should be bent and your back straight. Drop your body weight towards the floor until your front knee is bent at a 90° angle. You may have to tilt your pelvis forward to get this position right. Rise up and repeat.

Bicep curls strengthen the biceps – muscles in the upper arms that are used whenever you lift anything. Using hand weights or a weighted bar, stand upright,

HEALTHY LUNGS
Cardiovascular training builds up lung capacity, making snorkelling feel even more effortless.

LUNGE EXERCISE
Practising lunges in front of a mirror will help
you to get the position of your front leg right:
knee directly over foot, bent to a right-angle.

ABDOMINAL CRUNCH
Always keep your lower back flat on the floor and
never arched. For a harder workout, aim your right
elbow to your left knee, and vice versa.

with your back straight and knees slightly
soft, and hold the weights in your hands
with your palms facing upwards. Without
rocking or moving your shoulders, bend
the arms towards the chest and then
lower, taking care not to lock the elbows.

EXERCISING YOUR TORSO
Press-ups strengthen your shoulders,
upper body, and core muscles. Lying on
your front, bend your knees, curl your
toes under your feet, and place your
hands shoulder-width apart below your

shoulders. Press your body weight up
and down from this position. Keep your
back straight at all times and your
elbows pointing out to the sides.

Crunches strengthen abdominal
muscles, which will help protect your
lower back. Lying on your back, bend
your knees slightly and place the soles
of your feet on the floor. Place your
fingertips behind your ears and lift your
upper torso and shoulders off the floor.
Hold this for three to five seconds while
looking forward, then lower and repeat.

HYDRATION AND NUTRITION

During a dive, you can burn as much energy as you would playing an aerobic sport, such as squash or badminton. The precise amount will vary according to your fitness, the temperature of the water, and any prevailing currents. But while it is tempting to stoke up on a large cooked breakfast in preparation for a day's diving, better food choices before a dive are complex carbohydrates, which will keep you feeling fuller for longer and provide a steady supply of blood sugar to maximize energy levels while you are diving. Some foods may make you feel uncomfortable on a dive – commonly, greasy or hot and spicy dishes – so these are best avoided.

After a dive, you need to replace the energy you have burned with foods that release energy into your blood relatively quickly, such as refined carbohydrates. Have something to eat within an hour of surfacing, if possible. Energy-replacement drinks can be a quick fix, but avoid those with a high caffeine content.

GOOD DIVING FOODS
Wholegrain bread, pulses, and unrefined cereals and pasta release energy slowly during a dive. Dried fruit and nuts make good snacks.

Above all, the most important thing is to remain well hydrated before and after a dive. Your physical performance will be reduced if you become even mildly dehydrated and this is a big issue if you are diving in warm waters where the outside temperature is also high. Aim to drink at least 2 litres (3½ pints) of water during the course of the day (more if it is hot). This will help to reduce muscle cramps and fatigue, and also helps decrease the risk of DCS.

AVOIDING PROBLEMS

It is important to get plenty of sleep before and after diving, to give your body a chance to recharge. Diving is physically demanding, and if you are run down you are more susceptible to catching colds. If you do have a cough or a cold, you should not dive, because some symptoms of respiratory illness can prevent you from being able to equalize and may increase your vulnerability to DCS (*see pp.100–01*). Avoid taking decongestants as these can impair your performance underwater.

STAYING HYDRATED
Make sure you drink plenty of still water to maintain good hydration. Tea, coffee, and fizzy drinks are no substitute.

FOODS TO EAT WHEN DIVING

The following list gives examples of the sorts of foods it is good to include in meals and snacks before and after a dive:

BEFORE A DIVE Granary, wholemeal, or rye bread; wholemeal pasta; sweet potatoes; brown rice; porridge; bran-based cereals; sugar-free muesli; pulses and nuts; beans; leafy vegetables; and plain yogurt.

AFTER A DIVE Pasta and rice (ideally in a salad or low fat sauce); potatoes; fresh fruit; white bread or bagels.

AFTER A DIVE
It's tempting to make for the bar after a day's diving, but have something to eat, too. Even standing still in cold water burns calories.

So, too, can alcoholic drinks, which are best avoided the night before a dive as they can also contribute to dehydration. Divers sometimes experience minor ear infections, especially after days of continuous diving or if diving in slightly polluted waters. There are various ways of avoiding ear problems, including rinsing the ears with fresh water after every dive, or using an alcohol-based fluid designed for swimmer's ear.

Lastly, you should have a regular dive medical to check that you are in good enough shape to dive. If, between medicals, there have been any changes in your health since you last dived, then it is always best to have a checkup.

Going diving

Introduction

Becoming a qualified diver is a tremendously exciting experience, but the range of choices facing you post-qualification can be daunting. The joy of diving is that within one sport lies a host of different specialities, all requiring different skills, knowledge, and planning techniques.

RECREATIONAL DIVING

Upon qualification, the world of diving opens up to you. Whether you become a casual resort diver or an advanced technical diver with a liking for the more extreme elements of the sport, only time and experience will tell.

The broad spectrum of recreational diving encompasses many different environments and experiences, including reefs, caves and caverns, wreck diving, ice diving, freshwater diving, and night diving. There are also various specialist activities in which you can participate, such as filming and photography, wildlife and conservation diving, underwater archaeology, and free diving (diving without an air supply). The majority of divers find that they derive most enjoyment from sampling a range of different environments and activities, rather than limiting themselves to one specific aspect of diving.

Many new divers aim to acquire further specializations, badges, and qualifications from the moment they pass their initial training course. This urge, while understandable, should be tempered by the need to gain general diving experience. There is no substitute for time spent in the water – what was once intimidating becomes familiar, helpful routines start to emerge, skills and safety consciousness improve, and knowledge increases. You will also feel more confident and comfortable in the water as you learn to tailor your kit configuration to your own needs.

Only when you have served your "apprenticeship" by gaining experience of different environments and diving skills should you make any decisions about future specializations. Without putting in the hours underwater, you will find further training and courses more difficult, no matter how well structured and delivered they are. In addition, the more experience you have, the more aware you will be of your own likes, dislikes, and aptitudes, allowing you to make more informed choices for the future direction of your diving.

BEACH BRIEFING
Becoming confident enough to conduct your own dives without a guide or instructor gives you greater freedom. Always plan and brief dives thoroughly before entering the water.

Fortunately, gaining general diving experience is relatively easy, with dive groups and clubs springing up in abundance to meet the sport's growing appeal. Furthermore, dive travel is so well established that almost any region of the world is now accessible, and opportunities to dive exist in virtually every coastal resort around the world. A whole range of diving encounters are available – from a casual beach dive through to full-blown expeditions – all easy to arrange via the internet or through dedicated dive travel agencies.

PLOTTING YOUR FUTURE COURSE
The more experience you gain, the better informed you will be when deciding whether or not to pursue a particular aspect of diving.

PROFESSIONAL DIVING

The enjoyment of diving leads some people to consider a full-time career in which diving plays an essential part. Diving professionals range from recreational instructors and dive masters, whose main role is to introduce others to diving, through to military experts, commercial specialists, scientific divers, fishermen, and underwater cameramen and photographers.

Further skills are always needed to succeed in your chosen career – an underwater film-maker, for example, must be an accomplished camera operator as well as a superb diver, and an instructor needs good communication and teaching skills, in addition to first-class abilities in the water.

Professional diving can offer excellent rewards, both personal and financial, but they tend to be well earned. Professionals must dive in all conditions and at all times, and the work is often arduous and sometimes dangerous.

PREPARING FOR AN ICE DIVE
Diving under ice is thrilling, but it is not for beginners. The hazards of enclosed surroundings and extreme cold mean that special training is required.

Identifying your aims

Time spent researching a dive is time well spent. Not only does it help you to unearth new attractions and clarify the aims of the dive, but it is also likely to heighten anticipation, enhance safety, and maximize the pleasure and interest you derive from the trip.

ASSESSING AIMS

The nature of dive research will vary from trip to trip, but certain core issues should always be taken into consideration.

Identifying the divers is obviously one of the first items to be addressed. Diving is not, as a rule, an individual sport, so of necessity others will be involved in the dive itself. The experience and qualifications of divers within a group will vary, and what may be a comfortable dive for one person may be extreme for another. Time spent

BEGINNING RESEARCH
Use magazines, books, and maps to highlight basic issues that you can then investigate in depth on the internet.

discussing qualifications and experience levels may well prove invaluable in establishing the ideal dive location and activity for the group as a whole.

Along with making sure that you have the right mix of divers, you will need to ensure that their aims are not likely to conflict. Imagine the scenario, for example, of a keen photographer preparing to take an

TROPICAL CONSIDERATIONS
When planning tropical dives, consider the effect of local weather patterns. Run-off from tropical islands in the wet season, for example, may impair visibility.

DIVING WEBSITE
The internet is an invaluable research resource, allowing you to access the opinions and advice of authoritative dive organizations.

award-winning image of a sunken ship, when an impatient wreck-enthusiast swims in front of the camera lens and spoils the shot. Establishing the main aim of the dive at the outset, or even allocating buddy teams with the same interests, should prevent such problems.

When diving with a local operator, try to check out their credentials. In many parts of the world there are associations set up by groups of respectable operators to govern the local dive industry. Failing that, many tourist boards and even government agencies require dive operators to register – it is always worth getting an independent view of your potential host from these organizations.

LOCATION AND TIME

Conditions can vary greatly along even the most bland section of coastline or within the most innocuous looking body of water. Choosing an exact site in advance has the benefit of allowing very specific research into local issues. Key questions to be answered include: what are the hazards involved? Where are the established entry and exit points? What are the divers likely to encounter during the dive? What is the tidal range? What are the prevailing currents?

The timing of the trip is also important. Tides, for example, may affect not only visibility, but also the

marine life present, as well as entry and exit considerations. Marine life will also be influenced by seasonal variations, as will water temperatures. Furthermore, a different range of marine animals may well be present at night than during the day, while boat traffic and use of the area for other watersports will vary throughout the day and the week. Diving at the wrong time can make the event a disappointing experience.

Safety is the most important area of your research. You will need to assess the conditions you are likely to encounter – waves, currents, depth, and temperature – and the facilities available to you should an accident occur. You should not turn up at a dive site unless you know the exact location of the nearest medical centre, recompression chamber, and casualty evacuation facilities. Knowing how to contact these agencies in an emergency is also crucial – researching phone numbers in the comfort of your own home is infinitely better than trying to do it on a rocking boat whilst caring for an injured diver.

UNDER THE ICE
The possibilities for thrilling diving trips around the world are almost endless, limited only by time, budget, and imagination!

Planning a trip

Armed with the fruits of your research, you will have a clear idea of where you want to dive, when you want to go, who you will be diving with, and what you will see when you get there. The final task before your departure is to plan the trip in as much detail as possible.

REALISTIC TIMETABLING

Most trips revolve around a key moment in time – the instant when the divers enter the water. This is often determined by a certain phase in the tide when the diving is most favourable, or by the desire to dive at a specific time of the day or night, such as when the Sun is high for photography, or in the gathering dusk when the reef is at its most active. A realistic, workable timetable is thus vital to achieve such time-specific goals.

Devising a timetable, such as the chart below, by working backwards from the moment you aim to enter the water is the best way to plan your diving day. This method is used by many divers to

PACKING THE KIT
Checklists and routines will help to ensure that all your kit makes it to the dive site.

ensure that their diving is as stress-free and as enjoyable as possible.

PRESSURE TEST

Before you start packing your equipment for a dive, carry out a pressure test. This involves rigging the kit to a cylinder, and ensuring that the seals and regulators are all functioning as they ought to be. This is also a useful means of ensuring that your cylinder is full prior to departing for the dive site. There is no more sickening sensation than journeying to a dive site, looking out over perfect conditions, assembling your dive kit, and turning on the air to be greeted by a cacophony of hissing regulators and seals – or indeed the cylinder itself being empty.

REVERSE TIMETABLING

A diver knows they must enter the water at 3:00 pm to dive during slack water between the tides. They work backwards from this to calculate a realistic departure hour, building in a contingency to ensure arrival at the dive site in good time.

Activity	Time Taken	Actual time
Entering the water		3:00 pm
Kitting up and buddy checks	25 mins	2:35 pm
Site inspection and briefing	40 mins	1:55 pm
Arrival and parking	10 mins	1:45 pm
Journey to site	1 hour	12:45 pm
Loading car	30 mins	12:15 pm
Checking and packing dive gear	30 mins	11:45 am
Contingency time	30 mins	11:15 am

PACKING WITH CARE

The greatest cause of the postponement or cancellation of dives is forgetting items of kit. A fool-proof method of guaranteeing that you pack all of your equipment is to load your kit into your dive bag at home in the order that you will be putting it on at the dive site. Visualizing your arrival at the site and kitting up will see you load your kit bag in the following sequence: suit, bootees, knife, weight belt, cylinder, BCD, regulator, computer, hood, mask,

CAVE DIVING
For more complicated trips, such as cave dives, specialized equipment may be necessary, and this must be factored into your planning.

snorkel, fins, gloves, and finally any ancillary items (delayed SMB, torch, slate, and so on).

An alternative packing technique is to run through a checklist from head to toe, and again pack your gear in that order. The list then runs: hood, mask, snorkel, suit, regulator, BCD, cylinder, computer, gloves, weight belt, knife, bootees, fins.

There are innumerable ways of trying to ensure that no item of equipment is forgotten, but the most effective are those that are convenient, quickly become a habit, and take little time.

DIVERS ENTERING THE WATER
A realistic timetable will ensure that kitting up and briefing on site is not rushed, and that you do not miss your "window" of opportunity with the tide.

Site-specific planning

Pre-dive research is important, but there is no substitute for a thorough assessment of the site on the day of the dive. This may highlight issues not raised by your research, and allow you to make adjustments to accommodate changes in conditions before the dive commences.

FINALIZING YOUR PLAN

Once you know when and where you are going to dive, you must devise a practical plan for each of the dives you mean to conduct on the day. Whether you are planning for just yourself and a friend, or for a larger group, always take local conditions into account before settling on a final dive plan.

A dive plan must address the following key points. Firstly, it should broadly define the aim of the dive, the dive's entrance and exit points, and its general route, as well as describing an alternative exit in case the main choice is inaccessible. It should also define the dive's maximum depth and time, as well as decompression restrictions, and should specify the minimum reserve of air that divers must surface with at the conclusion of the dive.

Depending on the aim of the dive and the experience of the group, special signals may be required. It is imperative to select diver recall systems – the signals or sounds that will be used to indicate

UNLOADING THE KIT
Even if you feel sure that every item of kit was packed before the journey, double-check on site that you have everything you need.

that the dive should be aborted. Your plans for the dive should also identify any potential hazards that may be encountered. If an incident occurs, what procedures should be followed? Define what action to take if divers become separated – in murky waters, this is one of the most common reasons for dives being aborted. Make sure that any divers you intend to pair together as buddies share similar interests or levels of experience, so that there are no conflicts of interest during the dive.

Assess local conditions and examine weather reports; worsening weather conditions might dictate a move to a more sheltered site nearby, or rule out the use of a boat. Finally, ensure that the designated shore marshal or dive supervisor understands their duties, including recording cylinder pressures and the times that divers enter the water, and responding to incidents. Provide them with contact details of local agencies to be informed in the event of an emergency.

INSPECTING THE DIVE SITE
Resist the temptation to enter the water as quickly as possible. Assess the conditions and inspect the site, noting the dive's entry and exit points.

THE DIVE BRIEFING

The final task is to brief the entire dive crew. The briefing, which should ideally take place overlooking the dive site, must cover all aspects of the dive plan, and include not only divers, but also shore marshals, deck hands, and anyone else associated with the dive.

At the end of the briefing, ensure that all the divers clearly understand the constraints of the dive plan, and are fully prepared for the dive. After taking any final questions from the group, the dive is ready to commence.

The simple maxim "plan the dive, and dive the plan" is an old one, but its worth has been proven over time. Following it means that all of the divers will get the most they can from the dive, and, importantly, will enjoy it in safety.

ENTERING THE WATER
By the time you enter the water, everyone involved with the dive should be fully aware of the dive parameters.

Wreck diving

Exploring wrecks is – for many people – the main reason to dive. This activity is particularly popular in countries without coral reefs to dive on. However, it also has a general appeal, because wrecks give a historical context for a dive and demand mastery of specialist skills.

DIVING ON WRECKS

Sunken ships have an obvious attraction as sites of archaeological and historical interest. A wreck is a time capsule from a given period, and the waters around most countries contain thousands of them.

Although most known wrecks are metal-hulled vessels, unusual conditions will sometimes preserve wooden-hulled ships dating back hundreds of years. These provide an excellent opportunity to examine past shipbuilding techniques, and sometimes hold interesting and unusual artefacts. To explore significant wrecks, you should be properly trained and preferably work within an archaeological organization.

Information on recent wrecks, such as warships sunk during the two World Wars, is usually readily accessible. It is often possible to research the specifications and history of the vessel, along with details of her crew and

DESCENDING A SHOTLINE
Popular wrecks often have a buoy moored to their structure to make location and descent easier.

mission. Historical records may give details of the events surrounding the sinking of the ship.

Wrecks also make for good diving because they act as artificial reefs, attracting all sorts of marine life. Over time, the structure becomes encrusted with marine growth, especially filter-feeders, if it lies in a tidal stream. Fish exploit the safety and shelter that wrecks offer: smaller fish tend to shoal around wrecks; larger fish, such as moray or conger eels, can hide safely in nooks and crannies; and predators, such as sharks, may be found in the wreck's surroundings, because they feed off the smaller fish.

PREPARATION AND SKILLS

Wreck diving can be a fascinating activity, but it is not without risks. Under no circumstances go inside a wreck if you lack appropriate training and equipment; the danger of entrapment is very real, and specialist knowledge and skills are required to enter wrecks safely. Exploring the outside of wrecks is safer, but always treat such sites with respect.

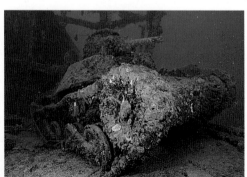

TANK IN TRUK LAGOON, SOUTH PACIFIC
Wreck diving is not just about ships; crashed aircraft and military vehicles carried by sunken vessels provide equally enthralling alternatives.

SUNKEN LEVIATHAN
The sight of a major wreck, such as the
Giannis D in the Red Sea, rarely fails to
send shivers down the spine.

FINNING TECHNIQUE

Wrecks often contain a lot of static silt and mud, which is easily disturbed by changes in water currents caused by divers finning overhead. Good visibility can suddenly and dramatically change to almost nil, so using a frog kick (*see p.123*), which generates relatively little turbulence, is recommended to minimize disruption of the silt. The best time for wreck diving is at slack water, but a small current can help sweep away any disturbed silt.

USING SHOTLINES

When you arrive at the dive site, ensure that your boat cover is moored to the wreck's marker buoy. If it doesn't have one, an experienced diver needs to swim down and attach a shotline directly to

DIVING IN CONFINED SPACES
Wreck penetration often involves exploring in dark, confined spaces. It is not recommended for those with claustrophobic tendencies.

the wreck, to act as a guide for other divers to follow. If you intend to return to the surface via the same shotline, it can be useful to use a distance line (*see p.127*) to help you find your way back to the bottom of the shotline, especially in poor visibility. If you plan to ascend from another part of the wreck, you should deploy a DSMB (*see pp.130–31*).

PENETRATING WRECKS

When wreck diving, you should carry back-ups of certain pieces of kit, such as your reel and your torch, as well as an independent air source, such as a pony cylinder (*see p.68*), in case of emergencies. You must also ensure that you follow the "Rule of Thirds" (*see p.117*) with your air consumption – a third of your air is used to descend to the site and

LEVEL POSITIONING
The frog kick is a gentle swimming stoke that mainly causes turbulence in the water behind and not below you, and so does not kick up silt.

explore, a third to return to the point of entry, and a third is left in reserve as a contingency. Allow extra time at the end of the dive to find the shotline, and do not take any unnecessary risks with your dive time, depth, or penetration.

EXPLORATION TIPS

It is a good idea to investigate the area around a wreck, as artefacts may well have spread over time and pieces of wreckage may have been knocked off that might be of interest, but take great care. Always be aware that the structure (both inside and outside a wreck) may be much degraded and potentially dangerous. Wear protective gloves, even in warm waters, as corroded metal can be sharp. Wrecks are often heavily fished, so carry a knife in case you become entangled in fishing line. You also need a powerful torch (and a back-up) to illuminate your way in poor visibility, and to signal to your buddy. In some very enclosed wrecks, it is advisable to wear a helmet and head torch.

DIVER USING WRECK KIT
Carrying extra air and Nitrox is a failsafe, and can help to extend dive times and shorten decompression stops. Good light sources and dive plan information are also essential.

THE GOLDEN RULE

Never remove items from a wreck. As with any artefact, marine finds are more useful to archaeologists when examined *in situ*, and their context provides more information about the wreck than if they are handed in without details of where they were located. Worse still is if they are lost forever in a diver's personal artefact collection.

US troopship artefacts

RESPONSIBILITIES WHEN DIVING

Wrecks are historical sites, and just as you would not remove artefacts on an historical site on land, such as a castle or monument, you should also respect a wreck and not damage it in any way. Be considerate of the enjoyment of others who may dive the wreck after you. Dive responsibly and with care, and do not remove anything without being given permission to do so. When you find an artefact, such as a ship's bell, after

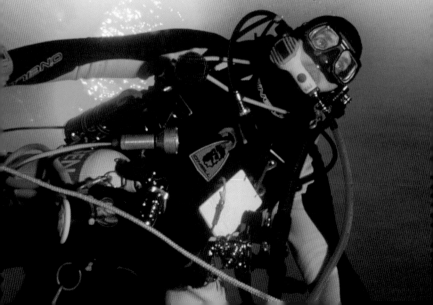

a long, hard search, you may feel that you deserve to be able to take it away as a trophy, but all such discoveries should remain where they were found, or be raised by trained archaeologists for preservation in a museum.

WOODEN-HULLED VESSELS

Most of the wrecks that you are likely to explore will be metal-hulled, but wooden ships are also preserved under some conditions. Avoid touching the wooden structure, as it is likely to be extremely fragile. Historic wooden vessels may have been lying protected under sand or silt for many hundreds of years. If you want to expose parts of the wreckage for any reason, you should do so by wafting your hand over it to remove the silt, creating a current to take the silt away.

WRECKED BY DESIGN
The former US Coastguard cutter *Keith Tibbetts* was sunk deliberately at Cayman Brac to provide an artificial reef for divers to explore.

LIVE AMMUNITION

Wrecks from the two World Wars can provide fascinating dive experiences for military history enthusiasts, but remember at all times that they may also contain live ammunition that could potentially be very dangerous. Never touch anything that resembles a shell or mine, and research what you are likely to find on the wreck before diving.

ARTIFICIAL REEFS

At some popular dive sites, wrecks have been sunk deliberately to provide a safe, interesting dive at a reasonable depth for recreational divers. Such wrecks quickly become colonized by marine life and provide a fantastic opportunity for diving and marine research. They are generally a good place to start wreck diving, as the structure will be intact and any hazards will have been removed. At some wreck sites there are special diving trails with underwater display boards to explain

the layout. There may also be laminated booklets that you can take with you on the dive, which enable you to read about the most interesting features of the wreck whilst on site.

VIRGIN WRECKS

Every wreck diver's dream is to find a previously undiscovered wreck – and there are certainly still plenty to be found. Before you embark on such a search, you should familiarize yourself with the law regarding wrecks, and any wreck you find should be reported to the authorities. Generally speaking, you can dive any wreck around the world apart from those that are designated as historic wrecks and war graves, which are restricted and require special permission to dive.

Locating a virgin wreck can be a difficult, lengthy task, and is liable to be expensive. But a modern hardboat with an experienced skipper and hi-tech equipment such as an echo sounder, 3D imaging of the seabed, and a GPS system, combined with charts and some good background research on your part, could help you hit the jackpot. Many undiscovered wrecks are found in very deep water, so ensure that you are fully qualified and appropriately trained before undertaking deep wreck dives.

RESPECTING HISTORY
Many wrecks sunk during conflict are official war graves and may not be dived.

FINDING OUT MORE

If your interest in a wreck goes beyond merely diving it and you wish to enhance your dive by finding out more about the wreck's history, there are a number of available sources of information. Good starting points include books on wrecks in the area that you are diving, and using the internet to do some background research. There are numerous websites and forums where you can discover more about wrecks, and also make contact with other divers interested in finding new wrecks. Furthermore, local museums may have displays of artefacts recovered from wrecks in the area, and local divers and boat skippers may be able to reveal information about the history of a wreck.

EXPLORING VIRGIN WRECKS

If you are searching for a particular undiscovered wreck, it is important to start your research in the archive. Studying the ship's specifications and plans will help you identify any remains that you find, and determine whether they belong to the subject of your search. It is a good idea to take video footage of anything you find on a dive, as this is a non-intrusive method of recording the remains, and the footage will be critical in identifying the wreck and for showing to experts.

Navigational chart

Nature and conservation diving

Recreational divers represent a huge pool of manpower that can potentially contribute to conservation work. Many divers take up the sport due to an inherent fascination with nature, and more and more are now applying their skills to organized conservation projects.

DIVING RESPONSIBLY

Most divers have a certain level of knowledge and enthusiasm for marine life and the ocean environment, and realize that along with the thrill of exploration comes responsibility. Divers are in a unique position to observe the deterioration of busy coastal margins around the world and, with the development of the modern eco-tourism market, are now also able to actively contribute to conservation projects in the same regions.

At the most basic level, conservation work simply means responsible diving by anyone taking up the sport in the first place. Always adhere to a "no-touch" rule when diving delicate reef systems;

GOOD PREPARATION
A group of divers at a conservation site discuss the work they will be conducting.

you will find this vigorously enforced by most dive operations around the world. Good buoyancy control, streamlined equipment, and a respect for the varied inhabitants of the sea are now widely taught as the only way to dive, and as a result even heavily dived areas experience less habitat disturbance than they used to.

MAKING A DIFFERENCE

Voluntary work, though often conducted at the most basic level, can nonetheless be extremely significant at a local and even international level. The efforts of one voluntary organization alone – Coral Cay Conservation – contributed greatly towards the establishment of the Belize Barrier Reef (*see pp.316–17*) as a World Heritage Site, and have seen eight Marine Protected Areas (MPAs) established around the world in the last 20 years.

Formally observing and recording marine life is not just the preserve of the scientific expedition. Significant work has been done by enthusiastic amateurs. Organized conservation and monitoring projects extend from casual one-day beach clean-ups run by local diving clubs, right through to multi-national operations setting up

USING ID SLATES
To familiarize themselves with marine life during a dive, divers use species identification slates – waterproof cards with pictures of the species likely to be found at the dive site.

nature reserves throughout the world. Diving conservation is now big business, with hundreds of organizations around the world claiming (with varying levels of accuracy) to run projects that contribute to scientific knowledge or the establishment of marine reserves and protected areas. Most organizations put volunteers through an intense training period before allowing them to take part in even relatively simple sampling or monitoring programmes.

REEF EXPOSED
A healthy reef at low tide. Rising global temperatures are harming coral, and sights like this may become less common in future years.

FIRST PRINCIPLES

There are two principal considerations that must be borne in mind by anyone working as a diver on a marine conservation project. The first is safety. You need good diving skills, and enough experience to be able to keep a watchful eye on the ever-present factors of depth, time, and potential hazards while simultaneously making meticulous observations. Enthusiasm for the work being undertaken must not distract you

PRESERVING HABITATS
Carrying out conservation work not only allows you to give something back to the marine environment, but may give you the opportunity to visit exotic destinations.

from the normal rules of safe diving. The second factor is consideration for marine life. Unless you are working under the direction of a well-recognized conservation group, you must only gather data without touching or harming the marine environment. Both marine algae and animals should be recorded only *in situ*.

WORKING TOWARDS OBJECTIVES

Good science starts with a clear means to identify the subject of the research. In the case of most amateur enthusiasts, this means reading up in accurate reference works and guides about the dive environment in question. A further, essential part of any observation programme is the need to record data effectively, requiring not only a means of noting down results, but a framework of headings and categories that remain the same for the entire observation

FINDING A PROJECT

Conservation, to paraphrase an old adage, begins at home. There are marine ecology programmes in most countries and interested divers can usually find groups in their area that contribute to protecting the local marine environment. Search the internet and specialist diving magazines to find suitable organizations local to you.

programme. Only by combining these two important factors – accurate identification and consistent record-keeping – can you accomplish truly effective research and monitoring. Repeated observation of species populations within a given area, for example, can provide invaluable data for analysis by research groups. Your recordings may help local initiatives, or possibly go forward to form part of a much larger-scale project, in which

CORAL MONITORING PROGRAMME
Advanced or potentially invasive techniques should only be used under the direction of a recognized conservation group.

DIVING AT A MARINE RESERVE
Even a little research into how and why an area is protected will add food for thought to your enjoyment of the dive.

complex statistical techniques may be used to draw conclusions with far greater significance than you perhaps imagined when gathering your data.

EQUIPPED FOR THE JOB

Although this is the age of the computer and of instant global communications, most scientific expeditions still use some fairly basic equipment to record data in the field. Observation strategies can begin with nothing more than a keen pair of eyes, an underwater slate, and a good guide book. An additional item that can be extremely useful is a magnifying glass. This simple piece of kit greatly enhances enjoyment and has become essential for many divers around the world when diving complex reefs.

Underwater photography and videography, if correctly documented, can provide potentially valuable information. In an organized programme, you may receive training in advanced techniques, such as the use of catch bags, nets, and quadrats, or in ways

to ensure that the target region is sampled effectively, such as GPS systems and datum lines. Effective sampling and observation does not necessarily require high-tech gadgets, but an effective strategy to ensure scientific integrity in the results you achieve is essential.

A CAREER IN CONSERVATION

Should you wish to develop your interest in conservation techniques, there are many courses and reference works available. Formal qualifications may be sought at undergraduate and postgraduate level, although demand for places is extremely high. Jobs in this area are also relatively difficult to come by. However, the rewards for persisting in either scientific or conservation work can be immense.

The loggerhead turtle, an endangered species

Photography and videography

Since the dawn of diving, there has been interest in capturing images of the remarkable ecosystems and animals of the sea. Although underwater photography was initially a complex process, advances in technology have seen it become an accessible, absorbing pastime.

EARLY PIONEERS

The development of underwater filming and photography has mirrored the evolution of diving itself. Early pioneers made their own waterproof housings for cameras, but the invention of the O-ring (enabling watertight hydraulic seals) in 1937 and the Aqua Lung in 1943 convinced camera companies that they should make and sell their own designs.

What prompted this was the huge appetite for images of the underwater world. The rapid growth of recreational diving, and growing interest in underwater films among cinema audiences, spurred on the development of underwater film and stills photography equipment. Although the first underwater film was made in 1939 by diving pioneer Hans Hass – an instructional documentary for spearfishermen called *Stalking Underwater* – the first truly commercial underwater movie was made by Jacques Cousteau in 1956. His feature film *The Silent World* was an Oscar-winning sensation that established him as the world's premier underwater filmmaker and explorer.

MINUTE SUBJECTS
One of the most interesting aspects of underwater photography is macro (close-up) work. Tiny creatures can make dramatic subjects.

GROWING MOVEMENT

Until the early 1980s, underwater stills photography and filming was seen as the preserve of either the dedicated amateur or full-time professional diver. Underwater photography was brought to the masses with the development of the Nikonos series of amphibious cameras – culminating in the Nikonos V, still viewed by many as the best underwater camera ever made. Underwater filming did not become a popular pastime until the mid-1990s, when digital video cameras came onto the market, making moving pictures cheaper and technically easier for amateurs to produce. Digital imaging also revolutionized stills photography underwater. Small, easy-to-use digital cameras with

STALKING A SUBJECT
Photographing marine species underwater requires guile and a good understanding of animal behaviour and habitats.

many automated functions have made it simpler for divers to record high-quality images of their underwater experiences.

Despite this, the jump to producing professional-standard material remains as great as ever. Light behaves very differently underwater than in air (*see p.183*), and there are myriad extra factors to take into consideration when aiming for truly professional results. The work that you see on the page or the screen may well have involved lengthy planning, complex equipment, and the specialized skills of a professional post-production studio.

However, the same principles that guide professionals can enhance amateur work. You must have knowledge of the underwater environment and the behaviour of target animals, and possess

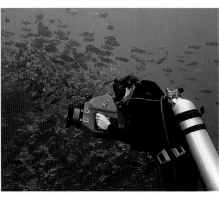

CAMERA CONTROL
Though cameras, especially digital models, have become smaller and easier to use, it still takes great skill to wield one effectively underwater, especially for video footage.

impeccable diving skills. Add to this mix some tips on technique when photographing and filming underwater, and you will be well placed to get the best from the dazzling range of camera and video gear available to divers.

USING LIGHT CREATIVELY
An understanding of how light behaves underwater is essential to capture a mood effectively.

STILLS PHOTOGRAPHY

The advent of the digital age has seen an explosion in the popularity of underwater photography, with more and more divers creating images of their dives for posterity. However, producing good results consistently is a craft, and this is what separates the professional from the amateur photographer.

CAMERA SYSTEMS

Underwater camera systems for stills photography can be divided into two categories. The first consists of truly amphibious cameras that do not require a housing to be used underwater, and can also operate on dry land. The pioneering Nikonos V camera is a famous example of the type. Amphibious cameras often have interchangeable lenses, and are available in both film and digital formats. These highly specialized cameras feature oversized controls for ease of operation underwater.

The second category, housed systems, are conventional cameras in waterproof cases. The cameras themselves can be divided into two sub-categories: compact devices, and SLR (single lens reflex) models.

Compacts come in film and digital formats, and are light and convenient to carry and use. Most models offer fully automated focus and exposure control. You cannot change the lens on a compact, but some have variable focal length (zoom) lenses. After-market add-on lenses that attach to the outside of camera housings are also available.

ANIMAL MAGIC
To capture the vibrant colours of marine creatures and environments, you will need a purpose-designed strobe lighting system.

SLR cameras, which are available in both digital and film versions, allow the use of a range of lenses and offer complete creative control over key functions such as aperture, shutter speed, and focus. For this reason they are invariably the choice of professional underwater photographers, although SLR-compatible ports, housings, and lighting systems can be very expensive.

CAMERA HOUSINGS

Both compacts and SLRs require a housing to protect them from water damage. These are normally made of plastic, though aluminium housings are also available for SLRs. Aluminium housings are strong and durable but expensive and bulky, and hide the camera within, making it harder to operate. Plastic housings are cheaper and allow you to see the camera, but can be less durable. They are especially vulnerable to scratches and abrasion.

NIKONOS CAMERA
Amphibious cameras like the Nikonos V have an integral water-resistant housing.

DIGITAL COMPACT
Fully automated functions make digital compacts easy to use, but limit creative control.

SLR CAMERA
Available in film and digital formats, SLRs are bulky but offer superior image control.

Flash hot-shoe

Flexible joint

Shutter-sync wire

Strobe arm mount

Strobe unit

Hand grip

SLR HOUSING (FRONT VIEW)
Serious investments in their own right, large SLR housings offer excellent access to key controls.

Shutter trigger

Dome port

Watertight controls

Viewing screen

COMPACT IN PLEXIGLAS HOUSING
The housing features push-button mechanical controls for taking, reviewing, and even editing images underwater.

COMPACT WITH STROBE
A diffuser lens placed over the strobe softens the light it casts.

Bare strobe unit

Add-on wide-angle lens

UNDERWATER LIGHTING SYSTEMS

Lighting is one area where compact digital cameras fall short. Their built-in flashes are too close to the lens to avoid "backscatter" (*see p.183*). You can distance the light source from the lens by using an auxiliary strobe light, bolted to the housing. SLR-based and amphibious systems often use strobes in pairs, mounted on flexible arms to allow the subject to be lit from different angles. Knowing how to position strobes to best advantage and manipulate power settings is essential, though many cameras will automatically trigger the strobe to fire for the correct duration for the exposure.

HOUSING MAINTENANCE

Maintaining a housing is relatively straightforward. O-ring integrity should always be checked and the ring lightly lubricated with silicone grease. Make a final visual check before diving. Housings should be rinsed in fresh water as soon as possible after a dive. Operate the mechanical controls during rinsing to prevent a build-up of salt crystals. If water penetrates the housing it will ruin the camera, so a few moments taken to prepare and rinse gear can prevent expensive damage.

Optical viewfinder

Shutter trigger

O-ring

Display screen

View port

Release catch

Digital compact in Plexiglas housing

MAKING FILMS UNDERWATER

Like underwater stills photography, videography has been revolutionized by the advent of digital cameras, which are small and easy to use, compared to film or analogue video. Basic point-and-shoot underwater videography is quite easy with consumer-grade digital cameras. To advance beyond the novice stage, however, you need specialized skills, more advanced equipment, and a flair for using video editing software.

CHOOSING A VIDEO SYSTEM

Choice of camera is the first decision for novice videographers. Though analogue video cameras are still available, digital is now the dominant technology. Digital cameras are available in digital tape, flash media, HDD (hard disk drive), and DVD recording formats. Look for cameras with three-chip processors (called 3CCD cameras). These divide red, green, and blue colour information into separate processing paths, offering richer colours than cheaper one-chip models. At the top end of the market are cameras with HD (high definition) imaging, which produce video of astonishing clarity, due to the high rate at which they scan visual information.

PRECISE POSITIONING
To be a good underwater film-maker you need to perfect your buoyancy control and finning.

A robust housing will be necessary to protect the camera from water damage, while a basic underwater lighting system is essential for capturing good colour footage, since water filters out various colours from natural light as depth increases (*see p.183*).

FILMING SKILLS

Creating high-quality underwater video requires you to do more than merely jump in with everything set to automatic, press record, and film throughout the dive. Many automatic systems perform poorly underwater. For example, autofocus becomes inaccurate in low-contrast environments, resulting in hazy images. Careful manual control of focus and manipulation of white balance (which sets the baseline for colour values in different light conditions) are key skills.

Your diving skills also must be excellent; you need to be a steady platform for the camera – camera shake is a common cause of ruined footage. The camera and housing should also be neutrally buoyant (they should neither sink nor rise underwater) for ease of

Auto-focus lens
Viewfinder
Manual controls

BASIC VIDEO CAMERA
Affordable cameras for home use usually feature automatic focus and exposure control, but may also have some manual options for skilled users.

Microphone
Viewing screen
Glare shield

ADVANCED DIGITAL CAMERA
Top-end video cameras have advanced features like High Definition, multi-chip processing, plus image stabilization systems for sharp images.

PRESSURE HOUSING AND LIGHTS
Housings fall into two categories – electronic or manually controlled. The latter use plungers, rods, pins, and cogs to allow the camera controls to be manipulated from outside the housing; they require more skill, but have the advantage of avoiding electronic systems that can go wrong or short out in the event that the housing is flooded.

Monitor screen with housing

Articulated arm

High-intensity video light

Basic light

Housing with lights

Battery power lead

Tough casing

Carrying handle

Bare housing

handling, and you should familiarize yourself completely with how your camera is operated, so its use becomes second nature underwater.

PRODUCTION AND EDITING
Thorough planning is the secret to good film-making, and video should be shot with an audience or editor in mind. Building a story around a given dive is not a complex process, but creates a target shoot list for the camera operator to work from, and gives the finished film an engaging narrative. You can place scenes in order and polish the results to a professional standard using video editing software that is commercially available for use on home computers.

KEEPING CLEAR
While filming, be careful to avoid causing physical damage to the organisms you have come to film. Avoid touching, or kneeling on, reefs.

KEY PRINCIPLES

Modern cameras and housings allow even the novice to achieve consistently good photographs and video footage. One key development of the last ten years has been the ability to immediately view the results – even during the course of the dive – and then make adjustments accordingly before the next shot. But throughout the history of underwater photography and videography, certain principles have applied as much to hardened professionals as they have to happy snappers. Following these simple rules can immeasurably improve even your first forays into photography and film-making underwater.

GETTING CLOSER

The first principle when shooting underwater is to get as close to the subject as is feasibly possible. Even the most crystal-clear water contains a mass of suspended particles, and even if your eyes cannot pick them out, you can be

LINING UP FOR A SHOT
Good positioning relative to your subject can help make subjects stand out from the background.

sure your lighting system or lens will. Getting close to the subject means greater clarity of the resulting image, and this is one of the reasons why "close-up wide-angle" is such a popular approach. This uses a wide-angle lens at close range, allowing the whole subject to be viewed with the lens only a short distance away. For the same reason, "macro" (close-up) photography is often a good place to start if you are a beginner since clear, well-lit macro images are relatively easy to achieve.

For the novice photographer or videographer, another excellent principle is to remember to take shots with an upward orientation. There is nothing worse than viewing an endless series of dull blue or green shots where the subject is lost in the background of reef or seabed. Shooting upwards isolates the

SUNLIGHT THROUGH WATER
The shifting light patterns encountered underwater can make for dramatic photography, but are challenging to expose correctly.

subject against the background of the open water, and creates a more striking contrast. The composition of such shots can still include reef or coral, wall or wreck; however, the subject itself should be consistently easier to spot.

WAITING FOR A SHOT
Many fish are inquisitive, but easily alarmed; good buoyancy control will allow you to keep still until a subject presents itself.

USING LIGHT SOURCES

Effectively lighting a subject is one area where most amateurs struggle. It is also one of the areas where modern compact digital cameras with built-in flashes will let a picture down. If the light source is too close to the lens, particles in the water will reflect the flash directly back into the lens. This creates a phenomenon known as "backscatter", a snowstorm effect of white dots on the photograph. One of the most basic

prerequisites of taking good underwater images in anything other than perfect underwater conditions is an ability to position a strobe away from the lens. This allows the flash to come in at an obtuse angle, and helps to prevent backscatter from spoiling a shot.

These simple principles do not, unfortunately, guarantee good images every time, but they are useful for anyone starting out in photography or filming. Trial and error will help to refine your skills over time, and the best advice is to jump in, remember the basics, snap or film away, and enjoy!

DEPTH AND COLOUR LOSS

Water absorbs different wavelengths of light as depth increases, causing images taken without artificial illumination to seem washed-out and dominated by blue tones. Reds fade from visibility at a depth of 3–5m (10–16ft), oranges at 10m (33ft), and yellows around 15m (49ft); by 25m (82ft) greens have almost disappeared, and by 30m (100ft) everything appears deep blue or black to the naked eye.

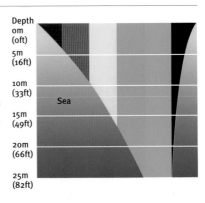

Depth
0m
(0ft)

5m
(16ft)

10m
(33ft)

Sea

15m
(49ft)

20m
(66ft)

25m
(82ft)

Night diving

To many, the idea of diving at night may seem a little crazy, but there is far more to it than just the thrill of exploring in the dark. Night diving reveals a whole host of underwater organisms that lie hidden during the day and only become active at dusk.

LIGHT AND COMMUNICATION

Night diving is obviously less simple than diving during the day, but when properly organized, it is relatively straightforward. A powerful torch will easily light your way and the creatures around you, revealing marine life in its true colours. However, if you cover up your torch (never switch it off; the bulb may blow when you turn it back on), you will be surprised at how much light there is underwater. Many creatures use phosphorescence at night, and as you move through the water, you will cause plankton to release tiny pulses of light, leaving beautiful glowing wakes trailing behind you.

NIGHT ON THE OCEAN
When diving on a clear, moonlit night such as this, you may be surprised at just how effectively the Moon is able to illuminate the underwater environment.

The main restrictions compared to daytime diving relate to communication, not only between divers, but also – and perhaps more importantly – between divers and boat cover. You will be able to monitor your buddy's location from the position of their torch beam. Signalling to your buddy can be done in the normal way, while shining your torch on to your hand as you make the sign. Attract your buddy's attention by waving your torch, but take great care not to shine it at their face, since it can take as long as 15 minutes for their eyes to fully readjust to the near-darkness and restore night vision.

At the surface, avoid flashing your light unless you need to alert the surface cover in an emergency. If you are diving from the shore, leave a light source there – for example, a bright boat light, torch, or beacon – so that you can easily find your way back to land after surfacing. Exit points should be highlighted with coloured lights, to distinguish them from any other light sources.

You will find that most gauges and computers are easily readable by torchlight, and just shining the beam directly on to your gauge will make it luminous for a while.

LIGHTING TIPS

It is vital that all divers carry a torch, and at least one other as a back up. Take spare batteries; if using rechargeables, make sure that they are topped up. Use hand-held torches, not head-mounted ones: one look at your buddy with a head-mounted torch will ruin their night vision. A glow-stick attached to the back of your suit, while not essential, will increase your own visibility.

Hand-held torch

TAKING PRECAUTIONS

Night-diving buddy pairs often link themselves together with a short line. While not essential, this is recommended for novice night divers and in poor visibility. If you are diving on a wreck to which a shotline and buoy is attached, secure a strobing marker light to the base of the line so that it can be easily located in the dark. When choosing a dive site, opt for something simple, such as a shallow wreck or reef with plenty of distinctive features. An interesting daytime dive may be worth revisiting

DIVING INTO DISCOVERY
A very different "night shift" of marine life can be seen during nocturnal dives, like this outlandish basket-star organism.

to investigate marine life that emerges at night. To minimize the risk of incidents, do not dive too deep, as any problems will be much harder to cope with in the gloom. If diving a more open site, use a surface marker buoy with marker light attached to identify it to any boat cover. Be careful not to lose contact with surface cover: getting lost at night could mean you are not recovered until morning.

TORCH SIGNALS

During a dive, your torch beam will alert your buddy to your position. You can also make simple signals with your torch beam on the seabed to communicate with your buddy. At the surface, wave your torch vigorously from side to side if you require immediate assistance.

SIGNALLING "OK"
Tracing a large circle on the seabed communicates to your buddy that you are OK.

SIGNALLING FOR ATTENTION
A rapid side-to-side movement means that you want to show or tell your buddy something.

Cavern diving

Rich with opportunities for dramatic dives, caverns offer a bridge between ordinary open-water diving and the far more specialized activity of cave diving. Nonetheless, diving in caverns demands careful preparation and respect for potential risks.

WHAT IS CAVERN DIVING?

A cavern is a large, enclosed area of rock or coral that is of sufficient size to allow a diver to enter and move around. These fascinating environments can be extremely dramatic, are often eerily lit, and may play host to an array of animals not encountered on the open reef.

Unlike the more extreme sport of cave diving, in which divers penetrate beyond the reach of natural light, in cavern diving the exit is always clearly within view. However, cavern diving still carries inherent risks because the diver does not have direct access to the surface in the event of an emergency. If simple safety drills are not followed at all times, there is the potential for very serious problems to develop when diving even in simple caverns.

CAVERN DIVING EQUIPMENT

A torch is an essential item of kit for cavern diving, but it is also sensible to bring along a back-up lamp. This need not be a large, bulky model but must be able to provide enough light if your main torch malfunctions. Be sure to keep batteries freshly charged. An alternative air source, such as a pony cylinder (see p.68), is also an excellent idea in caverns, as the diver cannot ascend directly to the surface if the primary air source suffers an unexpected failure.

A back-up torch

SAFETY AND SKILLS

The first rule of cavern diving is to prevent your natural curiosity from turning a cavern dive into a cave dive! The exit should be clearly visible at all times – if not directly in your line of sight, then at least the natural light of the cavern entrance should remain visible. For many divers, the temptation to explore deep into cave systems is strong, however, the moment the exit is lost from view and natural light fades, the dive becomes a cave exploration, which should not be attempted without appropriate equipment and specialized safety and skills training.

Certain skills are essential when diving larger caverns. Buoyancy control is important, particularly when there is a silty substrate on the cavern floor.

ON THE THRESHOLD

A diver hovers at the entrance of a freshwater cavern in Australia. Following basic safety rules is essential at such sites.

It is also advisable to use a finning technique known as the frog kick (*see p.123*). This is a gentle, circular fin-stroke that helps you avoid stirring up sediment. One misplaced kick from a fin can turn a cavern into an impenetrable soup of silt and lead to disorientation and panic. For this reason, and as a matter of plain common sense, it may also be appropriate to tie off a line at the entrance of larger caverns (*see p.127*) to provide a direct route to the exit in

INNER SPACE
A diver shines light on the interior of a sea-cave. Caverns have a mysterious ambience quite different from that of open diving environments.

case of reduced visibility. It is also strongly advisable not to enter a cavern without local knowledge or a guide – there may be specific issues about a cavern system and the hazards it contains – such as seasonal changes in visibility – that do not appear in any standard dive guidebooks.

Ice diving

Diving under ice might not sound an attractive proposition, but it is a uniquely exciting experience. Visibility is typically excellent beneath ice, with soft light filtering through from the world above. Ice diving can also take you to breathtakingly beautiful parts of the world.

UNIQUE ENVIRONMENT

Ice diving can be done in the sea or in frozen lakes. The aquatic life you encounter will depend on where you are in the world and whether you are in a marine or freshwater environment. Visibility is often stunning as the ice provides a protective layer over the

COLD-WATER KIT
A diver waits to enter the water wearing special equipment designed to cope with conditions of extreme cold.

Double hood protects head

Cold-water regulator set

Dry glove system keeps hands warm

Drysuit

water, so it is not churned up by the wind, and low light levels under the ice also help to inhibit algal growth.

KNOWING THE ROPES

If you are planning to go ice diving, you will need to undergo specialist training. This will teach you not only the safety aspects of diving while tethered on a rope under ice, but also how to cut the ice hole through which you enter the water, and how to tend safety ropes for other divers while you remain on the surface in a support role.

Ice diving requires a minimum of four to six people per dive. There will normally be two divers operating as a buddy pair (*see pp.110–11*), and two people to tend their lines. It is advisable to have at least one extra person on standby. It is standard practice for each diver to be tethered separately, and it is not advisable to tether two divers on one line, because if anything happens to this rope then both divers can be lost. Lines should always be tied using a bowline knot, which is very secure.

SIGNALS AND SAFETY

Signalling to your tender is an important part of ice diving. As you are diving in extreme conditions, it is vital that he or she knows you are OK throughout the dive. You will learn about giving rope signals during training.

Apart from the obvious dangers of diving in an enclosed environment, you must also be careful to monitor your core body temperature. Repeat dives

SPECIAL PROCEDURES
Ice divers rely on a surface support team (*above*) for safe diving under the ice.

should only be undertaken when you are fully warmed up. You should also ensure that you eat high-energy, hot food to replace the calories you will burn during the dive and in keeping warm afterwards.

SPECIALIST KIT

Ice diving requires special equipment. You will need an environmentally-sealed regulator set (*see p.63*), which is designed to be less susceptible to freezing. You will be taught to submerge this in the water before diving, to acclimatize it to the

FROZEN DEPTHS
A diver films the fascinating world beneath the surface. Many unique animals live in cold seas.

temperature. You must only breathe from it when submerged, to reduce the risk of free-flow (an uncontrolled release of air due to a frozen mechanism). It is also recommended that your primary air source and octopus are mounted on separate first stages (*see p.61*) to ensure that one will work if the other freezes. Your cylinder will need a special pillar valve to accommodate this.

You will need to wear warm undergarments beneath your drysuit, thick neoprene gloves or a pair of waterproof dry gloves (*see p.54*), and two thick hoods for extra warmth.

Freediving

Once simply a fishing technique, freediving – diving using only the air carried in the lungs – has become increasingly popular as a sport. Extreme athletes now constantly push the perceived limits of human performance, diving to remarkable depths on a single breath of air.

PURE SPORT

Freediving is not exclusively the preserve of the extreme athlete: anyone who has snorkelled and duck-dived to explore the seabed could describe themselves as a freediver, making this the most accessible of all diving disciplines. Many would argue that it is also the purest form of diving, requiring only the minimum amount of equipment and relying entirely on discipline, courage, and physical conditioning.

The roots of freediving stretch back to when the human race took its first tentative steps into the sea, diving into the water to harvest food and explore the seabed. Modern freediving, by contrast, is a disciplined sport, with record attempts highly regulated by the two governing bodies – A.I.D.A. (Association Internationale pour le Développement de l'Apnée) and F.R.E.E. (Freediving Regulations and Education Entity). Divers compete in a number of

EQUIPMENT

Freediving does not require much equipment, but specialized items, such as streamlined suits and fins of variable flexibility, are used to maximize the speed of movement through the water. Masks with low internal volume are also useful, as they allow divers to conserve air that would otherwise be used to exhale into a standard mask to counteract mask squeeze (*see p.115*).

Specialist mask

categories, two of which usually take place in a swimming pool: static breath hold – a simple endurance test with a timed immersion in a shallow pool – and dynamic breath hold, a test of the distance divers can swim using only a single breath. In open water, competitors are judged on the depths they can reach and return safely from.

Freediving naturally carries inherent risks – the most advanced and extreme disciplines demand that the body's supply of oxygen is completely used on a dive, and losing consciousness is always a danger. Exploration of freediving limits should never be conducted alone, and only after attending one of the many introductory courses available to those interested in taking up the sport.

STATIC BREATH HOLD COMPETITION
Divers compete for the length of time they can hold their breath. World-class competitors can achieve times of over seven minutes.

TOUCHING THE DEEP
A freediving competitor reaches for the tag that proves that the designated target depth has been reached – this must be presented at the surface for inspection by adjudicators.

DIVING DEPTHS

Competitive depth records are judged in strict categories, defined by precise given parameters such as the use of weights or fins. In "No Limits" – the category in which the highest profile records are set – the diver is dragged down by a weighted sled, and rockets to the surface using an airbag.

Depth obtainable by an average club freediver.

Competent amateur freediver

30m (98ft)

Depth obtainable by a competitor in the "Constant Weight" category, which allows the use of fins and ballast. Top divers can reach 100m (328ft) – roughly the height of Big Ben in London or the Statue of Liberty, New York.

Constant Weight

100m+ (328ft+)

Depth obtainable by the top "No Limit" class of freedivers.

200m+ (656ft+)

Underwater archaeology

While marine archaeology is mainly confined to the academic and scientific world, it could be said that every diver who explores a wreck has an archaeological interest and responsibility. Both the seabed and many freshwater sites hold compelling historical secrets.

RULES FOR THE AMATEUR

Although every dive has the potential to reveal historic artefacts, targeted methodical surveying is an altogether more serious business, as is the correct means of excavating and recording any finds. Archaeological divers can therefore be placed in one of two distinct categories – the serious professional diving archaeologist, and the enthusiastic amateur.

Although this is a field in which amateurs can make a very valuable contribution, it is essential that they do so only through involvement in an organized project, conducted by a recognized and authorized group. Far too many sites have been destroyed, and artefacts removed, by what amounts to

vandalism and theft – the equivalent on land might be digging up a historic site or burial ground without permission, which is unthinkable, of course.

There are many organizations that welcome help from amateur volunteers, and will supervise and guide you. The thrill of discovery really does reach a new level when it is shared with individuals who understand the full significance of a find. You may find that more scope for joining an organized project exists if you first undertake some training, perhaps by volunteering on digs on land.

Learning professional marine excavation and recovery techniques can be fascinating for the amateur. Archaeologists go to great lengths to avoid damaging a surveyed location, and even when they locate an item of interest, try to avoid intrusive collecting techniques or digging.

MORE THAN YOU BARGAINED FOR

By taking an artefact from a dive site you destroy its integrity and hinder efforts to learn about past peoples. And that may not be the end of the matter. In many parts of the world, sites of marine archaeological interest are strictly regulated. The recovery of artefacts is – quite rightly – taken very seriously, and penalties for illegal activity and for removing items can be severe.

Amphorae, used to store oil and wine, recovered from a Turkish site

RELIC OF CONFLICT
Divers inspect the remains of a Japanese fighter aircraft shot down in the Pacific during World War II.

WHAT TO EXPECT

Marine archaeological expeditions are usually initiated because research or local knowledge has pointed to a region that has archaeological potential. Modern GPS (Global Positioning Systems) equipment has made pinpointing such sites much easier. On reaching the site, a detailed survey is generally first carried out.

This may involve using a datum line (a fixed reference line on the seabed from which measurements are taken), or pegging out a grid. Precise recording of the location and state of the site before digging is vital, and is usually conducted through photography or extensive sketching. Small test digs may take place before a full-scale excavation occurs, with the exact site of each find carefully logged, and the finds themselves sketched or photographed. Preservation and restoration techniques are extremely specialized for such finds. Marine archaeology is a long way from the derring-do of Indiana Jones, requiring organization, attention to detail, fine diving skills, and persistence.

CAREFUL SURVEY
Meticulous recording of survey data is one way in which amateurs can help on a professional dig.

Technical diving

The desire for ever-deeper dives and longer periods underwater has led to the development of special gas mixtures. The use of these in technical diving offers an exciting range of new skills and marine environments for qualified technical divers to explore.

PUSHING BACK BOUNDARIES

Scuba divers are limited, by simple physical laws, to a certain amount of time under water (dependent on the depth of the dive) and an overall maximum depth. Training agencies recommend that recreational divers using compressed air go no deeper than 40–50m (130–165ft). Beyond this, nitrogen can build up dangerously quickly in the body, greatly increasing the risk of decompression sickness

(DCS; *see pp.142–43*). In addition, the increased levels of nitrogen in the bloodstream below 50m (165ft) can lead to severe nitrogen narcosis (*see pp.100–01*). The oxygen content of air, too, becomes increasingly toxic to the nervous system the deeper you dive (*see pp.96–97*).

To extend dive times and allow exploration to greater depths, special mixtures of gas have been developed in which the balance of oxygen and nitrogen has been altered, or that contain new gases to dilute the impact of either oxygen or nitrogen. The use of these mixes is known as technical diving, and involves three types of gas mix: Nitrox, which allows longer dive times, and Trimix and Heliox, to reach greater depths.

EXTENDING DIVE TIMES

Normal air is composed of around 21 per cent oxygen and 79 per cent nitrogen. Nitrox is a gas mixture that contains a higher percentage of oxygen and a lower nitrogen content than normal, allowing longer dive times before the diver's body stores up too much nitrogen, and also reducing diver fatigue after the dive. Nitrox can be mixed in various proportions,

Multiple light sources

Complex fastenings for extra kit

Heavy-lift BCD jacket

UNDERGROUND ODYSSEY
A diver emerges from the water wearing the complex equipment required for cave diving, including tanks filled with special gas mixes, and sophisticated dive computers.

Cylinders contain gas mixtures for specific depth ranges

Heavy-duty drysuit worn over a thermal undersuit insulates the diver from the low temperatures of extreme depths

BEYOND NORMAL LIMITS
A diver explores deep within a flooded cave system. Technical diving procedures enable divers to go further than ever before.

from 22 to 50 per cent oxygen. However, beyond a certain depth the increased oxygen in the Nitrox mix becomes toxic and can cause seizures. The more oxygen in the blend, the shallower this will occur. For this reason, diving with Nitrox requires special training, although courses are readily available to recreational divers.

GOING DEEPER

Divers wishing to travel deeper than 50m (165ft) use either Heliox or Trimix, both of which introduce helium into the breathing mixture. Heliox contains only helium and oxygen, whereas Trimix is a three-gas combination of helium, oxygen, and (usually) nitrogen. Heliox is used mainly by military and commercial divers, while Trimix is more often used by leisure divers. Both succeed in reducing the likelihood of nitrogen narcosis (*see p.101*),

TECHNICAL KIT

Diving at extreme depths or in extreme environments, like deep caves, requires special kit. Technical divers meticulously analyse their equipment, and try to eliminate weak points – there is little margin for error during a deep technical dive. To support the extra gas cylinders used during technical dives, most divers opt for high-lift "wing" style buoyancy compensators (*see p.59*). They also choose high-perfomance regulators that can handle the task of supplying breathing gas at extreme depths. Sophisticated dive computers are used to monitor how technical gas mixes are metabolized during a dive.

A multi-gas computer

oxygen toxicity, and DCS. However, as helium conducts heat six times faster than air, these mixes can cause the diver to feel very cold. Helium is also absorbed rapidly into the body, so lengthy decompression is necessary. Divers wishing to use these gas mixes must undergo appropriate training.

Careers in diving

Lots of people grow to love recreational diving and consider turning their passion into a profession. Work in diving is demanding, and earnings are often modest, but the personal satisfaction to be gained from a career in diving may make the hard work worthwhile.

GOING PROFESSIONAL

There are two common factors in the life of any diving professional: the work is invariably challenging, and there are always many more candidates for jobs than there are vacancies.

As a growth sector, the recreational diving industry offers the most career opportunities. Qualifying as a divemaster or instructor with a recognized training agency means that you will be able to work at dive centres in every corner of the globe. However, qualified instructors are responsible for the safety of their students, and the selection process is necessarily a rigorous one. Being a highly skilled diver is just one of the qualities an instructor must possess;

strong communication skills, maturity, and in-depth technical knowledge are also required. Becoming an instructor with a commercial agency can also be an expensive process, but it is a crucial first step toward gaining work in diving, and may open the door to a lifelong career.

COMMERCIAL DIVING

The world of commercial diving covers all activities outside of recreational instruction, and includes scientific, media, and industrial diving. The last of these represents the best-known face of the commercial diver – the hard-hatted aquanaut working on the rigs and pipelines of the oil industry. The demands of the job have changed from

DEEP-SEA EXPLORER
A diver in a mechanized pressure suit works on the deep ocean bed. Such jobs are very demanding and competition for new positions is high.

EXPERT GUIDANCE
An instructor shepherds a new student through his first dive. Resort guides are sought after in many areas.

UNDERWATER WORKER
A commercial diver repairs a steel frame on the sea floor. Such jobs require advanced knowledge of marine engineering techniques.

the pioneering days of oil exploration, and today's commercial divers must be able to master advanced surveying and engineering skills whilst working in the most difficult of environments.

SAFEGUARDING THE SEAS
A navy diver prepares to submerge for mine-clearance duties. Military divers face dangerous tasks and are trained to exacting standards.

JOINING THE SERVICES

Military and police diving present a different set of challenges for the aspiring professional, often requiring diving in appalling conditions, such as in confined spaces or very low visibility. Demand for diving jobs in the military or police is invariably high, and only the best candidates are accepted after a careful and exacting selection process.

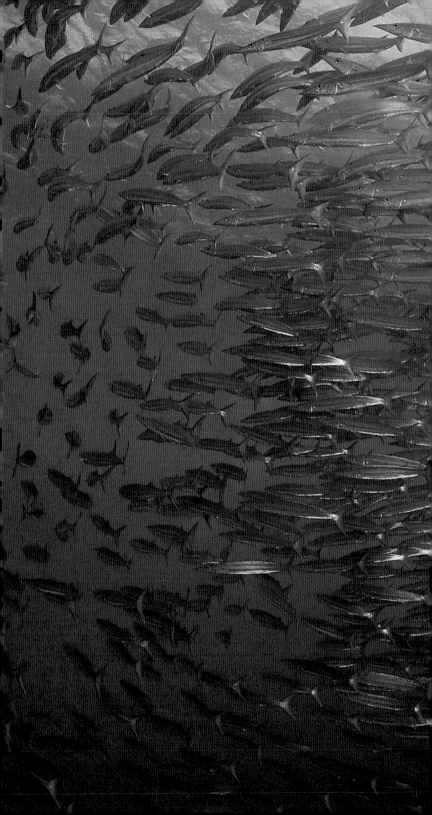

Underwater life

Introduction

Oceans cover 70 per cent of the world, yet we remain ignorant of much of what lives beyond the relatively shallow regions explored by man. The sea is a vast depository of life holding a bewildering array of animals and plants, from the massive to the microscopic.

PLUMBING THE DEPTHS

Although the majority of our planet is covered in water, only about 16 per cent of all known species live in the sea. This is more a reflection of our own inadequate knowledge than of a lack of diversity in the oceans: there are undoubtedly many thousands of unknown species lurking in the vastness of open sea that we have yet to encounter. Much of our exploration of the sea has, by necessity, taken place only in the shallow margins around land. The limits of our own physiology and technology make sustained exploration below 100m (330ft) both demanding and expensive,

MARINE MELTING POT
The ocean contains a diverse range of life-forms, such as this bizarrely patterned nudibranch.

but the average depth of the ocean is in the region of 3.8km (2.3 miles), leaving vast tracts of our own planet totally unexplored.

The coastal fringes that are the realm of the recreational diver reveal a wealth of life. Only two per cent of known marine species live in the open ocean, with the remaining 98 per cent burrowing, swimming, scuttling, and crawling over reef, rock, and muddy sea bed. Although recreational divers are confined to depths of around only 40m (130ft), the first 200m (656ft), known by scientists as the neritic province, hosts the greatest diversity of life in the sea.

ZONES OF LIFE

Four temperature bands define the basic zones of marine life on the planet. At the northern and southern extremities of the Earth are the polar seas, capped with ice. These graduate into temperate seas, which mostly range from 10 to 20°C (39–68°F). Subtropical seas form a loosely-defined buffer zone around the tropical seas of the equator, which are the world's warmest, rarely dropping below 20°C (68°F).

THERMAL RANGE
Sea surface temperatures vary from freezing point at the poles to more than 30°C (86°F) in the tropics.

KEY

Polar

Temperate

Subtropical

Tropical

ENDLESS VARIETY

Water is the perfect medium to support life, at once a means of transport, communication, support, and reproduction. The lives of countless numbers of people worldwide are dependent on the world's oceans and the life they support, which ranges from microscopic plankton to the immense bulk of the largest animal alive today – the blue whale.

Types of marine environment and the species that inhabit them vary with location around the world. The open ocean is roamed by giants, with large migratory species, filter feeders, and opportunistic predators. The latter, bold and inquisitive, provide many of the "big-animal encounters" that divers find so rewarding. Closer to shore, the warm, clear waters around the tropics are home to coral reefs, the most spectacular of all marine systems. More temperate coastal regions have richly populated marine "forests" of kelp – seaweeds that grow to immense lengths to reach the sunlit upper reaches of the water.

ENVIRONMENTAL CONCERNS
The sea supports countless livelihoods, and it is perhaps no surprise that overexploitation occurs. Here, an official apprehends shark-finners.

Colder waters are the province of migratory marine species, travelling the seas in search of new feeding opportunities as the seasons change. And although we tend to think of migrations taking place over great distances laterally, there is also a great vertical movement in the oceans. As the day and night change, a range of animals migrate through the water column, creating the largest daily movement of animals on Earth.

FLIGHT PATH
With a massive wingspan of up to 3m (10ft), the eagle ray is a magnificent marine species.

Tropical seas

If ever there was an image that sums up the magic of diving, it is that of a coral reef. Although coral reefs are the most famous feature of tropical seas, these warm clear waters have much more to offer, such as mangrove swamps, sea-grass beds, and vast tracts of open ocean.

WARM BELT

Tropical waters occupy the region within the "20°C isotherm" – the irregular band of water north and south of the Equator that seldom drops below 20°C (68°F). Although undeniably appealing to the diver, they actually present a less attractive environment for marine life. The warm equatorial sun heats the upper layers of the water column, creating a marked temperature difference between the surface water and deeper colder water. Such temperature stratification prevents mixing of the water column, so nutrients are not passed up from deeper water. Marine animals and plants have therefore had to adapt and evolve numerous strategies to cope with the lack of nutrients in the water around them. Perhaps the most

PERFECT SNORKELLING CONDITIONS
By happy chance for divers, tropical coral reefs require clear warm water with little seasonal variation to grow at an optimum rate.

remarkable of these is the coral reef. Primary production – the formation of organic compounds from inorganic material – is up to 100 times greater in coral reefs (*see p.204*) than in open tropical waters, and although they cover only 0.2 per cent of the ocean environment, they are home to 25–30 per cent of all fish species.

CORAL FORMATION
These complex and often huge structures are built by the tiniest of marine creatures.

LIFE ON THE REEF

The diversity of tropical regions is based to a large extent on coral reefs, although these vary in their diversity depending on location. The reefs with the most vibrant marine life are found in the Indo-Pacific, with up to 700 coral species playing host to 2,000 fish species. In contrast, Atlantic coral reefs have only 70 coral species and about 600 fish species.

Racoon butterflyfish

The reefs of the Indo-Pacific are the richest marine environments on Earth. Their beautiful structure and bright colours, combined with the splendour and variety of animals that inhabit them, make reefs irresistible to divers, and it is no coincidence that many of the world's best dive sites are found on coral reefs.

PARADISE ISLAND
Tropical beaches draw ever-increasing numbers of tourists, creating intense development pressures which, if uncontrolled, pose a significant threat to tropical seas.

COASTAL NURSERIES

Tropical waters are also home to mangrove swamps and sea grass beds, both arguably as important as coral reefs in the overall health of tropical seas. There are 40 species of mangrove – tropical trees and shrubs that grow in shallow and intertidal coastal waters – and they form flooded forests that act as nurseries for various reef and open-water fish species. The 50 species of sea grass form "meadows" in shallow waters that are feeding grounds and nurseries for many fish species. The eradication of sea grass beds and mangrove swamps around the world is a real concern, with undeniable impacts on coastal ecology as animal populations are denied crucial areas for the growth and development of their young.

REEFS UNDER THREAT

Coral reefs worldwide are under intense pressure. The continued development of coastal regions has caused silty water to run into the seas, smothering these delicate systems, and, coupled with the damage caused by destructive fishing methods, it is thought that up to 90 per cent of reefs have been impacted by humankind. There is also evidence that rising water temperatures are causing a phenomenon known as bleaching, which is fatal to reefs. This occurs when the coral polyps eject the minute algae that sustain them as a response to stress.

Diving a reef can be the highlight of a diver's life, but we have a very real responsibility when exploring reefs not to harm or disrupt them in any way. A considerate approach is vital if we are to preserve these wonderfully vibrant ecosystems.

BLEACHED CORAL
Coral bleaching is one of the more vivid consequences of global warming and increased pollution.

THE CORAL CYCLE

Reefs are formed because of the extraordinary symbiotic relationship between tiny animals – polyps – and minute algae. Polyps are colony-forming animals that construct coral reefs. The polyp has a hard exoskeleton made of calcium carbonate, and this forms the physical structure of reef systems. Minute single-celled algae called zooxanthellae live within the polyp, protected by its hard skeleton, and nourished by its waste products. In turn the zooxanthellae provide the polyp with nutrients and oxygen, which they produce, like plants, through photosynthesis. This process requires light, which is why tropical reefs are found only in waters less than 100m (330ft) deep – the so-called "photic zone", penetrated by sunlight. This relationship is vital: warm, clear water tends to be low in oxygen and nutrients, but the partnership of algae and polyp creates a highly efficient nutrient recycling system, and, in turn, sustains a rich array of marine life.

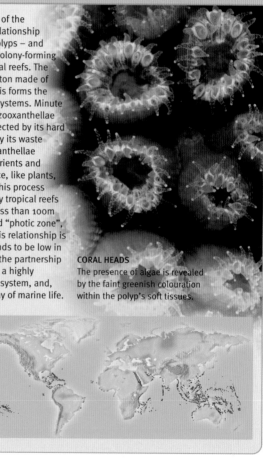

CORAL HEADS
The presence of algae is revealed by the faint greenish colouration within the polyp's soft tissues.

REEF DISTRIBUTION

Over 90 per cent of coral reefs are clustered in the Indo-Pacific region. Reefs do not form on coasts that experience cold or strong currents.

KEY
● Reef

REEFS AND RESPONSIBILITY
Low-impact "hands off" diving techniques are essential to avoid damaging coral reefs.

Subtropical seas

Although there is no strict definition, subtropical seas can be described as waters too consistently warm to support temperate marine life, but too cold for coral reefs to flourish. Also known as warm temperate waters, subtropical seas are found in all of the world's oceans except the Arctic.

BETWEEN TWO WORLDS

Subtropical waters are sandwiched between tropical ecosystems (generally identified by the presence of coral reefs and mangroves), and the temperate zone (identified by cold, rich waters supporting complex systems such as kelp forests). In subtropical marine systems, the water temperature is too high to contain large amounts of oxygen and nutrients (see pp.208–09), and yet too low to promote the recycling properties of coral reefs (see pp.204–05).

The most popular subtropical areas for diving are the Mediterranean and parts of the Gulf of California (also known as the Sea of Cortez). Other key sites include South Africa's Aliwal Shoal (p.259), Fernando de Noronha (see p.318) off the Brazilian coast, and the islands of Cocos, Malpelo (see p.319), and Roca Partida (see p.320) in the eastern Pacific.

RED GROUPER
These large predatory fish are typical of Mediterranean seas, but sadly, overfishing has depleted their numbers.

In terms of their marine life, there is a stark contrast between the Gulf of California and the Mediterranean. The former is famed throughout the diving world for its big-animal encounters, while the latter is a somewhat barren system. The cause of this difference is their topography. The Mediterranean is in effect an isolated bowl of deep water,

MEDITERRANEAN COASTLINE
The beauty of the coast and its clear waters are some recompense for a relative dearth of marine life.

whereas the Gulf of California is less enclosed and relatively shallow, with water and animals able to move freely to and from the Pacific.

Plankton, which are at the base of the food chain, thrive in waters in which mixing of the water layers brings nutrient-rich deep water to the surface (*see pp.214–15*). Most of the cold, nutrient-rich water from the Atlantic that enters the Mediterranean does so through the narrow Straits of Gibraltar, creating a plume of colder water that extends to the Sicilian Channel. The best dive sites in the Mediterranean lie along

this plume. Much of the rest of this sea experiences very little mixing of the water column, and while the result is very clear water, there is little to support life.

The Gulf of California is open at the southern end, with the Baja peninsula to the west and the Mexican mainland over 200km (124 miles) to the east. Much of it is less than 300m (984ft) deep, and these shallow waters are regularly mixed by water entering from the Pacific to the south, and are rich in marine life. This is one of the finest locations to encounter large animals such as humpback whales and manta rays.

OCTOPUS ENCOUNTER
Various species of this cephalopod can be encountered in subtropical waters worldwide.

Temperate seas

The richest of all marine ecosystems, temperate waters are the stretches of ocean between the poles and the tropics. These waters are hugely changeable, offering a seasonal range of conditions at any one dive-site, often accompanied by a variety of visiting migratory species.

THE TEMPERATE ZONE

It is difficult to define the temperate zone precisely, because major ocean currents can artificially extend temperate waters into tropical regions, or push temperate species into near-polar regions. The best definition is perhaps found in the temperature range of the water: true temperate waters rarely sink below about 10°C (39°F) or rise above 20°C (68°F).

The positioning of the temperate zone means that its waters see a greater change of conditions from season to season than tropical and subtropical seas. In particular, the amount of light hitting the surface of temperate waters varies considerably between winter and summer, and this leads to a seasonal variation in productivity – the sheer amount of life that an ecosystem can support. At the base of the food chain in the marine ecosystem are tiny organisms called plankton, which are dependent on light and nutrients for growth and reproduction. In the winter, when even water near the surface receives little light, conditions are poor for plankton growth, and so productivity is low. However, during the stormy winter months there is considerable mixing of cold, nutrient-rich deep water with the

FILTER FEEDER
The basking shark moves through the water with its huge mouth open, filtering plankton from the water.

surface layer (*see pp.214–15*), and so in spring, when the amount of light hitting the surface of the water vastly increases, conditions are perfect for the growth of plankton. Huge spring blooms develop, attracting plankton-feeding species and their predators, and the waters become rich in marine life. Productivity drops again in summer, because, even though light conditions are perfect for plankton growth, there is little mixing between the surface layer and deeper water, and so nutrients become scarce.

ROUGH SEAS
Temperate seas can be rougher and colder than tropical and subtropical waters, but those who brave them are rewarded by the wealth of marine life on display.

TEMPERATE DIVING

Diving in temperate waters is not the crystal-clear, warm-water experience beloved of the coral reef diver, and requires more equipment (*see p.45*) than diving in tropical regions. However, some of the localized ecosystems within temperate seas, such as the majestic kelp forests (*see pp.210–11*) found in certain coastal regions, are extremely dramatic. When dived at optimum times in the season, temperate waters are rich in life. The seasonal blooms of plankton draw a range of migratory species, and also attract impressive predatory species, such as shark and tuna.

PLANKTON BLOOMS

Plankton are free-floating animals (zooplankton) and plants (phytoplankton) at the base of the marine food chain. When environmental conditions are optimal for their reproduction, they can multiply very rapidly, creating huge "blooms" of many millions of individual plankton. Where massive blooms of phytoplankton develop, the sea can literally turn green in colour.

Cyclops zooplankton

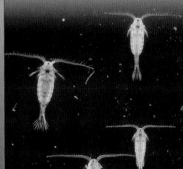

UNDERWATER FORESTS

The forests of giant kelp that grow in temperate seas are considered by some to be the most impressive marine environment of all. Although kelp – a brown alga – is extremely abundant in temperate waters throughout the world, true kelp forests are specific to the areas with marine conditions that support the growth of two kelp genera: *Macrocystis* and *Nereocystis*. These require reasonably clear water, a degree of water movement, a suitable substrate making up the sea bed, and a maximum temperature: most kelp forests will not flourish in water that exceeds 20°C (68°F) on a regular basis. Some species of kelp grow at a phenomenal rate, and to a truly colossal size. *Macrocystis pyrifera*, or giant kelp, can reach in excess of 50m (165ft), and can grow up to 60cm (25in) in a single day, making it the fastest growing alga on Earth.

The best areas for the growth of kelp forests are off the west coast of the US and Canada; in the Cape region of South Africa; in Southern Australia; along almost the entire length of the west coast of South America; around much of New Zealand; and in southern Japan. For the diver, the attraction of these biological wonders is not simply

SEA OTTER
A vital resident of kelp forests, sea otters help control populations of sea urchins, which if left to multiply, would otherwise decimate the kelp.

the forests themselves, but also their numerous residents. The analogy with a terrestrial forest is a good one: activity takes place from the seabed up to the canopy, from specialist molluscs that bore into the kelp itself, through to pelagic animals such as rays that soar through the upper levels. As well as permanent residents, a kelp forest provides a nursery for many open-ocean species and a hunting ground for impressive predators. To dive a kelp forest on a day with good visibility as the sun dapples through the canopy overhead is an unmatchable experience.

SUBMERGED CANOPY
Invariably dramatic and teeming with aquatic life, kelp forests are the temperate water equivalent to the bustling reefs of tropical seas.

KELP BEDS
Huge numbers of marine creatures, large and small, make their home among kelp.

Polar waters

Although both the Arctic and Antarctic conjure up visions of frozen desolation, below the ice and water surface lie regions of staggering abundance. Possibly the most challenging of all marine environments, the polar regions offer many surprises for the intrepid diver.

FROZEN ENVIRONMENT

Polar waters are found in the regions around the Arctic and Antarctic, though the precise lines of demarcation are blurred. Where polar waters start and temperate waters end varies between the poles. For the Arctic it is the 10°C (50°F) above-water July temperature boundary, while for the Antarctic it is seen as the line of the Antarctic Convergence, a zone where cold Antarctic waters sink below warmer northern currents.

Both the Antarctic and Arctic have quite consistent water temperatures, because the low angle of the sun and the reflective qualities of the ice minimize the impact of solar radiation. The temperature of the water hovers around an extremely chilly 0°C (32°F), only just

BELUGA WHALE
Arctic diving "safaris" provide opportunities to dive with animals such as beluga whales and a number of seal species.

above the freezing point for seawater, which is –1.8°C (29°F). However, although they may seem similar, the Antarctic and Arctic are actually quite different in terms of their physical geography and marine ecosystems.

POLES APART

The plants and animals of the Arctic and Antarctic differ considerably, situated as they are on opposite sides of the world. Antarctica has its own species of krill (some seven of them) – the small shrimp-like creatures that are the bedrock of the food chain here. Swarming in huge numbers on the surface, they draw in a host of feeders – including the mighty baleen whales – during seasonal migrations.

Krill

The Antarctic is an isolated continent covered largely in ice: its nearest land masses are over 1,000km (620 miles) away, and the entire continent is circled by an ocean current. The Antarctic Circumpolar Current is extremely significant, as it essentially cuts the Antarctic waters off from warmer waters further north. The Arctic, by contrast, is mainly an area of ocean covered in a thick layer of ice, bordered by the land masses of North America, Europe, and Asia, and as such its waters are affected by temperature changes, land run-off, and shallow coastal currents.

ICE DIVER
There are more diving opportunities in the Arctic than in Antarctic waters. Diving under the ice demands a high level of expertise and specialist skills (*see pp.188–89*).

LIFE ON THE ICE

The adaptations that have evolved in animal life to cope with extreme polar environments are remarkable. There is a tendency towards gigantism – a larger body size keeps the relative body surface area to a minimum, and therefore the effects of heat loss through the skin are less pronounced. Fish have a high body fat content, and mammals have blubber and fur to insulate them, while behaviour such as migration in the winter months means the worst conditions are avoided. The most extraordinary adaptations exist, perhaps, in the fish and invertebrates of polar waters: many have special "antifreeze" proteins in their blood to keep it liquid at low temperatures.

ICE SHELF CALVING SMALL ICEBERG
Up to 70 per cent of all freshwater on Earth is held in the Antarctic ice cap. It sits on a huge land mass, while the Arctic is largely floating ice.

The open ocean

Only a tiny proportion of the world's oceans cover the shallows around land. Beyond, great tracts of open water plunge to abyssal depths. At first glance a featureless marine desert, this is actually a fascinating ecosystem containing some of the most impressive marine creatures.

A LAYERED WORLD

The oceans of the world are divided not only geographically, but also vertically, descending through the water column in distinct zones defined by temperature. Only the upper 200m (650ft) or so are heated by the Sun. Below this warmer surface layer, the temperature of the water can fall dramatically with depth in a layer of water called the thermocline. This layer of rapid temperature change is present in tropical waters all year round and in temperate waters in summer, but

is not found in polar waters. Below the thermocline, the temperature continues to fall, but more slowly. Many animals find the dramatic change in temperature at the thermocline stressful, and are confined to either the warmer water above it, or the deep, cold water below it.

The deeper layers of the ocean are richer in nutrients than the surface layer, and are also colder, and so have a greater capacity for holding oxygen. Mixing of the layers – bringing oxygen-and nutrient-rich water into the surface layer – can be

LIFE IN THE OPEN SEA

Even in remote areas of open ocean, communities of living creatures thrive. In the Sargasso Sea in the North Atlantic, a vast rotating current propels floating *Sargassum* weed in an endless circular procession. The weed supports many invertebrate species and juvenile fish.

Sargassum weed

CAUGHT ON CAMERA
Open-water predators, like this blue shark, will investigate any new visitor to the environment.

caused by currents, storms, or other natural patterns of water circulation. When the nutrient-rich water is hit by sunlight, an explosion in plankton growth, or "bloom", occurs, creating regions of abundance as plankton feeders, and in turn their predators, congregate.

LIFE AT THE DEEP END

Pelagic animals (those of the open ocean) have developed remarkable physical and behavioural adaptations to suit their demanding environment. Massive vertical migrations take place at night, when marine animals move into the well-stocked surface layers, hidden under cover of darkness from predators that hunt by sight. However, many of the predators of the open ocean boast a battery of senses for detecting

prey at long range, and investigate any object in their vast territory for its food potential. These opportunistic hunters include the blue shark, marlin, and tuna – some of the most awesome and beautiful animals in the oceans. The cold-blooded tuna can heat its blood to warm its muscles, enabling deadly bursts of speed.

BUILT FOR SPEED
With their streamlined bodies and powerful sickle-shaped tails, dolphins are perfectly designed to hunt even the most fast-moving prey.

Freshwater environments

Branching out from the sea to explore freshwater environments opens up a whole new range of dive sites to discover, from Icelandic ravine lakes to Mexican caverns or the Florida swamps, each with fascinating, freshwater-specific animal and plant life.

LAKES AND RIVERS

The first thing any diver accustomed to seawater will notice in a freshwater system is the difference in buoyancy. The salt content of seawater – around 35 parts per thousand – makes it denser, and thus a naturally more buoyant environment for the diver than freshwater. Consequently, you will find that you need to carry considerably less weight. The lower salt content also means that equipment suffers less damage through corrosion.

There are a number of logistical and safety issues specific to freshwater diving. Some of the more adventurous dive sites are lakes at altitude, and require the use of specialized tables or a dive computer

PRIVATE PROPERTY
Some of the most scenic rivers and lakes are privately owned, so it is important to check whether permission is required before you dive.

to avoid decompression issues. Lakes are susceptible to land run-off, and may quickly become murky in poor weather, while rivers may swell rapidly in adverse conditions, creating dangerous currents. Rivers and lakes may also support disease, notably Weil's disease and bilharzia, particularly in regions of dense human population.

Despite these drawbacks, with some research and strategic preparation before a dive, local rivers and lakes can provide a perfectly viable and exciting alternative to sea diving. Freshwater systems become anoxic (lacking in oxygen) at depth, and subsequently support very little life. This means that shipwrecks do not deteriorate as quickly – because the organisms that would usually destroy them cannot function – so deep lakes can often offer impressive collections of well-preserved wrecks.

African lake fish

NATURE ON DISPLAY
Freshwater species are generally unaccustomed to divers, creating wonderful opportunities for close observation and encounters.

LAKE DIVING
Exploring a freshwater lake can provide a fascinating and exhilarating alternative to sea diving. Here, in the beautiful Blindsee mountain lake in Austria, divers can explore an underwater forest of fallen trees.

Mammals

Of the 5,000 species of mammals on the Earth, around 2.5 per cent are found in marine environments. These warm-blooded aquatic animals are perhaps among the most charismatic and approachable creatures you will encounter on any dive.

WARM-BLOODED LIVING

Mammals have a number of features that make them unique in the animal kingdom. Firstly, they are warm-blooded, which means that they are able to regulate their internal body temperature. Most are covered in hair (apart from Cetaceans) and all, except monotremes like the duck-billed platypus, give birth to live young and feed them on milk produced by milk-secreting glands. At least three orders of mammals include species that spend the majority, if not all, of their lives in water: Cetaceae, which includes whales, dolphins, and porpoises; Carnivora,

including the pinnipeds (seals, sea lions, and walruses) and otters; and Sirenia – manatees and dugongs.

WHALES, PORPOISES, AND DOLPHINS

Cetaceans spend their entire life in water even though, like other mammals, they have lungs and need to breathe air to live. They are divided into two main subgroups – Mysticeti and Odontoceti – based on their adaptions for feeding. Mysticeti are filter-feeding baleen whales, such as northern and southern right whales, humpback whales, and blue whales.

SOUTHERN RIGHT WHALE
There are few more impressive sights than a whale's flukes breaking the ocean's surface.

SUPREME PREDATOR
The majestic orca or killer whale is a versatile hunter, catching a range of prey from fish to seals and even whales and birds.

Odontoceti, by contrast, have teeth and include some species of whale and all dolphins and porpoises.

AQUATIC CARNIVORES

Pinnipeds are aquatic mammals that spend some time on land, particularly for breeding. There are 33 species, including seals and fur seals, sea lions, and walruses. These carnivorous mammals have webbed feet, enabling them to move on land and in the water. With their long front flippers, fur seals and sea lions are able to walk on all four flippers on land.

Sea otters are the largest members of the mustelid or weasel family and are most commonly found off the coasts of California, Alaska, and Russia. Unlike other marine mammals, they have no insulating layer of blubber, but have the thickest fur in the animal kingdom. They are one of the only mammals, other than primates, known to use tools, utilizing stones and other items to crack open shellfish and pry prey from cracks in rocks.

THE SIRENIANS

It is rare to encounter manatees (*see also p.309*) and dugongs. These fascinating migratory mammals, belonging to the order Sirenia, typically reach adult sizes of around 3m (10ft) in length, and have front limbs in the shape of flippers and no hind limbs. Despite their imposing size, manatees and dugongs are placid, herbivorous creatures that spend most of their time grazing.

SEALS

Commonly seen on dives and at the water surface, seals tend to be found close to shore and in the more remote areas of the world, such as the Arctic and Antarctic, where they can feed and reproduce without disturbance. There are 18 species, the largest of which is the elephant seal. Seals are efficient swimmers, using their rear flippers for propulsion and their front flippers for steering. These lively mammals are fun to swim with but have sharp teeth and can be aggressive during the pupping season.

Harbour seal

Sharks, skates, and rays

Like other cartilaginous fish (also known as the Chondrichthyes), sharks, skates, and rays have a skeleton made of flexible cartilage rather than bone. Collectively known as the elasmobranchs, they have between five and seven paired gill openings, and nostrils beneath the snout.

SHARK SPECIES

There are around 500 known species of shark, ranging in size from the giant whale shark, at up to 20m (66ft) in length, to the minute lantern shark, which measures just 30cm (12in). All sharks have pectoral fins attached behind the gill openings, a large caudal (tail) fin, and one or two dorsal fins – a basic body plan that has changed very little in hundreds of thousands of years. The jaws are lined with many rows of teeth, which are continually renewed throughout the shark's life. The tough, rough skin of a shark is covered by dermal denticles – tiny scales that minimize drag (friction with the water) when swimming. Sharks propel themselves by sweeping their caudal fin from side to side. Unlike most other fish, sharks have no swim bladder, so they must swim continuously or they will sink. They also need to maintain the flow of seawater over their gills so that they can extract oxygen for respiration.

Sharks have extraordinary sensory powers. Their highly developed senses of smell and taste are used to detect potential prey, and they have excellent vision. In addition, they can sense changes in water pressure caused by the movement of other animals using their lateral line system. This consists of fluid-filled channels along the sides of the body that are lined with sensory hair cells. Sharks can also detect the minute electrical fields produced by other living animals, using electrosensory organs called "ampullae of Lorenzi", which are located on the head.

LEOPARD SHARK
The leopard shark can be found at depths of up to 30m (100ft) and is often seen lying on sandy bottoms.

TIGER SHARK
Although rarely encountered, the tiger shark is one of the most voracious shark species. It feeds on large fish, turtles, and sea birds.

humans pose far more of a threat to sharks, with many shark species currently endangered, and some even facing extinction, due to overfishing.

FOOD AND FEEDING

All sharks are carnivores, but they feed on a wide range of prey and use a variety of feeding techniques. Filter feeders, such as basking, megamouth, and whale sharks, sift plankton from the water as they swim. Many bottom-dwellers, including wobbegongs and angelsharks, lie camouflaged on the seabed ready to ambush passing fish, while others, such as leopard sharks, feed largely on seabed invertebrates. Some species, such as white-tip reef sharks, feed cooperatively, hunting in packs and actively pursuing prey. The mako and the great white shark tackle large prey such as seals, swordfish, other sharks, porpoises, and sea turtles.

Although sharks are the top marine predators, only a few species are potentially dangerous to people, and attacks on humans are rare. In fact,

SHARK REPRODUCTION

During mating, the male uses his claspers (modified extensions to the pelvic fins) to transfer sperm to the female. The majority of sharks, including dogfish and leopard and tiger sharks, are viviparous, giving birth to fully formed offspring. Oviparous (egg-laying) species lay their eggs on the seabed, where the embryos are nourished by the yolk within the egg-case. Catshark egg-cases have long tendrils that twist around objects on the seabed. In other species, such as epaulette sharks, sticky filaments glue the egg-cases to a secure site. All young sharks fend for themselves from birth or hatching.

Egg-case

Spiny dogfish

SKATES AND RAYS

The 600 skate and ray species share many of the features of sharks, but have a very different body plan. The gill slits are on the underside of the body. The pectoral fins are positioned above the gill openings, not behind them as in sharks, and are greatly enlarged and flattened to form "wings", while the caudal fin is reduced or absent.

Most skates and rays are bottom-dwellers, and are well adapted for life on the seafloor. Their flat body shape enables them to lie on the seabed unnoticed, and they have a downward-pointing mouth and eyes on top of the head. Spiracles (breathing holes) behind the eyes enable them to "breathe" – take in water to extract oxygen – when half-buried in the substrate. Most rays and skates eat invertebrates, such as molluscs and crustaceans, and small fish, but some are

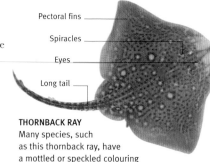

Pectoral fins
Spiracles
Eyes
Long tail

THORNBACK RAY
Many species, such as this thornback ray, have a mottled or speckled colouring that camouflages them against the seabed.

plankton feeders. They swim with strokes from their modified pectoral fins, in an undulating movement similar to a bird flapping its wings. Their tails are used for defence rather than propulsion: they have a stinger at the base of their tail, with short barbs that can inject venom into aggressors. Skates lack this tail barb.

Skates tend to be more common in temperate waters, and rays in the tropics, but the main distinction between them is in their reproduction. Rays produce live young, while skates lay eggs in leathery cases (often called "mermaid's purses").

MANTA RAYS
These large, filter-feeding rays sieve microscopic plankton from the water with their gill-rakers. Manta rays also eat small shoaling fish.

SPOTTED EAGLE RAY
This species uses its flattened, duckbill-like snout to dig up food from the seabed.

DIVING WITH RAYS

Manta rays, with their elegant, dance-like swimming motion, are perhaps the most popular ray species. They are also the largest of the rays, measuring up to 6m (20ft) across. They often congregate at special cleaning stations on the reef, where they allow smaller reef fish to pick tiny parasites off their skin. The flap-like lobes on either side of the mouth funnel plankton between their jaws as they swim. When not in use, the lobes are coiled up to make the ray more streamlined.

Other types of ray seen during dives include guitarfish, which have pointed heads and elongated bodies, and electric rays, which possess organs that can deliver an electric shock to incapacitate prey. Torpedo rays can discharge more than 200 volts – enough to stun a diver.

Circular-bodied stingray species should also be treated with caution, since they have venomous barbs at or near the base of the tail. The sting's effect can be mildly painful to potentially fatal, depending on the species. Eagle rays, which also have venomous barbs, can be identified by their distinctive beak-shaped snout. They have powerful crushing teeth, large "wings", and a long tail.

Rays are docile animals, and despite their self-defence mechanisms, pose no real threat to the diver if unprovoked.

Bony fish

Bony fish, or Osteichthyes, make up about 95 per cent of all fish species – more than 23,500 in number. These vary in every ocean that you will dive in, and there is a wealth of shapes, sizes, and colours, and intriguing behaviours and interactions for you to discover.

COMMON FEATURES

Typical bony fish are torpedo-shaped and streamlined with a muscular tail. They have a caudal fin at the base of the tail for propulsion; a pair of pectoral fins, just behind the gills for steering; an anal fin just below the tail; a pair of pelvic fins on the lower side; and, normally, one to three dorsal fins on the back. They are covered in a slimy secretion that reduces drag, and nearly all species have a covering of

ROLE REVERSAL
Male seahorses have a pouch in which they incubate the eggs produced by the female.

protective scales. They breathe using gills, although a few have evolved to use lungs as well as gills, and they are cold-blooded.

Bony fish are the most diverse and numerous of all the vertebrates. The earliest fossilized fish remains date from around 395 million years ago. All fish have a bony skeleton and a swim

NAPOLEON WRASSE
These lumbering open-water dwellers can become relatively tame in frequently dived sites.

bladder – an air-filled sac that aids buoyancy. The sexes are separate; most lay eggs, and fertilization is usually external.

There are two groups of bony fish. The Sarcopterygii (lobe-finned fishes), which have a fleshy lobe at the base of their fins that is leg-like in appearance, form a small group that includes the coelacanth and Australian lungfish. These ancient fish probably gave rise to the amphibians. But by far the majority of bony fish belong to the Actinopterygii (ray-finned fishes). These fish have jointed bony rays that support their fins, and a symmetrical caudal fin.

The species you see will vary depending on your location. Fish identification can be rather like bird watching and many divers make checklists of what they have seen on each dive. An identification guide to the fish in the area that you are diving in will help to identify them correctly.

SAFETY IN NUMBERS
Moving as part of a large group means that each member of this shoal of Barracuda – a ray-finned species of bony fish – is less likely to be eaten.

A WORLD TO DISCOVER

One of the greatest attractions of diving is the opportunity to observe an amazing range of fish species in their natural habitat. Bony fish species display a wide variety of colours and patterns, especially those species found around coral reefs. As in some bird species, the male is often brightly coloured and the female is drab in contrast. A male's vivid colouring may be used to attract a female in courtship displays. For example, the vivid markings of the male cuckoo wrasse become even more colourful in spring to attract females.

On reefs you may also have the opportunity to observe some fascinating interactions between species. Animals such as manta rays and turtles regularly visit "cleaning stations", where smaller fish, such as cleaner wrasse, pick off algae, parasites, and dead tissue from their skin and even from inside their mouths. Anemonefish (also called clownfish) are able to live among the stinging cells of host sea anemones because they secrete a special mucus that protects them from being stung. In return for their sheltered home, they drop pieces of food and attract other fish that the anemone can feed on.

AVOIDING PREDATORS

You'll need sharp eyes to spot some of the many fish species that are camouflaged or have unusual ways of avoiding predators. Some of these species are so elusive they have only recently been discovered. Masters of disguise include the scorpion fish, which hides on reefs and is virtually indistinguishable from the coral and algae that surround it, but can deliver a nasty sting should you step on it. You may encounter flatfish, such as plaice and flounder, when diving in areas with a sandy bottom, but many are so well camouflaged to match the seabed that they are extremely hard to spot.

The holes and crevices in many reefs and wrecks provide ideal hiding places for fish such as moray and conger eels,

BLUE RIBBON EEL
This small, elegant moray eel from the Indo-Pacific is a shy creature: although it seems to gape threateningly, in fact, it is simply breathing.

with their slender body shape, large mouths, and menacing-looking teeth. Their hiding place is revealed when they gape to breathe (they have restricted gill openings). Eels have no pectoral or pelvic fins and use their long, muscled bodies to dart in and out of their lairs.

SOCIABLE FISH

In open water you may encounter incredibly large fish like the napoleon wrasse, which can reach a weight of over 135kg (300lb). In some areas the wrasse have been hand fed so often that they are friendly towards divers, though feeding them is discouraged. In more open water and around wrecks, you will see great shoals of fish such as sardine, barracuda, glassfish, and mackerel. Such ocean-going, or pelagic, fish tend to have pale bellies, silvery flanks and dark-coloured backs. This makes it hard for prey and predators to spot them – when viewed from above, the darker shade blends in with the colour of the deep sea; viewed from below, the pale colouring merges with the light from the sky.

ADAPTIVE CAMOUFLAGE

Bizarrely, flatfish start off life with a "normal" fish shape but then undergo a metamorphosis into their characteristic flat body form. One eye migrates to the other side of the head, the skull deforms, and the mouth becomes asymmetrical. The side of the body that sits on the sea floor becomes lighter and the upper side becomes darker, camouflaging itself to the colour of the substrate.

Reptiles

Most reptiles live on land but some are aquatic, notably turtles, terrapins, crocodiles and the related alligators and gharials, and sea snakes. These cold-blooded, or ectothermic, animals are mostly found in tropical areas, but some live in temperate regions.

BIRTH AND HATCHING

Reptiles are typically oviparous (the females lay eggs in which the young develop), although a few species are ovoviviparous (the young hatch from eggs within the mother's body). Egg-laying reptiles often build a nest in which to incubate their clutch.

One of the most prolific reptilian egg-layers is the turtle (order Chelonia), which has a hard shell that encloses and protects its vital organs. The head, tail, and flippers protrude, but many species can draw them in when threatened. Although they are air-breathing creatures, they only leave the water to breed and can lay as many as 200 eggs in nests excavated in sandy beaches.

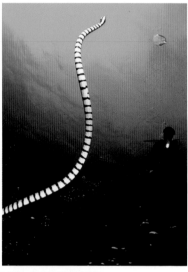

DIVER AND BANDED KRAIT
Related to cobras, sea snakes are venomous, but fortunately they are quite timid and if unprovoked are not inclined to attack humans.

THE SNEEZING IGUANA

The only lizard that forages for its food in the sea, the marine iguana has a curious habit of "sneezing" salt. The marine algae that form the main part of its diet contain a lot of salt. A gland connected to the nostrils removes the salt from the body, and the iguana then expels it by sneezing, leaving its face white. This is one of the unique adaptations that allows marine iguanas to live and feed in seawater.

SEA SNAKES AND LIZARDS

Although many snakes, such as the banded krait, swim in the sea, they usually return to land to breed. The yellow-bellied sea snake is the only true sea snake, the female giving birth in the water to up to ten live young, each about 25cm (10in) long. It can grow up to 1m (3¼ft) in length, and is black or dark brown in colour with a bright yellow underside. This sea snake has spread right across the Pacific from Southeast Asia to America, and gathers in huge numbers during the breeding season: a really big swarm can stretch for 115km (70 miles). Marine iguanas, from the Galápagos Islands, are the only lizards that can tolerate salt water. Males may grow to a length of 1.2m (4ft) or more (almost half of which is the tail). They are harmless herbivores, feeding exclusively on algae growing on rocks near the shore. When feeding, they can remain submerged for up to an hour, especially in the warmer shallows, though dives of five or ten minutes are more common.

SALTWATER CROCODILES
The saltwater crocodile is the world's largest living crocodile; record lengths have been up to 7m (23ft), but 4–5m (13–16½ft) is more common. This is the most dangerous species of crocodile, responsible for most crocodile attacks on people. It is found from eastern India and Bangladesh through Southeast Asia to Papua New Guinea and Australia, usually in brackish water in tropical estuaries, rivers, and swamps. The female lays eggs under a large mound of vegetation and stands guard over them for about 100 days. When the young hatch, she digs them out and carries them to the water. The hatchlings then live in crèche groups for about eight months, guarded by the adults.

RETURNING TO THE SURFACE
Turtles breathe air, like land-based reptiles. This one has a parasitic remora fish attached.

Marine invertebrates

Of all animal species on Earth, 95 per cent are invertebrates
(animals with no backbone), forming an incredibly numerous
but often overlooked section of the animal world. Every major
invertebrate group has an array of marine representatives.

AQUATIC ARTHROPODS

An arthropod is a type of invertebrate
that has its body encased in a hard outer
casing (the exoskeleton) and jointed
appendages. Land-based arthropods
include insects and arachnids, whereas
most underwater species are crustaceans,
a group that includes crabs, shrimps,
lobsters, water fleas, copepods, and
barnacles. There are about 39,000
species of crustacean, most of which are
marine, though some live in freshwater
environments. They vary in size from the
massive Japanese spider crab, with its leg
span of 3.7m (12ft), to the tiny water flea,
only about 0.25mm ($^9/_{1000}$ in) long. But
large or small, crustaceans all have certain
things in common. They possess two pairs
of antennae, three pairs of mouth
appendages, and compound eyes on
stalks. They also have three body
segments – the head and the thorax,
which are almost always fused and
covered by a carapace (an outer shield),
and the abdomen.

DRAWING NOURISHMENT FROM THE SEA
Bivalve molluscs, such as these mussels,
feed by filtering organic matter from the water.
Mussels live in nutrient-rich tidal areas.

MOLLUSCS

All molluscs, except the octopus, possess
some form of calcium carbonate shell.
There are three major marine classes of
this group of invertebrates. Gastropods,
with some 35,000 species, include
whelks, limpets, sea slugs, and conchs.
Many possess a shell but some, like the
sea slug (or nudibranch), have lost theirs
completely. Bivalves, such as clams,
mussels, oysters, and scallops have a shell
in two pieces. There are 20,000 marine
and freshwater species, the largest being
giant clams up to 1.2m (4ft) across.
Cepahalopods comprise around
600 species, including
nautilus, squid,
cuttlefish, and
octopus. The
cephalopods

SEA SCAVENGER
Crabs have a varied diet;
these crustaceans feed on
carrion, molluscs, and
even other crabs.

DELICATE DRIFTERS
Transparent and serene,
jellyfish are members of
the Cnidarian group
of invertebrates.

include the largest invertebrate of all, the giant squid, which grows to a size of 16m (52ft). Cephalopods can swim in short bursts by squirting water from their bodies, but many, like the squid, use undulating fins for locomotion. The only shelled species of cephalopod is the nautilus: squid and cuttlefish have internal shells and the octopus has no shell at all.

CREEPING BEAUTY
Nudibranchs are colourful molluscs related to the common garden snail.

ECHINODERMS

Marine bottom-dwelling invertebrates, echinoderms have a hard, spiny skin and five-part radial symmetry. They lack a head, are often brightly coloured, and are distributed throughout most of the world's seas. There are approximately 6,000 species of echinoderm, including starfish, brittle stars, sand dollars, sea urchins, and sea cucumbers, among others.

Most species of echinoderm reproduce sexually and have separate sexes. Fertilization is external – the eggs and sperm are shed into the water at spawning time. The floating embryo develops into a planktonic larval form. A few species reproduce asexually by fission (genetic copying of the parent organism into two or more clones).

Starfish may be circular, pentagonal, or the familiar star-shape, with radiating arms. Under each arm are tiny tube feet, which the animal uses for walking.

UNDERWATER CHAMELEON
Cuttlefish are molluscs that can camouflage themselves by changing the colour and texture of their skin.

The mouth is on the underside and the starfish feeds on living and dead animals as it moves along rocky surfaces and muddy bottoms.

Sea urchins, on the other hand, do not have arms. Instead they have a shell of tightly fused plates, forming a sphere. They have long prominent spines that protect them from predators, and have tube feet on their undersides, which are used for locomotion, respiration, and for trapping drifting particles of food.

CNIDARIANS

The cnidarian group of invertebrates, which includes the jellyfish, sea anemones, corals, and hydroids, are species with one of two basic body forms: medusae or polyps. Medusae, such as adult jellyfish, are bell-shaped with tentacles hanging down from the margins. They tend to be free-floating and solitary. Polyps, such as coral, sea anemones, and hydra, are tubular-shaped animals topped with tentacles. They frequently form colonies. Corals (*see also pp.204–05*) are unusual in that they depend on symbiotic algae to provide life-sustaining sugars. Medusae reproduce sexually, whereas most polyps reproduce by asexual fission. Cnidarians are unique in manufacturing cell-based stinging mechanisms, called nematocysts, in their tentacles, which are used to catch prey and in defence.

OTHER INVERTEBRATES

Comb jellies, which are bell-shaped creatures with vertical combs over their bodies, form another class of invertebrates – the ctenophores. The 5,000 species of sponge that live in both salt and fresh water belong to the phylum Porifera. Finally, there are over 8,000 species of segmented worms, which are classed as annelids.

PLANTS OR ANIMALS?

Many marine creatures stay rooted to a single spot for life. They posed a dilemma for early biologists who believed that mobility defined the animal state; this explains the common names of animals like the "lily of the sea" – in fact a crinoid. Other stationary animals include polyps, sponges, feather stars, and annelids such as fanworms. They are filter feeders, and contain toxins to deter predators.

Feather star

Places to dive

Introduction

With increasing numbers of dive centres opening up across the globe, virtually the entire world is now accessible to the travelling diver. Following a few basic travel tips can stand you in good stead when transporting yourself and your dive kit to your destination.

TRAVEL OPTIONS

Most holiday destinations in coastal regions around the world provide some sort of diving facility. Indeed, the sport is now so convenient that you can turn up on the day, certification card in hand, and be kitted out from head to toe with hired kit, before being guided around local dive sites. This is one of the greatest joys of the sport – the ability to visit different parts of the world and explore local sites with relative ease.

A step up from the more casual "just-passing-through" diving experience is the dedicated diving holiday. This is usually arranged through a resort-based dive operator, most of which will run a series of dives to local dive sites and offer a range of equipment for hire.

ICE DIVING
With many divers looking for more adventure in their diving, travel companies are offering challenging experiences, such as ice diving.

Developments in diving equipment over the last decade mean that most dive centres worldwide can offer a reasonable calibre of kit for hire. With the addition of local knowledge from a divemaster

who knows the waters well, you should be ensured of a reasonable diving experience, regardless of the location. While most dedicated dive operators work to a high standard, there are a few rogue operators around, and you should be wary of any that show a cavalier approach.

LIVEABOARD DIVE VESSEL
A liveaboard is essentially a floating dive centre, and as such should have all the facilities on board to guarantee safety, comfort, and a memorable diving adventure.

Liveaboards provide an even more intense diving holiday. These are dive vessels designed for long-range trips to more inaccessible places, and they provide non-stop diving throughout the voyage. Liveaboards often offer supplementary courses, such as photography or natural history, hosted by resident experts. There are few marine dive destinations on Earth that are not accessible via liveaboards, and for many this is the finest way to experience extensive reef systems, remote sites, or sprawling island groups.

There is also a range of diving expeditions available in the modern travel market. Some are conservation orientated and others more adventurous, such as seeking out big-animal encounters or spectacular wrecks. Take the time to investigate the results and credibility of the group co-ordinating your project, since some that claim high ethical standards in conservation and research fall well short of expectations. There are others, of course, who perform genuinely valuable work, and for many divers this is the most rewarding and educational aspect of their entire diving career.

LOCAL KNOWLEDGE
Most dive centres will be able to take you out on a boat and show you the best of the local dive spots.

TIPS AND PRECAUTIONS

Diving overseas involves putting a great deal of trust in your host, be it a local guide or dive operator, or a leader of a trip or expedition. Following a few simple rules and precautions will make this a less daunting prospect, and may also ease the logistical problem of transporting expensive equipment across the world.

Deciding on a destination is the first step in planning a successful trip. Finding a location that really appeals to you, yet

CHOOSING A DIVE BAG

While you can pack your gear in any case or bag you wish, most divers use bags specially designed to stand up to the rigours of dive travelling (*see p.79*). Soft bags, such as carryalls, can fold up and be stashed away at your destination. Semi-rigid trolleys make carrying easier, but they are less flexible. Rigid bags are heavier, but offer better protection for your kit.

Semi-rigid trolley dive bag

KIT HIRE
Hiring kit when you reach your destination is one way of lightening your travel burden and avoiding penalties for carrying excess baggage.

keeps within your budget, will make your trip more rewarding than simply opting for the most well-known sites or the cheapest deals. A brief period of research can reap huge rewards, and the range of information sources now available makes this a relatively simple exercise.

After identifying the aim of the dive trip, and the location to be visited, the next stage is to choose a host operator. Many local tourist boards can recommend registered operators who are known to work to a high standard. In addition, the PADI website (*see pp.34–35*) lists dive operators who have met a series of demanding criteria. This independent evaluation is invaluable in identifying the most professional centres and boats.

While hired equipment is generally of a good quality at resorts, many divers prefer to travel with their own gear. This is prudent, since unfamiliarity with hired kit can create an uncomfortable (and occasionally unsafe) diving experience. The diver also has the assurance of knowing that their own gear fits well, is functional, and has been tested recently.

Most airlines do not officially offer excess baggage allowances for dive gear (the dive industry is lobbying hard for a more reasonable approach to this issue), but a phone call in advance of the trip often works wonders – as does a courteous approach when checking in your kit. Carry delicate items, such as regulators and dive computers, as hand baggage; the latter, in particular, may be affected by pressure changes in the hold of the plane.

Dedicated diving insurance is vital, since you will not be covered by general travel policies. You need cover for damage to equipment in transit, medical care abroad (such as recompression treatment) and repatriation in the event of a serious diving incident. Policies usually cover divers down to a depth of 30 m (100 ft) – more than adequate for most trips.

ONWARD TRAVEL
If the final leg of your trip or any travel between islands involves flights on small aircraft, check if the carrier imposes their own luggage restrictions.

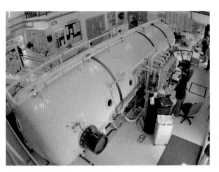

RECOMPRESSION CHAMBER
The costs of recompression – if it is available at all – can be exorbitant, and many chambers will not treat divers without proof of insurance.

On arrival at your target destination, it is always advisable to carry out a few simple checks when diving with the host operator. All dive operators should have emergency oxygen supplies appropriate to the range and scale of diving they provide, as well as first aid facilities and effective communications. It is worth making a quick visual inspection of the compressor facility – air certificates should be on display, but it is relatively easy to tell a clean, well-maintained compressor from a neglected one.

Europe

As a dive destination, Europe tends to be greatly underestimated by the international diving community. With an excellent diving infrastructure and well-established resorts and travel networks, Europe offers an eclectic mix of dive environments and a host of wrecks to explore.

TEMPERATE ZONE

Europe is, on the whole, a region of temperate waters, and this provides tremendous seasonal variation in the marine life around its coasts. The waters of western Europe are cold and rich in nutrients, and historically have been some of the richest fishing grounds on Earth. Migratory species move around the western edge of the continent, many borne on the undersea highway of the Gulf Stream. Consequently, the same divesite can be unrecognizable from winter to summer.

In diving terms, Europe is a continent of extremes, with Arctic diving to be had in the dramatic Norwegian fjords to the north, while subtropical diving can be enjoyed in the warm waters of the Mediterranean Sea to the south.

NORWEGIAN FJORD

Carved by glaciers millions of years ago, the fjords offer excellent dives in crystal-clear water, against a superb backdrop of snow-capped mountains.

FISHING BOATS AT ALBUFEIRA, PORTUGAL
Europe's fish stocks have been an important resource for millennia, but overfishing has now put the populations of some species at risk.

Europe has long been the scene of intense shipping activity, a fact reflected in the thousands of wrecks that today dot the seabed. These wrecks represent a history of seafaring itself – from Viking longships, to all types of fishing vessel, and merchant fleets that foundered in violent storms. Sunken warships from virtually all of the continent's navies bear witness to the many wars that have ravaged Europe through the ages.

WRECK OF THE *ZENOBIA*, CYPRUS
The Swedish ferry *Zenobia*, which sank in 40m (120ft) of water off Cyprus in 1980, is one of Europe's most impressive wrecks.

Wreck of the *Zenobia*

LARNACA HARBOUR, CYPRUS

Mediterranean Sea
CYPRUS
Larnaca
Zenobia

A wreck for all grades of diver, the *Zenobia* offers shallow and deep dives, and a range of penetrations from gentle investigations through to technical explorations. Readily accessible, this wreck is one of the most popular dive sites in Europe.

ACCIDENTAL SINKING

In June 1980, the 10,000-ton Swedish passenger ferry *Zenobia* ran into difficulties off the coast of Cyprus. A problem with the autopilot caused the vessel to gradually tilt over and sink over the course of several days, giving plenty of time for the passengers to be evacuated, but leaving her cargo, including 135 lorries, to sink with her.

REVERED WRECK

The *Zenobia* has become one of the most popular wrecks in diving because of her accessibility and the range of dives she offers. Divers can access the two main vehicle decks, the bridge, the accommodation area, and the restaurant. More extreme penetrations of the wreck include the engine room,

> ### ESSENTIAL INFORMATION
>
> **WATER TEMPERATURE** 21–26°C (70–79°F)
>
> **ECOSYSTEM** Subtropical
>
> **WHEN TO VISIT** Divers can visit all year round, but diving is at its best between March and October.
>
> **MUST SEES** Vehicle hold Number One; the bridge; the accommodation area.

although this is a multi-level, technical dive that requires careful planning and training. While not suitable for the novice, such dives are thrilling challenges. For those seeking a more sedate experience, the exterior of the wreck also provides a dramatic spectacle, with her props, huge hull, and superstructure still in excellent condition.

METAL MONSTER
The huge deck and holds are littered with fascinating debris from her former life as a ferry, including many intact vehicles.

Medas Islands

CATALONIA, SPAIN

The Medas Islands offer a glimpse of how Mediterranean marine life was in days of old – large fish shoals, passing pelagics, densely colonized reefs, and fine coral formations. Closely protected, the islands have much to offer visiting divers.

CONSERVATION AREA

The Medas Islands were granted the status of a Nature Reserve in 1983, and have therefore enjoyed more than 20 years of official protection. The life around the islands reflects this, with perhaps a greater abundance of marine life and range of species than anywhere else in the western Mediterranean.

DIVING THE ISLANDS

Located only 1.6km (1 mile) off the northeastern coast of Spain, the islands benefit from the nutrient rich run-off from the nearby River Ter. In addition, cold water upwellings on the craggy reefs around the islands create an oxygen-rich environment that allows marine life to thrive. As well as the usual Mediterranean species, such as

OUTWARD BOUND
A dive boat prepares to embark on the short voyage to the islands. Divers flock to the area to enjoy the profusion of marine life sheltering in the clear blue waters of the nature reserve.

scorpionfish, octopuses, and moray eels, local residents include large shoals of barracuda and bream, and there have even been sightings of eagle rays around the islands. Diving highlights include the famous Dolphin Cave – a 46m (150ft) tunnel set in a rock-face, and the tiny islet of Carall Bernat. It is also reassuring to note the return of red coral to the seas around the islands, a natural resource that was for many years exploited by the jewellery industry. Though a small fee is levied by the authorities for diving around the Medas Islands, the success of the ongoing conservation policy justifies the extra expense.

ESSENTIAL INFORMATION

WATER TEMPERATURE 14–25°C (57–77°F)

ECOSYSTEM Subtropical

WHEN TO VISIT The best time to visit the Medas Islands is between the months of March and September.

MUST SEES Dolphin Cave; Carall Bernat; red coral formations; rare sightings of eagle rays.

Dusky groupers are just one of the species living under protection at the islands

Sardinia

CENTRAL MEDITERRANEAN, ITALY

A rugged island in the middle of the Mediterranean, Sardinia has a dramatic geological past reflected in the caverns and caves that dot its coast. Although these are impressive features, Sardinia also has unique marine life and fascinating wrecks.

ROCKY COAST

The sharp reefs, dark overhangs, and craggy shoreline of Sardinia play host to an unusual array of marine life for the Mediterranean – a body of water not particularly famed for its marine diversity. Sardinia's geographical position means that it receives species from the Red Sea to the east (thought to be due to animals travelling through the Suez Canal), and the Atlantic to the west. Divers may encounter any of six species of wrasse, two species of grouper, wonderfully colourful sponges and corals encrusting rock walls, and a unique giant mollusc called the noble pen shell.

LOCAL CHARACTER
The common octopus is one of the key species found off the rocky Sardinian shoreline. This highly intelligent invertebrate is a common sight for divers.

NETWORK OF CAVERNS

This coastline is also famed for its caves and caverns. One system – Nereo Cave on the northwest coast – is particularly impressive, stretching for over 300m (1,000ft). As with all caves, caverns, and overhangs in Sardinia, such areas of low light are festooned in thick growths of red coral, for which the island is particularly well known.

There are also a number of fine wrecks to be dived. The best known of these is the wreck of the *Angelica*, a 4,400-ton freighter that ran aground on the island's jagged reefs in 1983, at Capo Falcone. The wreck lies at a maximum depth of 20m (66ft), so represents a relatively easy dive. The shallow location means that wind and weather have taken their toll on the wreck's structure over the years, but the site is well worth a visit should you desire a change of pace from the sea-caverns that dominate Sardinian diving. With many attractive beaches and towns along the coast, there is much to enjoy on shore, as well as beneath the waves.

ESSENTIAL INFORMATION

WATER TEMPERATURE 19–25°C (66–77°F)

ECOSYSTEM Subtropical

WHEN TO VISIT Sardinia can be dived all year round but the summer months offer warmer, if more crowded, seas.

MUST SEES Red coral; Nereo Cave; noble pen shells; wreck of the *Angelica*.

Ustica Island

SICILY, SOUTHERN ITALY

Ustica Island was described by no less authority than Jacques Cousteau as the most beautiful island dive site in the Mediterranean. A tiny volcanic outcrop off the coast of Sicily, its qualities have seen it established as a Marine Nature Reserve.

SMALL IS BEAUTIFUL

Ustica Island may owe its undisturbed ecosystem to the fact that it was a penal colony until 1950. A tiny island – it has a total surface area of 8 sq km (3 sq miles) – it is nonetheless one of the most significant sites in the Mediterranean, to the extent that Italy's Academy of Underwater Sciences and Techniques is based here. The volcanic origins of the island (seen in the name itself – the Latin *usta* translates as a burnt red colour) mean that the reefs around the island are particularly dramatic – with a craggy underwater topography featuring numerous caves, caverns, and overhangs.

SILVER SHOAL
Barracuda shoal in large numbers in the waters off Sicily, and are frequently sighted by divers visiting the Marine Reserve at Ustica.

> ### ESSENTIAL INFORMATION
>
> **WATER TEMPERATURE** 15–25°C (59–77°F)
>
> **ECOSYSTEM** Subtropical
>
> **WHEN TO VISIT** Diving takes place on Ustica Island all year round, but in winter the seas are relatively chilly.
>
> **MUST SEES** Red coral formations; the Colombara Bank; Medico Tunnel.

TOP DIVES

One of the best sites is Medico Tunnel off the northwest of the island, which consists of a tall pinnacle with a tunnel passing directly through it. Another site of particular note around the island is the Colombara Bank – well known for its beautiful reefs and aggregations of large fish, such as barracuda and tuna.

The Hebrides

WESTERN SCOTLAND

The islands of the Hebrides have the feel of genuine wilderness about them. Precipitous mountains plunge into dark bays and craggy lochs, and white beaches lead to waving kelp forests, creating one of the finest diving regions in Europe.

RICH SEAS

The topography of the Hebrides lends itself readily to abundant marine life, with steep walls in the lochs, convoluted rocky reefs in the open water, and strong tidal movements through numerous narrow channels connecting the islands. Washed in oxygen-rich cold water, the islands are host to a dazzling array of marine life both large and small. Notable sites in the region include dives around Skye (particularly the small island of An Dubh Sgeir), the wrecks and reefs of the Sound of Mull, the famous dives around Oban (home to one of the most established and respected dive operations in the UK), and the newly discovered dive sites of the remote Summer Isles. The last include the wreck of the *Fairweather V*, a fishing vessel that sank in 1991 and which is still intact and in good condition.

SURVIVING WILDERNESS
The characteristic rocky coastlines of the Hebrides are perhaps one of the last truly wild places in the United Kingdom.

TEMPERATE-WATER ECOSYSTEM

The Hebridean islands provide one of the richest and most complete insights into the marine life of a temperate-water zone. Visitors to the islands' rocky shores include itinerant whale and dolphin species, ling, conger eel, and a profusion of smaller native fish species. Colonial and encrusting organisms coat the rock walls, with anemones and sponges creating colourful and dramatic reefs. These are patrolled by otters – the Hebrides is one of the few dive sites in the United Kingdom where these fascinating mammals have largely taken to the sea. If conditions do not permit diving, the Scottish Sealife and Marine Sanctuary near Oban is well worth a visit. It has a spectacular aquarium and a busy otter and seal sanctuary.

A diver examines an undersea wall covered in dead men's fingers and plumose anemones

In the winter months, the islands of the Hebrides are subject to wild weather and cold water, with many dives becoming very demanding due to dark water and strong tides. In the summer months, the region really comes to life, with some of the beaches on the more remote islands becoming gateways to absolutely top-class shallow dives.

ANIMAL MAGIC

The shallow reefs just offshore in the Hebrides are some of the busiest temperate reefs anywhere in Europe, playing host to large edible crabs and lobsters, various species of cephalopod including cuttlefish and octopus, colourful nudibranchs, and an array of fish species including some spectacular wrasse.

Larger animals encountered in the open seas around the Hebridean archipelago, as well as in its many dramatic coves and bays, include both the common and the Atlantic seal. Bottlenose dolphins are regular visitors to these shores, as are the more rarely seen rissos and white-beaked dolphins. Whale species that can be spotted include minke and pilot whales, orcas, especially around the islands of Coll and Tiree, and, if you are very lucky, sperm whales and humpback whales. There are large gatherings of basking sharks late in the year, although predicting when and where these will take place is almost impossible. Occasionally, sunfish and leatherback turtles also visit the region.

It is not only the animals that provide the excitement for divers visiting this region. The third largest whirlpool on Earth can be seen at the Gulf of Corryvreckan, between the islands of Scarba and Jura.

ESSENTIAL INFORMATION

WATER TEMPERATURE 8–18°C (46–64°F)

ECOSYSTEM Temperate

WHEN TO VISIT Diving is possible all year round, but can be stormy in winter.

MUST SEES Otters; wreck of the *Fairweather V* in the Summer Isles; An Dubh Sgeir in Skye.

Scapa Flow

ORKNEY ISLANDS, GREAT BRITAIN

The most famous wreck-diving location in Europe, Scapa Flow is a huge natural harbour amid the islands of Orkney off northern Scotland. Its fame stems from the fact that it was the site of the largest ship-scuttling action in maritime history.

ANCIENT HARBOUR

Although Scapa Flow has been used as an anchorage since Viking times (the name derives from the Old Norse *Skalpeidfloi* – the Bay of the Long Isthmus), one event ensured its fame in the diving world. After World War I, the German High Seas Fleet was impounded in Scapa Flow by the Allies. The fleet, consisting of 79 vessels, was imprisoned there for over a year. On June 21st 1919, Admiral Von Reuter, the German commanding officer, misread a newspaper headline and assumed that hostilities were about to recommence and ordered his ships to be sunk by their own crews rather than let them fall into the hands of Allied forces.

GRAVEYARD OF SHIPS

The subsequent mass scuttling saw the majority of the fleet sunk, although the Allies managed to save 22 vessels by towing them into the shallows. Several of the German ships were salvaged in the intervening years, but three battleships,

ESSENTIAL INFORMATION
WATER TEMPERATURE 8–20°C (46–68°F)
ECOSYSTEM Temperate
WHEN TO VISIT Best diving conditions are between March and September.
MUST SEES Wrecks of *Koln*; *Kronprinz Wilhelm*; *James Barrie*; *Gobernador Bories*; basking sharks; seals.

four light cruisers, and five torpedo boats still lie on the seabed. In addition to this rich array of wrecks, the British Admiralty sank 50,000 tons of shipping during World Wars I and II as blockships in the narrow entrances of the Flow to prevent raids by German submarines.

With several other wrecks of varying origins scattered throughout the Flow, the site has become a mecca for serious wreck divers. Although the larger German wrecks can be demanding dives, there are many easier options for the less experienced. The blockships in particular are splendid dives, sitting in shallow tidal channels, washed by cold nutrient-rich waters and teeming with marine life.

Notable wrecks in Scapa are the *Kronprinz Wilhelm*, the *Brummer*, and

RUST IN PEACE
Not all of Scapa Flow's historic wrecks lie beneath the sea. Sandy beaches also bear witness to the past.

the *Koenig*. Amongst the blockships the *Gobernador Bories* has become particularly renowned, and the wreck of the trawler *James Barrie* is a magnificent sight at 40m (131ft) – sitting almost perfectly preserved on the sea floor.

WILD SCAPA

Scapa Flow has an extensive array of marine life, with the shallow wrecks in particular playing host to huge numbers of ballen and cuckoo wrasse, lobsters, conger eels, octopuses, and beautiful nudibranchs. Larger residents include grey seals, dolphins, and basking sharks in the summer months, and also the occasional visiting pod of orcas. Though the wrecks of Scapa Flow are, naturally, its greatest attraction, the marine life here is a welcome bonus.

VALUABLE SALVAGE

During the 1920s, the British salvage firm Cox & Danks raised many of the scuttled German battleships for scrap. Metal from the wrecks is still used today to make sensitive scientific instruments, as their steel was forged before the age of atomic weapons tests, and so is a rare source of high-grade metal that is completely free of radioactive particles.

Salvage work at Scapa Flow

GLIMPSE INTO HISTORY
Divers at Scapa Flow can inspect the urchin-covered remains of German battleships scuttled shortly after the close of World War I.

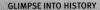

The Isles of Scilly

ENGLISH CHANNEL, GREAT BRITAIN

Something of a well-kept secret amongst British divers, the Isles of Scilly are a cluster of tiny islands that sit at the tail end of the Gulf Stream. Rich marine life, lively reefs, and an abundance of wrecks make this archipelago a diver's paradise.

SPARSELY POPULATED

The Isles of Scilly (or the Scillies as they are universally known) consist of 300 granite islands 45km (28 miles) off the southwestern tip of England. Only six of the islands are inhabited, and even these could hardly be described as crowded. The islands are low lying and very beautiful, with white sandy beaches fringing green islands.

The islands' position in one of the world's busiest shipping channels means that wrecks are abundant. The most

AZURE WATERS
The seas around the Scillies have a clarity more typical of southern France than southern England. This makes for excellent diving.

recent wreck here was the cargo ship *Cita*, which foundered on 26th March 1997, leading to a bonanza of free goods for enterprising locals. This vessel is now an excellent dive, lying in 35m (115ft) of clear water. By contrast, the wreck of the *Eagle*, a British warship that sank in 1707, offers a glimpse into naval history, with cannons still visible on the seabed.

OTHER ATTRACTIONS

As well as numerous wrecks to explore, divers also have access to splendidly busy reefs, and may even encounter larger species such as seals, as well as seasonal visitors, including basking sharks.

ESSENTIAL INFORMATION

WATER TEMPERATURE 8–18°C (46–64°F)

ECOSYSTEM Temperate

WHEN TO VISIT Diving is possible all year round, although in winter there can be violent storms.

MUST SEES Inner Gilstone Rock; *Cita* and *Eagle* wrecks; grey seals.

Seals are often encountered by divers off the Scillies

The Skelligs

COUNTY CORK, IRELAND

Two rocks that jut out of the Atlantic at the eastern end of the Gulf Stream, the Skelligs are a beacon for wildlife in the rich seas off southwestern Ireland. This has created a world-class dive site in one of the finest dive regions to be found anywhere in Europe.

TWIN ISLANDS

The Skelligs sit 18km (11 miles) off the southwestern coast of Ireland, and rise almost 213m (700ft) above the wild Atlantic waters below. They consist of two huge rocks – Skellig Michael and Little Skellig – around 1.6km (1 mile) apart. The craggy faces and reefs of the rocks are washed by the waters of the North Atlantic Current, a flow of water that carries the tail end of the Gulf Stream. This brings warm waters from the mid-Atlantic, accompanied by occasional large species, such as dolphins. This current is the secret of the area's richness.

HAVEN FOR MARINE LIFE

The rock-faces of the Skelligs are coated in colourful encrusting organisms, such as anemones, sponges, and dead man's fingers. Every nook and cranny has an occupant, with huge edible crabs, lobsters, conger eels, and rocklings all jostling for position. In the kelp forests, wrasse and dogfish lurk, whilst mackerel and bass cruise the open waters. Larger residents include a healthy grey seal colony, as well as visiting basking sharks.

SHELTERING STONE

The isolated, rugged setting of Skellig Michael may look inhospitable, but beneath the water's surface the area teems with vibrant marine life.

ESSENTIAL INFORMATION

WATER TEMPERATURE 9–22°C (48–72°F)

ECOSYSTEM Temperate

WHEN TO VISIT Best time to dive on the Skelligs is between the months of April and September.

MUST SEES The Pinnacle dive site; seal colony; gannets on Little Skellig.

Lundy

BRISTOL CHANNEL, SOUTHWESTERN ENGLAND

Lundy Island sits amid the powerful tidal stream of the Bristol Channel. Washed constantly by waters rich in nutrients, it is host to wonderfully busy reefs and the occasional larger visitor arriving from the great waters of the Atlantic, to the west.

PIONEERING RESERVE

Lying 16km (10 miles) off the coast of Devon, Lundy is a craggy granite outcrop approximately 5km (3 miles) in length. The richness of its reefs and the abundance of marine life saw Lundy established as the first Marine Nature Reserve in the United Kingdom.

There are two distinct faces to Lundy – the more exposed western shore, which faces the swells and storms of the Atlantic, and the more benign eastern shore. The topography of the granite creates wonderfully dramatic cliffs and reefs, with the regular tidal movement in the channel bathing these rock faces in nutrient-rich water.

REEF POPULATIONS

Divers will encounter an array of British reef life around the island – lobsters, several species of wrasse, huge shoals of bib and pollack, bass, conger eel, and octopus. More unusual Lundy residents

GENTLE GIANT
The gaping mouth of the basking shark nets only the tiniest plankton for its food. The species is often encountered off Lundy in summer.

include anglerfish and red-banded fish – the latter being unique to the island. The island is also frequently visited by basking sharks and dolphins during summer months.

The wreck of the British warship *Montague* can be found on Shutter Reef at a depth of 5–15m (16–49ft). A 14,000-ton battleship, she ran aground in fog in 1906 while on exercises in the Bristol Channel. Massive efforts to refloat her failed. Although the wreckage is scattered and broken, there remain piles of armour plate amid the kelp. The *Montague* was armed when she sank, so beware of live shells.

ESSENTIAL INFORMATION

WATER TEMPERATURE 8–22°C (46–72°F)

ECOSYSTEM Temperate

WHEN TO VISIT Visit Lundy from April to September for the best diving.

MUST SEES Basking sharks and dolphins; the wreck of the *Montague*; Gannets Rock; Knoll Pins.

Norwegian Fjords

NORTHWESTERN COAST, NORWAY

Cold water, steep walls, and strong currents may not be everyone's ideal diving experience, but for some marine life these are ideal conditions. Diving the Norwegian fjords is not for the faint-hearted, but the rewards are well worth the effort.

WILD COASTLINE

Norway's convoluted coast stretches for around 22,000km (14,000 miles) in a series of jagged inlets, bays, and fjords, and is dotted with over 50,000 islands. Norway also has, in Sognefjord, the longest (225km/140 miles) and deepest (1,350m/4,430ft) fjord on Earth.

There are many great dive sites along this gloriously wild coastline: one of the finest regions – and one that is gaining an international reputation for the quality of its diving – is Ryfylke, to the southwest. Diving the fjords requires previous experience and competence in cold-water diving, along with the relevant

DRAMATIC HORIZON
The plunging walls of the fjords, both above and below the water's surface, set the tone for this rugged and beautiful destination.

cold-water gear. The topography of the fjords creates steep walls colonized by kelp, dead men's fingers, sponges, and some rare deep water corals. Piked dogfish, skate, catfish, and numerous crustaceans are particularly abundant in Ryfylke. Seasonal highlights include migratory visits from salmon and their attendant predators, such as orcas.

ESSENTIAL INFORMATION

WATER TEMPERATURE 2–20°C (36–68°F)

ECOSYSTEM Temperate

WHEN TO VISIT The fjords can be dived all year round, but winter months can present cold, challenging conditions.

MUST SEES Pulpit Rock; Kjerag Wall; Lysefjord; visiting orcas.

Iceland

NORTH ATLANTIC

Born from the depths of the sea itself, Iceland is still a youngster in geological terms. The country's volcanic past provides some unique dive sites, including the opportunity to explore the marine life around a hydrothermal vent.

VOLCANIC BIRTH

Iceland was formed by volcanic action on the Mid-Atlantic Ridge, and has a surface area of just over 100,000 sq km (38,610 sq miles). The island is still experiencing an extraordinary level of volcanic activity, with 30 eruptions recorded in the last 200 years. Iceland's coastline is classically volcanic, bristling with craggy inlets, dramatic cliff and rock formations, and fissured reefs.

There are two diving experiences in Iceland that are not found anywhere else in the world. The first is the legendary Strytan hydrothermal vent, which rises from a depth of 70m (230ft) to within 15m (50ft) of the water's surface. Divers can see – and indeed feel – the hot water rising from the vent while enjoying the

ICELANDIC COASTLINE
The dramatic geological eruptions that gave birth to Iceland are evident in its craggy and forbidding cliffs and wild shores.

> **ESSENTIAL INFORMATION**
>
> **WATER TEMPERATURE** 1–8°C (34–46°F)
>
> **ECOSYSTEM** Temperate
>
> **WHEN TO VISIT** Diving in Iceland is at its best in summer, between the months of June and September.
>
> **MUST SEES** Strytan hydrothermal vent; Silfra in Thingvellir National Park.

diverse invertebrate and fish life drawn into this oasis of warmth in an icy sea. The second is Silfra, a water-filled ravine in Thingvellir National Park. This is another dive that gives a marvellous insight into Iceland's fiery origins. Part of a huge rift in the Earth's crust between the Eurasian and American continental plates, Silfra is filled with glacial meltwater that has been filtered through lava for decades, giving famously crystal-clear visibility.

White Sea, Russia

NORTHEASTERN RUSSIA

The White Sea is one of the most beautiful of the seas of northern Russia, and the only place in Russia where you can dive under the ice. The marine environment here is relatively untouched by human activity and the diving is superb.

FROZEN WORLD

Diving beneath ice is exciting and adventurous, and the visibility – anything from 15 to 50m (50–164ft) – can be stunning. The water is not affected by waves (due to the protection of the ice), and low light conditions mean that algal growth is minimal. The water in the White Sea, which lies across the Arctic Circle, is frozen from November until April, but the best time to go is in mid-March. Any earlier and the temperatures are very cold, far below zero; any later and the ice has retreated and you cannot get to the best dive sites. The Gulf Stream warms some of the waters further north, preventing them from freezing over.

DENIZEN OF THE ICY DEEP
A diver comes face to face with a gorgonocephalus – or, more dramatically, "gorgon's head" – a bizarre form of basket-star common in the White Sea.

RARE ORGANISMS

The White Sea offers plenty of life to see and photograph: for example there are some 80 species of fish, around 30 species of nudibranchs, and five species of seal. Shoals of tiny comb-jellyfish also form an extraordinary sight – the light glinting off them in a million tiny rainbows. It is possible to encounter beluga whales, and occasionally orcas and Greenland sharks, which venture into these waters.

In addition to some great diving, there are possibilities of ice snorkelling in fast-flowing rivers and among the icebergs and, looking to the skies, witnessing the stunning beauty of the atmospheric phenomenon known as the Aurora Borealis, or Northern Lights. Also within excursion distance of dive sites on the east coast is Star City, the Russian cosmonaut training facility; you can even arrange to dive at the hydrospace laboratory at the MIR Space Centre, used to prepare cosmonauts for the weightless conditions of space.

ESSENTIAL INFORMATION

WATER TEMPERATURE −0.5°C (31°F) at the surface to −3°C (27°F) at depth

ECOSYSTEM Polar

WHEN TO VISIT Diving is best in mid-March (see also, above).

MUST SEES Beluga whales; seals; Aurora Borealis; cosmonaut facility.

Africa and the Middle East

A continent synonymous with adventure and exploration, Africa offers spectacular shark encounters and many miles of unexplored reef. The Middle East boasts the Red Sea, perhaps the most famous of all places to dive, with a highly developed dive industry to match.

AFRICAN HIGHLIGHTS

South Africa is renowned throughout the world for big-animal encounters – in particular with the great white sharks of the Cape – and for the epic shark dives to be had off Natal. The latter is also the scene of one of the greatest spectacles in the marine world – the legendary Sardine

DESERT MEETS SEA
At many sites in Africa, the warm blue sea laps agains a harsh, arid landscape of bleached rock.

VIBRANT ECOSYSTEM
Africa's varied reefs sport a profusion of colourful soft corals, which play host to a stunning array of marine life.

Run, where gigantic sardine shoals move slowly up the coast, harried by dolphins, whales, sharks, seals, and gannets.

Lying to the northeast of the African coast are the magnificently wild beaches and reefs of Mozambique and the islands off Kenya and Tanzania. Further out to sea lie Mauritius, the Seychelles, and the Comoros, all offering diving of real quality on reefs influenced by the abundant marine life of the Indo-Pacific region to the east.

RED SEA RICHES

The outstanding gem of the Middle East is the Red Sea, perhaps the most heavily dived body of water in the world.

From the northern resorts of Eilat, Ras Mohammed, Sharm El Sheik, and Dahab, through to the wilder southern sites like the Brothers and the coast of Sudan, this region provides superb reef diving, as well as varied wrecks, such as the famous *Thistlegorm*.

Despite its popularity, the Red Sea still has unexplored regions, and new dive sites continue to be opened, so it will always have much to attract divers.

CRYSTAL-CLEAR WATERS
One of the saltiest bodies of water in the world, the Red Sea is also renowned for its superb visibility.

Gansbaai

WESTERN CAPE, SOUTH AFRICA

Gansbaai offers a rare chance to see the ultimate marine predator. With an island packed with breeding seals just offshore, Gansbaai is one of the finest locations on Earth to get up close and personal with the great white shark.

SHARK CENTRE

Gansbaai initially appears to offer little as a dive destination, with a small harbour on a rocky shore that is frequently battered by large swells. It is only when the diver stands on the quay and squints into the middle distance that the reason for this site's global fame emerges. A low island several miles offshore is the home of 60–90,000 fur seals, and proves irresistible to the great whites that cruise this region of South Africa. Great whites are one of the ocean's most formidable predators,

AWESOME ANIMAL
Great white sharks cruise the cold waters near Dyer Island, on the hunt for their preferred prey, fur seals.

growing up to 6m (20ft) in length. The great white's notoriety as a man-eater, however, is a misrepresentation of this fascinating creature, about which surprisingly little is known.

MAIN ATTRACTION

The presence of the sharks has spawned a thriving industry, with thrill-seekers coming from all over the world to dive with the great whites. Only cage diving is permitted with the sharks, but it is possible to dive within the seal colonies around the island in certain regions that are considered safe by local dive operators. Further afield there are beautiful cold-water reefs covered in swaying fields of kelp, but there is really only one reason why divers visit Gansbaai – that most magnificent of marine predators, the great white shark.

ESSENTIAL INFORMATION

WATER TEMPERATURE 11–17°C (52–63°F)

ECOSYSTEM Temperate

WHEN TO VISIT Year-round shark activity; numbers peak May to September.

MUST SEES Cage diving with great white sharks at Dyer Island, plus seal dives in a few recommended areas.

Aliwal Shoal

KWAZULU-NATAL, SOUTH AFRICA

Aliwal Shoal is one of the greatest adventure dive sites on Earth. The excitement begins on the beach, with perhaps the most dramatic surf launch in the diving world, and ends with outstanding shark encounters above a thriving reef system.

CROSSROADS IN THE SEA

Aliwal Shoal is a mountain of sandstone that juts into the underwater highway of the Agulhas Current. The site is renowned for shark encounters, in particular the famous ragged-tooth sharks that lurk within the caves and caverns of the reef. There are also Zambezi sharks in great numbers at the right time of year, as well as more occasional encounters with tiger sharks, and, thrillingly, there are a few rare sightings of great whites. However, Aliwal Shoal has so much more to offer than shark encounters, as the mixture of warm water reef fish and temperate species creates one of the most diverse reef systems in the whole of southern Africa.

VISITING SPECIES

Added to the array of life are transient visitors, such as migrating humpback and right whales, as well as turtles and huge brindle bass. The dive site is also directly in the path of the Sardine Run, one of the most impressive marine migrations anywhere in the world's oceans. Sardine shoals travel more than 1,600km (1,000 miles) in this great annual exodus.

ESSENTIAL INFORMATION

WATER TEMPERATURE 19–26°C (66–79°F)

ECOSYSTEM Subtropical

WHEN TO VISIT Ragged-tooth sharks in residence from July to October; Zambezi sharks can be seen October–April.

MUST SEES Ragged-tooth sharks; Sardine Run; migrating whales.

SURF SAFARI
Dive boats often encounter heavy surf on their way to Aliwal Shoal, some distance off shore. Launching in these conditions is exhilarating.

Sodwana Bay

KWAZULU-NATAL, SOUTH AFRICA

AFRICA
Maputo
Sodwana Bay
SOUTH
AFRICA   Durban   Indian
Ocean

The only coral reef dive site in South Africa, Sodwana is set in the heart of a National Park in northern Natal. The reefs host more than 1,000 species of fish, as well as impressive transients, such as whale sharks, billfish, manta rays, and whales.

REMOTE REEFS

Sodwana lies in a beautifully remote region of South Africa, nestling right up against the border with Mozambique to the north. Simply getting to the site is something of an adventure, requiring a journey by four-wheel drive vehicle through wild bush and bumpy dirt tracks. Although the dive industry in Sodwana is well established, it is also closely monitored. Only three dive centres are allowed to operate in the region to limit the number of divers on the reef and so protect the delicate coral reef ecosystem.

ESSENTIAL INFORMATION

WATER TEMPERATURE 21–29°C (70–84°F)

ECOSYSTEM Tropical reef

WHEN TO VISIT Year-round diving, but visit October to February for a chance of sighting whale sharks at Sodwana.

MUST SEES Seven Mile Reef; Nine Mile Reef; surf launch; whale sharks, mantas, and other visiting species.

Turtles of several species visit Sodwana

DIVERSE ATTRACTIONS

The four established reefs off Sodwana are named after their distance from the launch site, and are called Two, Five, Seven, and Nine Mile Reef. Each offers something slightly different, ranging from the most delicate of hard corals through to encounters with large ocean-going species including whale sharks. Although the journey to Sodwana is a considerable undertaking, the reward is nothing less than one of the finest coral reef dives on the continent.

SURF AND SAND

Despite the fact that Sodwana Bay is fairly remote, the site can be busy. Dive boats often launch with an audience of waiting divers.

Protea Banks

KWAZULU-NATAL, SOUTH AFRICA

Even within the singularly robust South African diving community, Protea Banks is a dive site famed for thrills. A reef cut with deep gullies, overhangs, and caverns, and notable for its shark encounters, this is not a site for the faint-hearted.

ON THE PROWL
The tiger shark is a species quite regularly sighted around Protea Banks, often with remora fish in tow.

CHALLENGING SITE
Although Protea Banks does not boast the dramatic topography of nearby Aliwal Shoal (*see p.259*), it lacks none of the excitement. Indeed there are many in the local diving community who consider Protea Banks more extreme than Aliwal – the reasons being the depth, the currents, and the terrific shark encounters. The top of the reef is, on average, deeper than Aliwal Shoal, with several dives in excess of 30m (98ft). The currents that sweep over the flat reef-crest are also stronger, and several of the dives are exhilarating drifts over a considerable distance of undersea terrain.

SHARK SPOTTING
The final reason Protea Banks is so revered amongst the dive community in South Africa is its shark encounters.

Not only can large numbers of ragged-tooth sharks be found here during their mating season, but there is a strong possibility of encountering tiger sharks or hammerheads. For several months of the year divers can also be confronted in mid-water by large numbers of the Zambezi shark. These magnificent predators follow game fish that arrive during the summer months.

ESSENTIAL INFORMATION

WATER TEMPERATURE 19–26°C (66–79°F)

ECOSYSTEM Subtropical

WHEN TO VISIT Ragged-tooth sharks can be seen from July to October; Zambezi sharks from October to April.

MUST SEES Ragged-tooth sharks; Zambezi sharks; migrating whales.

Mozambique

SOUTHEAST AFRICA

Wracked by decades of civil war, Mozambique was once a forgotten destination in world diving. The end of the conflict in 1992 prompted the gradual return of divers, and revealed the riches that lie in the blue waters off one of Africa's wildest coastlines.

NURTURING SEAS

The fast-moving waters of the Agulhas Current, which pass through the gap between the east coast of Mozambique and the island of Madagascar, are the source of much of Mozambique's great marine diversity. The reefs in this region are teeming with life, and although the entire coastline has dive sites of merit, there are certain regions that stand out, including Inhaca Island, Ponta do Ouro, the Bazaruto Archipelago, and Cabo San Sebastian.

FAR-FLUNG LOCATION

Mozambique is by no means an easy dive destination to access. Many of the sites to the south of the country require

a sturdy four-wheel drive vehicle to cope with the dirt and sand roads, and the isolated operators and resorts are tucked in behind long stretches of deserted beach. However, Mozambique's dive sites offer ample reward. The southern region of the country has become well

known for encounters with huge potato bass and ragged-tooth sharks, whereas further north encounters with bull and tiger sharks are a distinct possibility. Humpback whales move through the area in the summer months, and the occasional dugong is sighted in the shallow estuaries along the coast.

The Bazaruto Archipelago on Mozambique's central coast is an excellent place to see whale sharks, while nearby Vilnaculos is an excellent site to encounter manta rays and dolphins.

BRIGHT FUTURE

Mozambique still has a primitive tourist infrastructure, particularly in the northern regions of the country. Malaria is also a significant factor, with most of the country affected at certain times of the year. Nonetheless, Mozambique is making tremendous progress as a tourist destination, with the country's diving rapidly establishing itself as truly world class. Diving here can present challenges for the intrepid traveller, but the isolation and low tourist traffic can be seen as a real advantage in one of Africa's most rapidly developing dive destinations.

WAVE-SWEPT WILDERNESS

Mozambique has over 2,414km (1,500 miles) of coastline, much of it sparsely inhabited. The southern stretches of coast are dominated by sandbars, estuaries, and swamps, whilst the wilder north is characterized by long beaches and cliffs. The entire coastline is tremendously dramatic and wild, and even the capital Maputo has the famous Inhaca Island – a site famed in the diving world for its large animal encounters – directly offshore. Dolphins, whale sharks, and manta rays all frequent this site.

Surf breaks on a stretch of coast

LARGER THAN LIFE
Enormous potato bass are often found patrolling the bustling reefs of Mozambique. This imposing species can be extremely inquisitive, and individuals often approach divers.

Seychelles

WESTERN INDIAN OCEAN

The clear waters of the Seychelles teem with abundant marine life, and offer those prepared to travel that bit further a range of gentle reef dives on the inner islands. The outer islands have big walls, wild drifts, and large-animal encounters.

A PATTERN OF ISLANDS

The Seychelles archipelago numbers 115 islands in total, although these are spread over a vast area of ocean hundreds of kilometres off the east coast of Africa. The Seychelles is divided into the inner islands and the outer islands, with the two groups over 1,100km (680 miles) apart. The inner islands – including Mahe, the main island in the Seychelles – sit on a huge natural platform rising from the deep ocean around them. As such, diving here tends to be within the 10–30m (33–100ft) range, and takes place on shallow protected reef systems. Further afield are the outer islands, including the Aldabras, a group of islands known as the

TROPICAL VISTA
Balmy tropical beaches are typical of the Seychelles. Though remote, the islands offer tremendous attractions for the diver.

ESSENTIAL INFORMATION

WATER TEMPERATURE 27–29°C (81–84°F)

ECOSYSTEM Tropical

WHEN TO VISIT May to October.

MUST SEES Large pelagic species in the Aldabra Group; shallow reefs and marine life around the inner islands, including Mahe.

Powder blue tang

"Galápagos of the Indian Ocean" due to their isolation and diversity of marine life. The diving here is more intense and suitable only for experienced divers. The reef cuts and walls create opportunities for tremendous drift-dives, in which divers are carried along by underwater currents.

Mauritius

WESTERN INDIAN OCEAN

The islands of Mauritius in the Indian Ocean are a popular holiday destination, but are not well known for diving. This is something of an oversight, as the islands' stark volcanic reefs harbour a rich tropical ecosystem and offer dives of real quality.

VOLCANIC ORIGINS

Mauritius consists of two islands, and numerous smaller islets, located 800km (500 miles) east of Madagascar. Although relatively small, the islands have nearly 400km (250 miles) of undulating coastline due to the craggy nature of the volcanic rock that makes up the island group. The seas are colonized by over 200 species of coral, creating reefs inhabited by around 450 fish species – a rich tropical ecosystem.

ESSENTIAL INFORMATION

WATER TEMPERATURE 21–28°C (70–82°F)

ECOSYSTEM Tropical

WHEN TO VISIT Diving takes place in Mauritius all year round.

MUST SEES The Rempart Serpent and Cathedral dive sites; the unspoilt reefs around Rodrigues Island.

PLACE IN THE SUN
The shallow coastal waters and white sands of Mauritius make it a leading holiday destination, but it also offers great diving experiences.

TOP LOCATIONS

Most diving in Mauritius takes place on the western coast of the main island, as the eastern end of the island is exposed to the wind and waves of the open ocean. The Cathedral cavern with its resident porcupine fish is a must-see, and the Rempart Serpent site boasts a huge number of moray eels (it is reputed that 32 species have been seen here!). The region north of the main island, however, is becoming known as a good spot for encounters with some of the larger pelagic species, with regular sightings of tuna, wahoo, and marlin. The remote island of Rodrigues to the east offers a glimpse of some of the region's most pristine reefs – making an excursion well worth the effort.

The Brothers

NORTHERN RED SEA, EGYPT

Spectacular coral gardens have grown undisturbed around these two remote pinnacles of rock for thousands of years. Only accessible by liveaboard (*see p.237*), the Brothers dive site offers steep drop-offs and some terrific shark action.

ISOLATED OUTCROPS

The Brothers consist of two large rocks, named Little Brother and Big Brother, around 1.6km (1 mile) apart and 58km (36 miles) offshore in the northern Red Sea. Rising from deep water, they provide dramatically steep walls as a foundation for bustling reefs, and the upwellings of nutrient-rich waters and swirling currents draw in fish species both large and small.

SHARK SPOTTING

In addition to the diversity and colour of the reefs themselves, there are some tremendous shark encounters off the walls of the Brothers. Common species

REMOTE ROCK
Big Brother, the larger and more northerly of the two islands, is 400m (1,300ft) long and 90m (295ft) wide, and dominated by a lighthouse.

in the area include white-tip and grey reef sharks, although silver-tips, scalloped hammerheads, and oceanic white-tips are also frequently seen. If you are lucky, you may even encounter a thresher shark. Its scythe-shaped tail fin makes this species an unmistakable, if very infrequent, sight.

WRECKED ON THE REEF

As an additional attraction to the site, two wrecks – the *Aida* and the *Numidia* – cling to the precipitous sides of Big Brother. The *Numidia*, a former cargo vessel, lies at a very steep angle on the northern tip of the rock, with which she collided in 1901. Her bow can be found in just 8m (26ft) of water, but her stern lies in the depths, at 80m (262ft).

Another victim of Big brother was the Italian supply ship *Aida*, which sank in 1957 while carrying troops. Almost as impressive as *Numidia* and surprisingly intact, *Aida* is now heavily colonized.

ESSENTIAL INFORMATION

WATER TEMPERATURE 21–29°C (70–84°F)

ECOSYSTEM Tropical

WHEN TO VISIT Diving takes place on the Brothers all year round.

MUST SEES Oceanic white-tip sharks; scalloped hammerheads; wreck of the *Numidia*; (occasionally) thresher sharks.

Dahab

NORTHERN RED SEA, EGYPT

The coastal town of Dahab in southern Sinai is ringed by mountains and desert. The inhospitable landscape is in striking contrast to the splendid reefs and coral formations to be found just offshore – among which is the infamous Blue Hole.

DESERT HAMLET

Dahab lies on the Gulf of Aqaba, in the northeast of the Red Sea, only 80km (50 miles) north of the busy dive resort of Sharm El Sheik. Clinging to the shore in a harsh, arid landscape, the town has a faintly frontier feel to it. There are several dive centres in Dahab, offering training to all levels of ability.

DIVING IN DAHAB

Within a short drive of Dahab are many excellent sites accessible from the shore, including the Canyon and the Bells. Both of these sites are dramatic examples of the twisted coral formations that seem to characterize this stretch of coastline, with deep gullies, impressive overhangs, arches, and swim-throughs. The legendary Blue Hole site is actually the top of a massive shaft that sinks 300m (984ft) into the reef. The lure of diving through a long passage to the outer reef at a depth of 50m (164ft) has caused many divers to perish in the Blue Hole, and the received wisdom for diving this deep arch is that it should only be attempted using technical dive techniques and equipment (*see pp.194–95*).

ESSENTIAL INFORMATION

WATER TEMPERATURE 21–28°C (70–82°F)

ECOSYSTEM Tropical

WHEN TO VISIT Diving takes place in Dahab all year round, with water temperatures high throughout.

MUST SEES The Blue Hole; The Canyon and The Bells; Gabr El Bint (by boat only).

SHELL GAME
A diver follows a turtle – at a respectful distance – as it conducts a slow tour of one of Dahab's colourful reefs.

Wreck of the *Thistlegorm*

NORTHERN RED SEA, EGYPT

Packed full of artefacts and lying in the clear waters of the Red Sea, the *Thistlegorm* is perhaps the most famous of all shipwrecks for divers. Her fame comes at a price, however, with great numbers of divers clambering through the structure every day.

THE CLASSIC WRECK

The *Thistlegorm* first came to the attention of the global diving community in the 1950s, when she was discovered and filmed by Jacques Cousteau. Her location remained a secret until 1992, when she was rediscovered by recreational divers, and she has since become the most popular diving wreck in the entire Red Sea.

The *Thistlegorm* was a World War II armed merchant vessel, 126m (413ft) in length, carrying supplies to the British 8th Army in North Africa. Packed with machinery and ammunition, she was spotted in the northern Red Sea by a German bomber on the 6th October 1941. Two bombs entered her Number Four hold, causing a huge explosion that cut her in half; she sank immediately with the loss of nine souls.

DIVE EXPERIENCE

In many ways, the *Thistlegorm* is the perfect wreck dive. Her bow lies just 15m (50ft) below the surface in clear waters, and no part of the vessel is

TIME CAPSULE

A diver examines military hardware inside the wreck of the *Thistlegorm*

For many years after the *Thistlegorm* was sunk, British vessels would lower their flag as they passed her wreck, but today she has a happier role, having become a focus for diving in the Red Sea. The vessel's real treasure is its outstanding cargo of military equipment, which ranges from Lee Enfield Mark 3 rifles, wellington boots, Bedford trucks, and two Rolls Royce armoured cars, to – perhaps most famously of all – racks of BSA motorcycles. On the deck stands one locomotive; another lies on the sea bed beside the wreck.

below 30m (100ft); however, currents may be strong, and descent is usually made down mooring lines tied by the guide. Once inside the wreck there is a vast, serene, yet poignant underwater museum to explore, and the sheer size of the vessel means that thorough exploration requires several visits.

The *Thistlegorm* holds a unique place in divers' affections, though her popularity has become a drawback. She is only a

ESSENTIAL INFORMATION

WATER TEMPERATURE 20–29°C (68–84°F)

ECOSYSTEM Tropical

WHEN TO VISIT Year round. The wreck is best dived from a liveaboard.

MUST SEES The captain's bath; BSA motorcycles; locomotive on deck; Bedford trucks; armoured cars.

five-hour cruise away from the Red Sea's busy diving centre of Sharm el Sheikh, and in peak season it is not uncommon for more than 20 diving vessels to be moored over her at one time. The best time to dive is at dawn, when there is a chance to see this grand old lady of a wreck with few others around, although this means finding a skipper who will travel through the night.

Although not as densely colonized as one might expect, the *Thistlegorm* wreck still has abundant marine life. This region has approximately 1,000 fish species, 17 per cent of which are endemic to the Red Sea. Of particular note on the *Thistlegorm* are large numbers of lionfish, which lie in wait ready to ambush shoals of unsuspecting glassy sweepers, whilst overhead jack and barracuda sweep the superstructure for prey.

WEAPON OF WAR

A diver hovers above the distinctive deck gun on *Thistlegorm's* stern. There are strict penalties for wreck-stripping, so never be tempted to take a souvenir.

Asia

The tropical regions of this vast continent have always been highly praised by divers for the staggering richness of their marine life and their glorious reefs, but adventurous new diving opportunities are also beginning to open up to the north – even in Siberia.

REEFS UNDER THREAT

The geographical span of Asia, the largest continent, is reflected in the vast range of diving available. For many divers and marine biologists, the highlight is the famed "Triangle of Diversity" – a region in the Indo-Pacific that boasts the world's greatest diversity of coral and fish species.

The many thousands of islands of the Philippines, Indonesia, Papua New Guinea, and Malaysia are host to some legendary dive sites, with evocative names such as Sipadan, Lembeh, Tubbutaha, Komodo, and Kimbe. Sadly, while these are all dream destinations for any diver, destructive fishing techniques in the Indo-Pacific region, such as

dynamite and cyanide fishing, are damaging some of these delicate ecosystems. In the Philippines, only 4 per cent of all reefs remain unaffected by human activity, with up to 30 per cent reported to be impacted beyond recovery. Beautiful pristine reefs can still be found in the Indo-Pacific, but when diving on these threatened reef systems, be mindful of your responsibility to minimize any impact your presence could have.

BEACH BASE
A dive base on a sun-kissed tropical beach can provide the ideal "chill-out" spot after an exhilarating dive.

RESPONSIBLE REEF DIVING
With Asia's reefs at risk, it is vital that divers follow the rules of responsible reef diving to conserve them for future generations.

BEYOND THE TROPICS

The classic perception of Asian diving tends to be the archetypal tropical island chain fringed by glorious technicolour reefs. Dive sites throughout the region, including the Maldives, the Andaman Islands, and the Similan Islands, are all justifiably famed for their extraordinary diversity and beauty, both above and below the surface.

PYGMY SEA HORSE
A rare species found only on *Muricella* coral in Southeast Asia and Australia, the pygmy seahorse wraps its tail around coral branches and lies in wait for tiny crustaceans and larvae.

However, although much of the diving in Asia tends to be concentrated in the tropics, there are some excellent dive sites to be explored further north. One of the most notable is Lake Baikal in Siberia. This is the world's deepest lake, and the largest reservoir of freshwater on the planet's surface. Because of its size and varying depths, Lake Baikal contains a huge variety of ecosystems.

The Maldives

INDIAN OCEAN

Arabian Sea
INDIA
Maldives
SRI LANKA
Indian Ocean

Coming to prominence as a dive destination in the 1970s, the Maldives swiftly became established as a dream diving location. The extent of the archipelago, and its range of dive sites, ensures that it remains an essential stop-off at least once in a diver's lifetime.

RICH ARCHIPELAGO

The islands of the Maldives are the crests of an undersea mountain range that plunges over 2km (1¼ miles) into the deep waters of the Indian Ocean. The archipelago extends 764km (475 miles) from north to south, and is 129km (80 miles) across. This vast collection of islands is loosely divided into 26 major atolls, and although the islands are spread over 98,000 sq km (38,000 sq miles) of ocean, their land mass covers only 300 sq km (115 sq miles).

The Maldives offer a huge range of diving activities for those lucky enough to visit. Such is the abundance and delicacy of the remarkable reef systems throughout the Maldives that there are no less than 25 nature reserves and protected areas within the island group. The marine life around the islands is colourful and diverse, and includes over 700 fish species.

ESSENTIAL INFORMATION

WATER TEMPERATURE 24–29°C (75–84°F)

ECOSYSTEM Tropical

WHEN TO VISIT Diving takes place all year-round in the Maldives.

MUST SEES Grey reef sharks; hammerhead sharks; manta rays; whale sharks; turtles.

TOUGH CHALLENGES

Tourism and diving are vital to the economy of the Maldives, but both industries have had to recover from major natural disasters in the late 20th and early 21st centuries. El Niño – a periodic warming event in the Pacific Ocean – had a severe impact in 1997–98, when the hard coral on many reefs was bleached and killed by the rise in ocean temperatures. The islands were also hit by the 2004 tsunami, which destroyed much of the tourist infrastructure.

Fishing and diving boats ready for business on a Maldives quayside

Diving in the Maldives tends to be divided into drift dives on the outer reef, and dive sites within the atolls. The latter contain thilas, a local word meaning a coral platform rising almost to the water's surface, and kandus, which are smaller isolated coral outcrops and coral heads. The best drift diving is where cuts in the coral walls leading to the open sea channel tidal water through narrow gaps.

Most dives in the Maldives seem to include at least one encounter with white-tip reef sharks, and there are several sites where grey and black-tip reef sharks, as well as hammerheads, may be seen. Eagle rays and manta rays, too, are regularly encountered at the right time of year at certain sites, with whale sharks also returning to the same sites to make the most of seasonal feeding grounds. There are also five different species of turtle in the Maldives, the most common of which are the green and hawksbill turtles.

COLOURFUL CORAL
A diver examines soft corals on one of the region's flourishing reef systems. The Maldives offer an incredible variety of quality dives.

Similan Islands

ANDAMAN SEA, INDIAN OCEAN

A tiny string of granite islands sitting off the coast of Thailand, the Similans are best explored by liveaboard dive boat, but with some of the best beaches in Thailand, they have a great deal to offer both above and below the water.

STONE AND SEA

The Similan Islands consist of nine large granite outcrops sitting 64km (40 miles) off the coast of Thailand. They rise from the depths of the Andaman Sea, and run for 24km (15 miles) north to south. Although the islands do have individual names, they are commonly known simply by numbers, starting in the south with Number 1 (Koh Huyong), and continuing to Number 9 (Koh Bangu) in the north.

They are characterized by steep granite undersea cliffs on their western shores, with more gentle slopes to the east, where, sheltered from the summer monsoon winds, the coral growth is particularly lush. Over 1,000 fish species swarm over reefs colonized by a dazzling array of soft corals. Brightly coloured species, such as coral grouper, sweetlips, snapper, and blue triggerfish are present in great numbers and, from October to May, whale sharks and manta rays are frequently encountered.

The thriving reef systems around the islands were once threatened by overfishing as well as "dynamite fishing"

SHARK SPOTTING
A diver observes a leopard shark, hovering above this beautifully patterned predator, which frequents the waters of the Similans.

– the use of explosives to kill and collect large numbers of fish – but the islands were declared a National Park in 1982, and commercial fishing is now banned. The sweeping coral fields of Christmas Point are particularly spectacular, although they were slightly damaged in the tsunami of 2004. Other notable attractions include a dramatic maze of huge boulder formations at Elephant's Head Rock. The Similans remain well worth every hour of sea-crossing required to visit them.

ESSENTIAL INFORMATION

WATER TEMPERATURE 26–29°C (79–84°F)

ECOSYSTEM Tropical

WHEN TO VISIT Visit the Similan Islands between October and May.

MUST SEES Whale sharks and manta rays; boulder formations at Elephant's Head Rock; Christmas Point.

Andaman Islands

ANDAMAN SEA, INDIAN OCEAN

INDIA
THAILAND
Bangkok
Andaman Islands
MALAYSIA
Indian Ocean

One of the last great diving wildernesses, the Andamans are a truly unspoilt string of volcanic islands in the Bay of Bengal. Cloaked in rainforest and home to some of the last untouched tribes on Earth, they offer genuine diving exploration.

ISOLATED IDYLL

The Andaman Islands are sprinkled over 700km (435 miles) of ocean, and define the western edge of the Andaman Sea. Although the archipelago consists of 572 islands, only 36 are inhabited. Over 80 per cent of the land mass is covered in rainforest, home to tribes that have had very little contact with the outside world; in some cases, none at all.

The islanders do not run any commercial fishing operations to speak of, and therefore the steep walls and rich reefs of the region are home to a range of large marine animals in healthy populations not encountered anywhere else in the Andaman Sea.

DIVER'S PARADISE
With no large-scale fishing fleet, the Andaman Islands have well-preserved reefs stocked with a fascinating diversity of marine life.

ESSENTIAL INFORMATION

WATER TEMPERATURE 28–31°C (82–88°F)

ECOSYSTEM Tropical

WHEN TO VISIT Visit beween the months of November and May.

MUST SEES Barren Island; Passage Island; large manta ray aggregations; steep lava walls; dog-tooth tuna.

Diving takes place from November through to May, and can either be from liveaboard dive vessels, or through a small number of operators based in the islands. Notable sites include the outlying islands of Passage Island, Narcondam, and Barren Island, which have barely been dived at all. Expect encounters with a range of shark species, huge dog-tooth tuna, and feeding manta rays.

North Sulawesi

CELEBES SEA, INDONESIA

Indonesia has been termed the "Cradle of Diversity" by marine biologists, and with good reason. A recent survey counted more than 3,000 fish species here. Crowning it all is North Sulawesi, and the jewel in that crown is the Lembeh Straits.

CONSERVATION IN ACTION

North Sulawesi is formed by the long thin peninsula that juts out from Sulawesi Island into the Celebes Sea. The marine species diversity of this region is unparalleled, a fact recognized by the locals, who have set up a number of reserves, and by the divers who flock here. The careful approach to the marine environment here by local government means that 90 per cent of the coral cover is live and in good condition, a remarkable statistic considering the pressure the remainder of the Indonesian archipelago experiences from destructive fishing methods.

ESSENTIAL INFORMATION

WATER TEMPERATURE 23–28°C (74–82°F)

ECOSYSTEM Tropical

WHEN TO VISIT Year-round; optimum period between May and November.

MUST SEES Panguilingan; Lejuan II; Mandolin; muck diving for ghost pipefish; pygmy sea horses; mimic octopus.

Camera in water-tight plastic housing

a shallow body of water – ranging in depth from 5m (16ft) to a maximum of 30m (98ft) – so divers need to be aware of the large vessels that pass regularly overhead, as well as the periodic strong currents.

But while at first glance this may seem merely an unprepossessing shipping channel, closer inspection reveals a world of tiny riches.

NATURAL TREASURES

The Lembeh Straits is the channel between the island of Lembeh and the northern tip of Sulawesi. It is quite

MACRO LIFE IN SULAWESI

The magic that draws divers to this area is the extraordinary range of tiny but beautiful reef animals that can be found in the shallow coastal seas off North Sulawesi. The sheer diversity of "macro life" (small marine creatures) here, and the sometimes bizarre forms it takes, has led to the area being dubbed "God's dustbin". Outlandish species like the hairy frogfish make amazing photographic subjects.

A hairy frogfish gapes in the current

The Straits have a big name for small things – this is the finest site in the world for encountering the most exquisite, delicate, and unusual inhabitants of tropical seas. Diving in the Lembeh Straits goes by the unpromising name of "muck diving" – so called because of the dark sand that covers the seabed and the necessity to examine it closely for target species during the course of a dive. But the effort involved in diving here is well rewarded. Mimic octopus, pygmy sea horses, ghost pipefish, leaf fish, frog fish, and blue-ringed octopus can all be found here.

CONSERVATION AREA

The Bunaken Marine Park is one of the driving forces for conservation on North Sulawesi. It surrounds five islands, on which are a few small fishing villages, and covers over 750 sq km (290 sq miles). The park offers fantastic muck diving and also some tremendous walls, the most notable of which are Lekuan II and Mandolin on Bunaken, and Panguilingan in Mahado Tua.

VOYAGE OF DISCOVERY
An indigenous fisherman setting out in a traditional canoe. Many divers eschew the clear surface waters for the pleasures of muck diving.

Papua New Guinea

WESTERN PACIFIC

A location that still epitomizes diving exploration, Papua New Guinea offers a hugely exciting diving experience for the intrepid dive tourist. A vast region with numerous undived reefs and islands, Papua New Guinea is a real adventure.

OUTER LIMITS

For many years Papua New Guinea drew only the very boldest pioneers of adventure diving and extreme tourism. Made up of 600 islands, the reputation of this region as a wild and untamed part of the world is well founded. Papua New Guinea has 4 million inhabitants, divided into 1,000 tribes that speak 700 different languages. Spread over the 460,000 sq km (177,600 sq miles) of the island group, many of these indigenous tribes knew nothing of the modern world until very recently, with one tribe only making contact with the outside world in the late 20th century. Doubtless, others – as yet unknown – exist in the rugged Highlands, with much of the main island of New Guinea consisting of mountainous rainforest with a maximum elevation of 4,500m (14,760ft). While most visits to Papua New Guinea are trouble free, travel after dark is not advised, and in towns such as the capital, Port Moresby, the risk of robbery and violent crime must be taken seriously. Trips are best arranged with well-established diving operations who can provide guides and transport to the coastal diving regions, where the risks are significantly lower than in poor urban areas.

PRISTINE REEFS

The shallower regions of Papua New Guinea's coastline are the site of some fantastically complex reef formations, with perhaps the most famous being Kimbe Bay on the western coast of New Britain. Another dive site that has gained a reputation for providing particularly dramatic reefs and tremendous diversity is Eastern Fields, in the northern limits of the Coral Sea. This remote site can only be reached by ocean-going vessels and remains relatively unexplored.

Vibrant coral reef in Papua New Guinea

RICH SEAS

The good news is that the rugged terrain of the land frequently extends below the surface of the water, and Papua New Guinea is notable for the fact that its seas reach abyssal depths only a short distance from shore. This creates tremendous drop-offs and steep walls, which are inhabited by a bewildering array of species. The region has twice the number of fish species as the Red Sea, and ten times the coral species of the Caribbean.

SUNKEN HISTORY

In addition to this extraordinary species-diversity is a number of extremely fine wrecks, most of them relics of fierce

ESSENTIAL INFORMATION

WATER TEMPERATURE 24–28°C (75–82°F)

ECOSYSTEM Tropical

WHEN TO VISIT Diving takes place all year round in Papua New Guinea.

MUST SEES Submerged atoll at Eastern Fields; marine life in Kimbe Bay; World War II aircraft wrecks in Milne Bay.

fighting in the region during World War II. Rabaul, Kavieng, Loboata, and Madang all provide excellent wreck diving, with aircraft debris littering the seabed in certain areas, like Milne Bay.

Diving throughout the archipelago is becoming more accessible due to the presence of a number of established diving operators in the more renowned dive sites, and the increasing range of liveaboard operators now pushing into some truly remote regions. Nonetheless, there are still underwater areas of this extraordinary island group that remain completely unexplored. In a world that seems to become smaller and smaller with each passing day, it is an exciting thought that such places still exist for us to discover. By taking a responsible approach to venturing off the beaten track, divers can help preserve this region, and by doing so ensure a steady stream of new adventures for many years to come.

GHOSTLY REMAINS
Wreckage of aircraft lost during World War II is a notable sight in the waters off Papua New Guinea. The area was the scene of battles between Allied and Japanese forces.

The Philippines

SOUTHEAST ASIA

The Philippines undoubtedly offer a world of diving possibilities. Although destructive fishing techniques have taken their toll on many reefs, local legislation and a realization of the benefits dive tourism can bring to the local economy offer a chance of recovery.

RESTORING LOST REEFS

Consisting of 7,107 islands spread over 300,000 sq km (116,000 sq miles), the Philippines comprise one of the most bountiful regions on Earth in terms of species diversity, with at least 2,000 fish species recorded throughout the archipelago. However, in many areas, complex and delicate reef systems have been almost completely destroyed by dynamite and cyanide fishing. A recent survey noted that "excellent" reefs – those classified as having more than 75 per cent healthy coral cover – are

> ### ESSENTIAL INFORMATION
>
> **WATER TEMPERATURE** 24–27°C (75–81°F)
>
> **ECOSYSTEM** Tropical
>
> **WHEN TO VISIT** Best diving conditions are between April and November.
>
> **MUST SEES** Tubbutaha Reef; Jessie Beazley reef; Coron Bay; Apo Island; Puerto Galera.

now present in only 4.3 per cent of the total reef area surveyed. This is an issue that the Philippines authorities are, thankfully, attempting to address, and certain regions now have energetic conservation programmes in place.

LIVEABOARD EXCURSIONS

The remote Tubbutaha and Jessie Beazley Reefs in the Sulu Sea remain relatively undamaged, and provide some world-class diving. All diving at Tubbutaha is from liveaboards, although many of the shallow reef crests provide excellent snorkelling opportunities. The steep walls of Tubbutaha are swept by strong currents and have crystal-clear visibility. Of particular quality is North End, a dive that combines spur and groove reef formations with some classic walls. Jessie Beazley Reef is essentially a massive pillar of rock rising from deep water, providing a beacon for groupers, manta rays, barracuda, and eagle rays.

Quality diving can also be found at the Visayas, a small cluster of islands accessed via Cebu City. Malapuscua

HOLIDAY HOTSPOT
Indigenous water craft pulled up at a palm-fringed beach in the region. The Philippines appeal to both divers and non-divers alike.

HISTORIC FINDS
A diver inspects a wreck off the Philippines.
Palawan Island is the departure point for Coron
Bay, with its extensive World War II wrecks.

has become particularly famous for providing one of the most unusual of all shark dives, at a site where thresher sharks congregate to be "groomed" by cleaner fish (*see pp.225–26*). Apo Island is a fine example of a progressive conservation project, where local people have become involved in policing the reefs around the island.

MUCK AND WRECK DIVING

Further north at Puerto Galera, readily accessible from Manila, is some of the finest diving in the Philippines, with some outstanding "muck diving" (*see p.279*). Palawan also offers some wilder diving, with Coron Bay containing some particularly fine Japanese wrecks sunk during an attack by US aircraft on 24th September 1944.

Barracuda Lake offers a genuinely different diving experience, requiring a short jungle hike that is rewarded by an exploration of a system in which freshwater sits on top of seawater. A large barracuda in the lake is said to guide divers through his territory.

MARINE LIFE

The diversity of this archipelago is truly remarkable, with 1,499 crustacean species, 462 types of mollusc, and 22 different types of beach vegetation. Of the 500 known coral species worldwide, 488 are found here. This biological diversity was recognized in 1993, when the Tubbataha Reef Marine Park was made a World Heritage site.

The mandarin fish, one of over 2,000 fish species recorded in the Philippines

Australasia

The vast coastline of Australia offers superb coral reefs as well as spine-tingling cold-water encounters with giant marine predators. New Zealand, to the southeast, is rapidly emerging as a dive destination of real quality, with some of the world's best temperate dive sites.

BARRIER REEF AND MORE

For the uninitiated, the notion of diving in Australasia is limited to exploring the Great Barrier Reef, which lies on the northeastern coast of Australia. One of the most impressive natural features on the planet, it is a site of remarkable species diversity.

While the fame of the reef is fully justified, there are also many other rewarding dive sites in Australia and New Zealand. East of the tourist hotspots of the Great Barrier Reef lies the Coral Sea, equally beautiful and with fabulous marine life to be seen. To the south of Australia, the cold waters of Dangerous Reef and the Neptune Islands offer thrilling encounters with great white sharks. Further south still is Tasmania, home to lush kelp forests. On the sparsely populated western coast of Australia is Ningaloo Reef, one of the best locations for encountering the mighty whale shark.

VOLCANIC REEF
The temperate reefs of New Zealand's Poor Knights Islands teem with colourful marine life.

NEW ZEALAND

The jewel in New Zealand's diving crown is the Poor Knights Islands, which for many (including the late Jacques Cousteau) ranks as the finest temperate-water dive site in the world. The unique topography of the site means that this is a breathtaking place to dive, with vast shoals of fish swarming over craggy volcanic reefs and through atmospheric cavern systems. Protected by both traditional Maori law and modern legislation, the islands are a magnet for divers the world over.

New Zealand boasts some impressive wrecks, including the world-famous *Rainbow Warrior* and the dramatic *Mikhail Lermentov*. It is also rapidly developing a reputation for providing big-animal encounters with numerous whale species, as well as with iconic sharks such as the mako and the bronze whaler. To cap it all, New Zealand also offers stunning scenery, crystal clear rivers and springs, and magnificent fjords.

SOUTHERN FJORDS
The fauna of New Zealand's fjords includes red and black corals, penguins, fur seals, and bottlenose dolphins.

LIFE ON THE REEF
The Great Barrier Reef hosts a vast array of flora and fauna, including more than 1,500 fish species and 4,000 different types of mollusc.

Great Barrier Reef

Great Barrier Reef
Cairns
AUSTRALIA
Perth   Sydney
Southern Ocean

One of the true natural wonders of the world, the Great Barrier Reef is the longest reef of its kind on Earth. Home to a spectacular diversity of animal and plant life, recent legislation has granted even greater protection for this abundant natural habitat.

VAST ECOSYSTEM

The Great Barrier Reef is so extensive that its precise size has never been recorded, although it is estimated that it stretches for 2,250km (1,400 miles), and covers around 350,000 sq km (135,000 sq miles) – about the same surface area as Ireland. It is made up of 2,000 individual reefs, and around 71 coral islands are spread along its length.

In broad terms the Great Barrier Reef can be said to be divided into two regions – the inner reef, known as the

> ### ESSENTIAL INFORMATION
>
> **WATER TEMPERATURE** 24–29°C (77–84°F)
>
> **ECOSYSTEM** Tropical
>
> **WHEN TO VISIT** The Great Barrier Reef can be dived throughout the year.
>
> **MUST SEES** Ribbon Reefs (particularly Ribbon Reef Number 10); Cod Hole; Pixie's Pinnacle.

Great Shallow, and the outer reef, consisting of deeper reef systems and sloping walls leading to the open sea beyond. The reef itself is made up of over 400 species of coral, and supports around 1,500 species of fish. Approximately 4,000 species of mollusc inhabit the flats and nooks and crannies of the reef, whilst 23 species of marine mammal may be encountered along the vast length of this complex ecosystem.

GLOBAL IMPORTANCE

Certain areas of the Great Barrier Reef have enjoyed protected status since 1973, when it was established as a Marine Park. This was enhanced in 1981 when the reef was recognized as a World Heritage Site. More recent legislation has seen 71 per cent of the total area of the reef covered by some sort of

WORLD OF COLOUR
The range of marine life inhabiting the Great Barrier Reef is staggering in its variety and splendour, but divers must be careful not to touch delicate corals.

DEEPER INTO THE REEF

Certain parts of the Great Barrier Reef have been noticeably degraded or damaged by the high volume of dive traffic. This is no great surprise, given the delicacy of the reef's ecosystem and the inexperience of the many divers exploring it. Although there are still some fine dives to be had in these busy areas – especially for those new to the sport – many dive operators have moved further out into the reef system, offering packages on liveaboard boats that allow more experienced divers to explore remote and less spoilt sites.

Eye-stripe surgeonfish

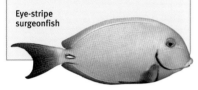

protective status – an optimistic sign for the future of a reef that is larger than any other coral system, but just as vulnerable to misuse and exploitation.

DIVING IN THE REGION

There is a mass market for diving the Great Barrier Reef, operating out of Cairns and Townsville in day boats containing very large numbers of divers. There have been a number of well-publicized incidents where divers have been missed when boats have departed back to shore, and although this is now very well regulated indeed, it is still worth, on the larger vessels at least, ensuring that the correct procedures are in place before diving. The other main diving activity on the reef takes place from liveaboards that venture further afield to more remote sites.

Divers on the reef are assured of reasonable hard coral and colourful fish-life almost anywhere along its length, but there are also a number of notable individual sites. Ribbon Reef Number 10 is particularly rich and diverse, even by the Great Barrier Reef's high standards, and is the location for dive sites such as Cod Hole – famous for encounters with giant potato cod – and Pixie's Pinnacle, renowned for its diversity of large-animal encounters.

ARTIFICIAL ISLAND
Some sites on the Great Barrier Reef have a permanently anchored observation platform, which visitors can travel to by tour boat.

The Coral Sea

WESTERN PACIFIC OCEAN

In the early 1970s, the first liveaboard operators began to explore the waters to the east of the Great Barrier Reef. Here they found the Coral Sea – a region of beautiful pristine hard coral formations and precipitous drop-offs.

REMOTE LOCATION

The Coral Sea begins about 160km (100 miles) east of Townsville, in the territory of Queensland, Australia. It stretches for another 160km (100 miles), covering an area of 98,500 sq km (38,000 sq miles). The dive sites consist of a series of undersea mountain-tops that rise from a great depth creating atolls, ridges, and reefs. The visibility in the region is some of the best in the diving world.

TEEMING WITH LIFE

The crossing to the Coral Sea through the rough waters of the inner reef can be demanding, however divers with the budget and time to make the journey are rarely disappointed. The area is

renowned for its big animal encounters, with tiger sharks and hammerheads mixing with more abundant species, such as grey reef sharks and white-tips. Manta and eagle rays are frequently seen off the steeper reef walls, while sea snakes can be seen on Marion Reef.

ESSENTIAL INFORMATION

WATER TEMPERATURE 24–27°C (75–81°F)

ECOSYSTEM Tropical

WHEN TO VISIT Conditions are suitable for diving all year round, but a lengthy boat trip is required to reach the area.

MUST SEES Cod Wall; Watnabe Bommie; Marion Reef; manta rays; sea snakes.

REEF DWELLERS
Bumphead wrasse cruise over the sandy seafloor of the Coral Sea. These large fish graze in "herds" over the area's reefs.

Wreck of the *Yongala*

QUEENSLAND, AUSTRALIA

The *Yongala* is a biological wonder – one of the most heavily colonized shipwrecks on Earth. Sitting amidst miles of featureless plains of sandy seabed next to the Great Barrier Reef, over time she too has become a teeming coral reef.

FATAL STORM

Lost in a typhoon on 24th March 1911, the *Yongala* was a 109m (357ft) steamer carrying 121 passengers north along the Queensland coast. All hands were lost as she foundered, and now she lies in 30m (100ft) of water, listing to starboard but still resolutely facing her original northerly direction of travel. Her isolated position, and the fact that she lay undiscovered for over 40 years after sinking, means that she is very heavily colonized with marine life.

MARINE SANCTUARY

The entire food chain of the coral reef is packed into the length of the *Yongala's* short hull. Schools of jack and trevally hunt clouds of bait fish on her port hull, whilst in her superstructure lurk turtles, morays, coral trout, and huge numbers of sea snakes. Potato cod skulk beneath the bow of the wreck, and very large bull rays nestle in the sand beside the wreck, ever watchful for the tiger and bull sharks that circle out in the blue, just beyond sight.

OCEAN WILDERNESS
Divers can encounter potato cod patrolling the bow section of the *Yongala*. The wreck is a magnet for marine life, attracting a range of species from sharks to turtles.

PROTECTED STATUS

Despite the popularity of the *Yongala* wreck among divers, exploration of the wreck's interior is strictly forbidden by Australian authorities under the country's Historic Shipwrecks Act. It may be, however, that the resident population of grouper are protection enough. In 2002 it was reported that a 2m- (6½ft-) long giant grouper had seized a diver's head before releasing him, shaken, but without serious injury, shortly afterward.

ESSENTIAL INFORMATION

WATER TEMPERATURE 24–28°C (75–82°F)

ECOSYSTEM Tropical reef

WHEN TO VISIT There is year-round diving on the *Yongala*, but conditions can be rough from May to August.

MUST SEES Sea snakes; potato cod by the wreck's bow; bull rays; bull sharks.

Tasmania

TASMAN SEA, AUSTRALIA

Tasmania offers a diving experience far removed from that of the usual coral reefs and warm waters of Australia. Nonetheless, this tiny island off the southern coast holds a host of diving possibilities for those prepared to travel a little further afield.

UNSUNG ISLAND

Tasmania is a small island dwarfed by the immensity of mainland Australia to the north. It measures only 300km (186 miles) from north to south, and is frequently overlooked by divers visiting Australia, distracted by the magnitude of the Great Barrier Reef and the big animals of Ningaloo Reef.

Tasmanian divers are delighted at this relative anonymity, as the island offers some of the finest kelp forests on Earth and some gloriously colourful and diverse cold-water dives. Currents rich in oxygen and nutrients sweep up from the icy waters to the south, giving life to wonderfully dense kelp forests and heavily colonized rock walls.

PERFECT CONCEALMENT
Sea dragons, such as this leafy variety, can be found in the kelp forests off Tasmania and South Australia. Its shape mimics the weed fronds.

ESSENTIAL INFORMATION

WATER TEMPERATURE 12–18°C (54–64°F)

ECOSYSTEM Temperate

WHEN TO VISIT The best time to visit Tasmania for diving is between the months of June and September.

MUST SEES Red handfish; kelp forests; Eaglehawk Neck.

SMALL WONDERS

Of particular note is the abundance of smaller animals, such as red handfish, although the island also plays host to numerous penguins, Australian fur seals, a number of different types of shark, and a variety of visiting whale and dolphin species. This rich diversity means that divers visiting Tasmania come to appreciate the true breadth of Australia's natural heritage.

Ningaloo Reef

WESTERN AUSTRALIA

A beautiful coral reef stretching for 280km (174 miles) off the coast of Western Australia, Ningaloo has much to offer the visiting diver. Its fame, however, lies with the abundance of a single animal – Ningaloo is the whale shark capital of the world.

MAGNET FOR DIVERS

Ningaloo Reef is approximately 1,200km (750 miles) north of Perth, Australia, and lies along a beautifully remote stretch of coastline.

The diving on the reef is centred around the small town of Exmouth – the population of which doubles during whale shark season, as divers flock there from around the world. Ningaloo Reef is splendidly rich in its own right – with 500 fish species and 200 types of coral. Such is the scale of diversity and the integrity of the ecosystem, that the region was declared a National Park in 1987; now over 3,885 sq km (1,500 sq miles) enjoys protected status.

WEALTH OF WILDLIFE

Although the whale sharks are less abundant from July through to February, they are replaced by other great attractions – between May and October huge numbers of manta rays can be seen, and from July to November, migrating whales pass along the coast. In addition, a survey in 1994 counted more than 1,000 dugongs along this stretch of coast – one of the most significant populations on Earth.

ESSENTIAL INFORMATION

WATER TEMPERATURE 24–29°C (75–84°F)

ECOSYSTEM Tropical

WHEN TO VISIT Year round diving, but whale sharks present March to June.

MUST SEES Whale sharks; manta rays; migrating whales; shore dive at Point Murat Navy Pier.

CLOSE ENCOUNTER
Touching whale sharks may distress them, and only those with specialist training, such as this marine biologist, should do so.

Poor Knights Islands

NORTH ISLAND, NEW ZEALAND

A mystical set of islands, sacred in Maori legend, the Poor Knights lie 23km (14 miles) off the coast of North Island in New Zealand. Honeycombed with caves and caverns, they are host to some truly remarkable gatherings of marine animals.

FORBIDDEN LAND

The Poor Knights Islands consist of stark volcanic rock pockmarked with overhangs, ridges, caves, and arches. The dramatic topography of the islands evokes their bloody history, as they were the site of a terrible Maori massacre in 1820, causing them to be declared *tapu* (forbidden) in Maori law. No one has set foot on the islands since, and this combined with Marine Park status since 1977 has created a wonderfully pristine environment both above and below the waves, which has drawn divers to this site from all over the world. Boats run to the islands from nearby Whangerai.

REMOTE LOCATION

The islands are only accessible by boat, so visits involve a short voyage aboard one of the many dive charter boats based on the mainland.

ESSENTIAL INFORMATION

WATER TEMPERATURE 15–24°C (59–75°F)

ECOSYSTEM Temperate reef

WHEN TO VISIT Year round diving, but rainy season runs from July to October.

MUST SEES Gatherings of southern sting rays; Blue Mao Mao Arch; bronze whaler sharks on deep ridges.

WEALTH OF MARINE LIFE

There are approximately 120 fish species around the Poor Knights, but it is the sheer numbers of fish present that are the main attraction. Vast shoals of species such as blue mao mao inhabit the overhangs and caverns around the islands, while the stark reefs are coated in an extraordinary diversity of

encrusting organisms, with brightly coloured sponges jostling for position with sea squirts and bryozoans. Thick carpets of kelp provide perfect hunting grounds for brightly coloured wrasse species, scorpion fish, and several different types of moray eel. In March, the dark waters under the Southern Arch host huge mating congregations of short-tailed southern sting rays. As well as this spectacular annual gathering, there is also a resident population of bronze whaler sharks, and regular transient visitors including orcas, dolphins, and several whale species.

Jacques Cousteau was so impressed when he visited the Poor Knights in the 1960s that he described the islands as the finest temperate water dive destination on Earth, and one of the top ten overall. The range of dive sites and sheer abundance of marine life provide a compelling argument that this applies as much today as it did then. This is an essential dive site if visiting New Zealand.

ODD ONE OUT
A lone wrasse swims at the centre of a swirling shoal of blue mao mao. The Poor Knights Islands are famous for their abundance of fish life.

EXPLORING CAVERNS

The marine life of the Poor Knights Islands teems amid dramatic underwater caves and arches, including the largest sea cave in the world – Rikoriko Cave. Visiting divers should equip with torches, including a reliable back up, and ensure that basic cavern safety rules are followed (*see pp.186–87*).

A diver explores a sea cave

Wreck of the *Rainbow Warrior*

CAVALLI ISLANDS, NEW ZEALAND

Perhaps no other shipwreck on Earth has the poignancy of the *Rainbow Warrior*. Sunk in an act of international espionage that shocked the world, she now lies off the Cavalli Islands, in one of the most beautiful regions of New Zealand.

TRAGIC FATE

The conservation vessel *Rainbow Warrior* was moored in Auckland harbour on the night of 10th July 1985. Shortly before midnight two explosions ripped through her, killing the vessel's photographer, Fernando Pereiro. This senseless act of terrorism was traced to the French Secret Service, leading to international condemnation and lengthy jail sentences for the two agents who planted the explosives.

PEACEFUL RELOCATION

The *Rainbow Warrior* wreck remained in Auckland for many months, before being refloated and towed further north to the Cavalli Islands, a beautiful marine sanctuary granted sacred status in Maori law. Here she was sunk as an artificial reef, and has become a popular dive site.

The *Rainbow Warrior* is a small vessel, and so can easily be covered in a single dive. She sits almost upright on the bottom, and her superstructure rises to within 15m (50ft) of the surface, with the seabed below at 26m (85ft). Her bow

FINAL RESTING PLACE
A diver surveys the wreckage of the former Greenpeace vessel *Rainbow Warrior*, which was badly damaged by a violent act of sabotage.

section is still largely intact, creating the illusion that she is sailing across the white sands of the seafloor beneath her hull.

REFUGE FOR MARINE LIFE

The *Rainbow Warrior's* hull is covered in a multi-coloured carpet of jewel anemones, and the vibrancy of colour on display here is remarkable. Her superstructure is now a home for scorpionfish, blue cod, and shoals of golden snapper, plus kingfish, and the distinctively shaped john dory. It seems fitting that this former conservation vessel now serves as a home for so many fascinating marine species.

ESSENTIAL INFORMATION

WATER TEMPERATURE 14–24°C (57–75°F)

ECOSYSTEM Temperate

WHEN TO VISIT Year round, but September to April is best.

MUST SEES Scorpionfish; the prow; the Rainbow Warrior Memorial; the ship's propeller and stern.

Wreck of the *Mikhail Lermentov*

MARLBOROUGH SOUND, NEW ZEALAND

The gloomy passageways and silty spaces of the *Mikhail Lermentov* are mute witnesses to one of the great mysteries of modern sea travel. Sunk under the strangest of circumstances, she now lies in the cold waters of Marlborough Sound, New Zealand.

ENIGMATIC WRECK

The 20,000-ton Russian cruise liner *Mikhail Lermentov* was driven hard onto rocks by an experienced local pilot on 16th February 1986. It was a clear, calm day, and theories abound as to the factors behind the sinking – bribes, alcohol, and espionage have all been blamed at one time or another. The mystery remains to this day, but the wreck represents a tremendous diving experience, although perhaps not one for the faint-hearted.

DIVING THE *LERMENTOV*

She lies on her starboard side in 37m (121ft) of water, although the sheer size of the vessel means that her port side can be reached at only 20m (66ft). Dives on her external superstructure are recommended, with highlights including the magnificent bow, the bridge, and the stern. For the more adventurous there is the famous ballroom, although this dive should only be undertaken by those with appropriate training and equipment (*see pp.166–71*). Marine life on the wreck includes scorpionfish, conger eels, and blue cod; occasionally pods of orcas hunt in the Sound itself.

> **ESSENTIAL INFORMATION**
>
> **WATER TEMPERATURE** 14–22°C (57–72°F)
>
> **ECOSYSTEM** Temperate
>
> **WHEN TO VISIT** Year round, but September to April is best.
>
> **MUST SEES** Bridge; swimming pool; stern; ballroom, provided you have the right gear and level of experience.

SERIOUS ADVENTURE

A diver explores in conditions of reduced visibility, often encountered on the *Mikhail Lermentov*. The wreck lies in deep coastal waters.

Oceania

The beauty of the estimated 20,000 islands that make up Oceania is unmatched anywhere else on Earth. The region holds tremendous riches, particularly for those confident enough to venture off the beaten track to visit the more far-flung islands and reefs.

WRECK DIVING IN PARADISE

Oceania is the collective name for the islands of the Pacific, generally considered synonymous with the South Sea Islands of Melanesia, Micronesia, and Polynesia. The region is typified by tranquil beaches with sugar-white sand and swaying palms, and, below water, powerful and intense diving experiences. Some of the world's most diverse reefs are in Micronesia, and the fierce fighting that raged through much of the region during World War II has created some impressive wreck sites.

Truk Lagoon in Micronesia, with its array of sunken Japanese ships, was viewed by many as the finest of all wreck diving locations until the establishment of a dive operation on Bikini Atoll in the Marshall Islands in 1996. From Bikini Atoll, divers can explore the remains of the fleet of ships sunk during the testing of hydrogen bombs by the US from 1946.

Palau has many magnificent dive sites, including Blue Corner, a coral ridge that juts out into the ocean and

UNDERWATER WONDERS
The coral gardens of Micronesia, among the healthiest on the planet, are home to butterflyfish, wrasses, angelfish, and puffers.

VOLCANIC CREATION
Many of the worlds atolls are located in the Pacific Ocean. These are created as a coral reef builds up around a subsiding volcanic island.

plunges more than 300m (1,000ft), and
the Ngemelis Wall, one of the best wall
dives in the world. There is also Jellyfish
Lake, an inland saltwater lake swarming
with jellyfish that have lost their ability
to sting. The nearby island of Yap boasts
one of the finest sites for manta ray
encounters. Yap is one of the more
popular destinations in Micronesia, yet
80 per cent of the reefs remain undived.
For those who have the time to explore
the remote islands of Oceania, they offer
a truly original dive experience.

TRADITIONAL ISLAND LIFE
Unspoilt islands offer the possibility of
fascinating cultural encounters and more
fulfilling diving experiences.

Palau

MICRONESIA, SOUTH PACIFIC

Divers constantly argue about what they consider to be the ultimate dive destination, but Palau will always be a strong contender. Consisting of 307 scattered islands, Palau has it all – wrecks, caves, and some of the busiest coral reefs on Earth.

A WORLD OF VARIETY

One of the great draws of Palau is the vast range of diving available. Like other island groups in Micronesia, it has colourful reefs cruised by large predators and impressive oceanic species. What gives Palau the edge over other sites in the region is that the geology and recent history of the islands have combined to create a diver's paradise. Caves and caverns honeycomb walls and reefs throughout the island chain; and fierce battles between American and Japanese forces during World War II mean that aircraft and shipwrecks abound.

Palau also has a number of rare natural phenomena, the most famous being Jellyfish Lake. This is a large volcanic crater filled with brackish water containing the pulsating forms of over 20 million mastigia jellyfish. To snorkel there is a surreal experience.

DIVING PALAU

Perhaps the most famous of all dive sites in Palau is Blue Corner. Jutting into deep water at the western edge of the island chain, this site has it all: swirling schools of barracuda, patrolling sharks, elegant eagle rays, and bustling Napoleon wrasse. Close to Blue Corner is another highlight, showing off Palau's renowned cavern diving – the Blue Holes. Here, divers enter a vast chamber illuminated only by pillars of light streaming through great gaps in the reef above. The Temple of Doom chamber, found at the rear of the Blue Holes, is a more serious dive that requires considerable experience and skill. The floor here is littered with the shells of sea turtles that were unable to find their way out of the chamber and perished. Chandelier Cave in Malakal Harbour is a more sedate alternative for those wishing to explore an easy cave system.

RELICS OF CONFLICT

In addition to the great natural diversity on show at Palau there are many fascinating relics from World War II.

One of the best shipwrecks from that era is that of the Japanese fleet tanker *Iro*. At 145m (475ft) in length, the *Iro* is large and exceptionally well preserved. She lies in moderate depths in a lagoon near the central town of Koror. Visiting divers should also see the wreck of the Aichi E13-A1 (codename "Jake") seaplane. Discovered a decade ago, this wonderfully intact aircraft lies in shallow water, and is an easy dive with many layers of interest.

The wreck of the "Jake" seaplane

ESSENTIAL INFORMATION

WATER TEMPERATURE 25–28°C (77–82°F)

ECOSYSTEM Tropical

WHEN TO VISIT Year round diving. Rainy season between July and October.

MUST SEES Blue Corner; Blue Holes; Jellyfish Lake; the wreck of the *Iro*; the "Jake" seaplane wreck.

PATTERN OF ISLANDS
An aerial view of a cluster of islets at Palau, ringed with white coral sand and azure seas.

Yap

CAROLINE ISLANDS, NORTH PACIFIC

A remote island paradise, Yap has become a magnet for divers seeking close encounters with manta rays. However, there is a great deal more to this tiny Micronesian island, with plenty of sharks on patrol, including grey, white-tip, and black-tip reef species.

PACIFIC IDYLL

With its lush mangroves and rolling green hills, Yap lies in clear waters that abound with tuna and dolphins. It has one of Micronesia's most vibrant indigenous cultures, and retains a genuinely remote island feel in all aspects of daily life.

MEETINGS WITH MANTAS

The real attraction, however, lies beneath the waves. Yap is one of the very few dive destinations on Earth where encounters with manta rays are guaranteed. Two shallow tidal channels cut through the islands, and it is here that the mantas gather at cleaning stations that dot the sandy sea floor. At these sites, divers can observe the activity of smaller fish called remoras, which use suckers to attach themselves to the rays and remove irritating parasites by

ESSENTIAL INFORMATION

WATER TEMPERATURE Around 28°C (82°F) year-round.

ECOSYSTEM Tropical

WHEN TO VISIT Year-round, but December to April by preference.

MUST SEES Manta rays visiting cleaning stations; shark dives; Yap Caverns.

nibbling them off. Divers crouch by the stations – normally isolated coral heads – and await the arrival of the star attraction. Manta rays can grow to more than 1,000kg (2,200lbs) in weight, and their wingspan can sometimes exceed 6m (20ft) from tip to tip.

PROTECTED ENVIRONMENT

Other dives in Yap should not be overlooked – there is some tremendous shark action here, and the reefs are in pristine condition due to a strictly adhered-to agreement to use traditional fishing techniques. Such forward-thinking legislation is of great benefit to both marine life and visiting divers, and is an admirable example of responsible stewardship of the seas. Nearly 80 per cent of the reefs around Yap remain undived due to local conservation by-laws, although the remaining 20 per cent are well worth exploring.

ON THE WING
Despite their impressive and imposing size, manta rays are a docile species that feed on microscopic plankton life.

Bikini Atoll

MARSHALL ISLANDS, CENTRAL PACIFIC

Bikini Atoll vies with Truk Lagoon to be the finest wreck diving location on Earth. This tiny collection of coral islands and lagoons is the site of spectacular and dramatic wrecks, with a truly extraordinary story behind their sinking.

ATOMIC TEST SITE

As World War II ended and the Cold War began, America chose a tiny atoll at the northern end of the Marshall Islands to conduct a massive programme of nuclear weapons testing. Ships of varying size, nationality, and vintage made up the 84 vessels of a dummy fleet, the vast majority of which were sunk in tests running from 1946 to 1958. Included in the fleet was the US aircraft carrier *Saratoga* – weighing 33,000 tonnes and now the largest shipwreck accessible to divers anywhere on Earth. Also at Bikini is the *Nagato*, the flagship of the Japanese fleet, and the first warship in the world to be armed with 16-inch guns. The last

ESSENTIAL INFORMATION

WATER TEMPERATURE Around 29°C (84°F) year-round.

ECOSYSTEM Tropical

WHEN TO VISIT Best time to visit is between April and September.

MUST SEES The US carrier *Saratoga*; Japanese battleship *Nagato*.

GHOSTS FROM THE PAST

The wreckage of a naval aircraft destroyed during US nuclear bomb tests (*inset*) at Bikini Atoll. Residual radiation has since dropped to negligible levels at this dive site.

active Japanese battleship, the *Nagato* saw action as late as July 1945, when she was attacked by US torpedo bombers.

The ships lie in deep water, with depths averaging 50–55m (160–180ft), but with 1,500 or so fish species swarming over the stunning remains, the rewards are well worth it for divers with sufficient training and experience. No dive site can offer a more dramatic insight into history.

Bora Bora

SOCIETY ISLANDS, SOUTH PACIFIC

Renowned as one of the most beautiful islands in the Pacific, Bora Bora is a huge lagoon dominated by an island at its centre. The lagoon and surrounding reef provide a dazzling array of dives against the stunning backdrop of volcanic peaks.

PACIFIC PARADISE

Bora Bora is part of the Society Islands, and is located 274km (170 miles) northwest of Tahiti. An atoll of sparkling beauty that has long entranced writers and artists alike, the main island is only 10km (6 miles) long, and sits at the heart of a lagoon three times its size. The reef around the lagoon has only one navigable channel, which is criss-crossed by smaller channels and gullies, most of which provide excellent dive sites.

ABUNDANCE OF LIFE

Bora Bora's lagoon and surrounding reefs are home to a huge variety of fish – a recent survey documented 500

ESSENTIAL INFORMATION

WATER TEMPERATURE 26–29°C (79–84°F)

ECOSYSTEM Tropical

WHEN TO VISIT Thanks to its balmy climate, diving in Bora Bora can be enjoyed all year round.

MUST SEES Manta ray encounters at Anua; shark dives at Tupitipiti.

ANATOMY OF AN ISLAND

Bora Bora is dominated by the jagged remains of a volcano, and encircled by a great lagoon. This remote atoll is widely considered to be one of the most beautiful spots on Earth.

different species, although the real number is almost certainly higher. Larger animals encountered on the outer reef and in the cuts in the atoll walls are grey reef sharks, white-tip reef sharks, groups of black-tip reef sharks, lemon sharks, and silvertips. Numerous species of ray can be encountered in the central lagoon, including the groups of manta rays for which the site has become justifiably famous.

Wreck of the *President Coolidge*

VANUATU, SOUTH PACIFIC

A relic of an elegant age of sea travel, the *President Coolidge* is a strong candidate for the most exciting wreck now accessible to recreational divers. Perched on a reef in Vanuatu, she hides one of the most famous icons in diving in her dark interior.

BEACHED BEHEMOTH

The *President Coolidge* sank on 26th October 1942 while carrying 4,800 American troops to the Pacific during World War II. She struck floating mines, laid by "friendly" forces in the area, and when it became clear she would not make it into the nearby harbour of Luganville, her captain beached the huge vessel on a reef. Here she remains today, with her stern submerged in 72m (236ft) of water, although her bow lies at a depth of just 15m (49ft).

DIVING THE *COOLIDGE*

The wreck is accessed directly from the shore. Within her bulk is a network of passageways and enormous holds containing the paraphernalia associated with equipping an army for war. Although converted for duty as a troop ship, there are still traces of her time as one of the world's most luxurious ocean liners.

An essential stop for any diver visiting this magnificent wreck is the statue of the Lady, in one of the first-class dining rooms. This once stood on the mantelpiece of the smoking-room, but a small earthquake dislodged it from its perch, and it was later moved further up the wreck. Other highlights include the promenade deck and a beautiful mosaic fountain, once the centrepiece of a gracious lobby.

ESSENTIAL INFORMATION

WATER TEMPERATURE 24–28°C (75–82°F)

ECOSYSTEM Tropical

WHEN TO VISIT There is year-round diving on the wreck.

MUST SEES The Lady; the swimming pool; lobby mosaic; the promenade deck; lampfish dive.

CASUALTY OF CONFLICT
The *President Coolidge* ran aground at Vanuatu during World War II. The wreck is still filled with corroding relics from that era.

Truk Lagoon

CAROLINE ISLANDS, NORTH PACIFIC

Regarded by many as the finest of all wreck sites, Truk Lagoon is the resting place for an eclectic mix of Japanese vessels sunk in a single raid by American aircraft in 1944. With many wrecks still in good condition, Truk Lagoon offers unforgettable diving.

WITNESS TO WAR

Truk Lagoon is a massive natural atoll almost 64km (40 miles) across; it is ringed by 225km (140 miles) of reef and small coral islands, forming one of the largest natural harbours of this type on Earth. The presence of 15 larger islands in the centre of the lagoon made it an ideal base for military operations, a fact not lost on the Japanese Imperial Navy, which amassed a vast number of warships, merchant vessels, and fleet tenders here in the latter stages of World War II, in readiness for further deployment.

ESSENTIAL INFORMATION

WATER TEMPERATURE 29°C (84°F)

ECOSYSTEM Tropical

WHEN TO VISIT Year-round diving, but rainy season from July to October.

MUST SEES The wrecks of the *Fujikawa Maru*, *Shinkoku Maru*, *San Francisco Maru*, and the "Betty" bomber aircraft.

Such an assembly of enemy vessels proved irresistible to American forces, which carried out a daring raid on 17th and 18th February 1944, launching 450 aircraft from nine aircraft carriers beyond the horizon. The raid was a complete success, with over 60 Japanese vessels sunk in a savage 48 hours.

SECRET SITES

The "ghost fleet" of Japanese ships lies on the seabed in Truk Lagoon, although only 38 of them have been charted. The others have been left unmarked for fear of looting and illegal diving (to dive the wrecks in Truk, a local guide is a legal and practical necessity). Highlights include the *Fujikawa Maru*, complete with Zero fighter aircraft still in her holds, and the *San Francisco Maru* – a huge freighter with an array of cargo including two tanks on her deck, so outstanding she is known as the "Million Dollar Wreck".

DIVING TRUK LAGOON

Wreck diving in Truk is deep, with the majority of the wrecks lying in depths of 30m (100ft) or more. The local operators are, however, well set up to cope with deep air diving, and have established effective drills and techniques to cope with repeated deep dives. Nonetheless a certain level of qualifications and experience is advisable before diving the fascinating wrecks of Truk Lagoon. Contact local operators for details.

Marine life at Truk

RELICS FROM THE PAST

A diver hovers over the ghostly remains of a Japanese ship sunk at Truk Lagoon. Aircraft and submarines also fell victim to aerial attack here.

Fiji

SOUTH PACIFIC

Pacific Ocean
AUSTRALIA   Fiji ✈
NEW ZEALAND

Simply hearing the name Fiji summons up images of an exquisite tropical paradise. With 800 islands sprawling over 207,000 sq km (80,000 sq miles) of ocean, the reality is just as exciting. Fiji offers a wealth of different experiences for the diver.

IDYLLIC ISLANDS

Perhaps one of the most notable features of Fiji for the visiting diver is that only 12 per cent of the islands in the archipelago are inhabited – and 75 per cent of the entire population live on just one island, Viti Levu. Fiji truly offers a wealth of different diving opportunities around a huge variety of reefs, channels, and islands. Coral reefs cover a staggering 15,540 sq km (6,000 sq miles); they include at least 398 species of coral and are home to over 1,200 species of fish.

UNDERSEA GARDENS

Fiji is particularly famous for its beautiful soft-coral gardens, the most renowned of which is the White Wall in the Somosomo Strait. The region's rich waters mean that filter-feeding invertebrates thrive in the coral lagoons. Sea fans, whip-corals, and a myriad of other species vie for space on the brilliantly coloured reef walls.

REEF RESIDENT
Sharks of many species, including grey reef sharks, patrol the soft-coral reefs of Fiji's scattered islands.

There are also many spectacular fish species in Fijian waters. For the thrill-seeker, there is plenty of large-animal action. The best-known shark dive here is known as "Aqua Trek 3D", after the operator that runs it, and offers the opportunity to see up to seven species of shark on a single dive, including bull, black-tip reef, white-tip, and lemon sharks. The dive is one of 100 recognized dive sites in Beqa Lagoon – an indication of the sheer variety of diving in this beautiful tropical archipelago. Happily, the area has been designated a Marine Park and enjoys protection from overfishing; the small fees asked of divers who experience its underwater environment are used to help fund conservation measures. Such careful stewardship ensures that Fiji's diving will remain outstanding for years to come.

ESSENTIAL INFORMATION

WATER TEMPERATURE 26–31°C (79–88°F)

ECOSYSTEM Tropical

WHEN TO VISIT Year round, but the best time to visit Fiji is between the months of April and November.

MUST SEES Somosomo Straight and the White Wall; Beqa Lagoon; Naingora Pass.

Anemonefish

Tonga

FRIENDLY ISLANDS, SOUTH PACIFIC

Tonga is a dramatic chain of volcanic islands to the east of Fiji. The grandeur of its scenery is matched by one of the most amazing encounters with a marine mammal that a diver can have anywhere on Earth – snorkelling with humpback whales.

PACIFIC OUTPOST

Diving in Tonga is based mainly in the central island group of Ha'apai, and in Vava'u further to the north. Port of Refuge in Vava'u, which for many divers is their first experience of Tongan diving, contains a particularly fine wreck in the form of the *Clan McWilliam*, a large merchant vessel sunk in the 1920s.

STAR SITES

Other sites of note in the region are Tuangasika Island, the location of an exciting cavern called Mariners Cave, and the steep walls of Hunga Magic – an undersea peninsula jutting into the blue water from Hunga island. Tonga's

ANNUAL MIGRATION
A humpback whale raises its massive flukes above the surface. Large numbers of this magnificent animal pass by Tonga each year.

> ### ESSENTIAL INFORMATION
>
> **WATER TEMPERATURE** 22–30°C (72–86°F)
>
> **ECOSYSTEM** Tropical
>
> **WHEN TO VISIT** July to October for humpback whales; avoid typhoon season from November to April.
>
> **MUST SEES** Humpback whales; Hunga Magic; Mariners Cave; *Clan McWilliam*.

fame in the diving world is, however, based around encounters with humpback whales. From July through to October, around 700 humpbacks move into warm waters around the island group. Although local conservation groups do not allow scuba diving with the whales (to minimize disturbance to them), snorkelling alongside these amazing mammals is a unique experience.

The Americas

As befits a land mass that spans virtually all latitudes of the globe, the Americas boasts a staggering range of dive sites. Great ocean currents beset both North and South America, combining with local conditions to create something for divers of every level of expertise.

COASTAL DIVIDE

The coasts of the North American continent offer very different, but equally thrilling, diving environments. To the west, you can enjoy magnificent wild diving in the fjords of Alaska and British Colombia, explore vast kelp forests off the Californian coast, and experience glorious encounters with humpback whales and whale sharks in the Gulf of California.

EASILY EXPLORED
The superb visibility and calm, warm waters of the Caribbean provide ideal conditions for reef diving.

The eastern coast features wrecks and raggedtooth sharks on the Outer Banks off North Carolina – the region where technical diving made its greatest leaps forward. The Florida Keys provide reef diving of the highest quality, and are popular as a training ground for thousands of divers who try the sport while on holiday.

The Caribbean offers classic coral reef diving. With its well-developed diving infrastructure, it has long been a favourite dive destination. To the south, in Central America, is the Belize barrier reef – the longest in the northern hemisphere. Off the coast of Venezuela lies Bonaire, in the Dutch Antilles, a beacon of marine conservation. Further south still is the island of Fernando de Noronha off Brazil, perhaps the finest dive site in the whole of South America.

SEA SAFARI
Even snorkelling over sandbars in the Cayman Islands, western Caribbean, can bring you face-to-face with fascinating marine animals.

ENCHANTED FOREST
The towering kelp forests in the shallow waters off California are among the most beautiful and biologically rich of all marine habitats.

Florida Keys

FLORIDA, UNITED STATES

The Florida Keys are a string of coral and limestone islands stretching 193km (120 miles) into the Gulf of Mexico. For many, this popular holiday destination represents a first introduction to diving, and there are dive sites of real quality and variety here.

SUNKEN TREASURES
The wreck of a tug boat lying in clear blue water. The Keys are famed for good underwater visibility and excellent areas for training.

PROTECTED ECOSYSTEM

The Florida Keys consist of 200 small islands, the largest of which are connected by the 42 bridges of US Highway One. The importance of the Florida Keys as a vibrant marine ecosystem was recognized as long ago as 1960, with the John Pennecamp Coral Reef State Park established as the first ever Marine Park in the USA. More followed, and the region now boasts 18 protected areas, providing cover out to 5km (3 miles) beyond the reef.

UNDERSEA ATTRACTIONS

The reef itself runs parallel to the island chain, roughly 8km (5 miles) offshore. As such, most of the diving here is from boats, and there are many experienced operators. There are some excellent wrecks, as well as classic spur and groove reef formations, with the outer reef inhabited by a diverse range of Caribbean species. The shallow inner reef also hosts manatees, as well as providing a nursery for smaller species and huge numbers of trainee divers.

ESSENTIAL INFORMATION

WATER TEMPERATURE 21–29°C (70–84°F)

ECOSYSTEM Tropical

WHEN TO VISIT Year-round diving, but hurricane season October to November.

MUST SEES Molasses Reef, wreck of the *Adolphus Busch Sr*; the Christ of the Deep Statue at Key Largo.

Crystal River

FLORIDA, UNITED STATES

The Crystal River in northwest Florida is parent to a network of channels and tributaries snaking through the swamps. What draws divers to the region is the chance to swim with manatees – one of the great animal encounters in the underwater world.

WEB OF WATERWAYS

The Crystal River stems from a series of inland upwellings through porous rock, creating a natural filtering system that results in some of the clearest water on Earth. What this meeting of rock and water also creates is a honeycomb of caverns, caves, and tunnels. Although these are frequently occupied by huge catfish (a draw in themselves), the real attraction for the diver is the presence of the West Indian manatee.

GENTLE GIANTS

These huge and placid animals – measuring up to 3m (14ft) long and weighing up to a ton-and-a-half – have been using the shallow pools and warm streams of the Crystal River to feed and

CLEAR ADVANTAGE
The stunning clarity of the water at Crystal River stems from geological conditions in the area. Such waters are perfect for observing manatees.

ESSENTIAL INFORMATION

WATER TEMPERATURE 20–27°C (68–81°F)

ECOSYSTEM Freshwater

WHEN TO VISIT Crystal River can be visited all year round, but for snorkelling with manatees the best time is between the months of December and April.

MUST SEES Devil's Den, King's Cavern; swimming with manatees.

A manatee

breed for thousands of years. Speedboats and habitat destruction have exacted a terrible toll on the manatees, which are now on the endangered list. Diving with the manatees is not permitted, but nonetheless snorkelling next to one of these huge animals in crystal-clear water is a tremendous experience.

Little Bahamas Bank

BAHAMAS, WESTERN ATLANTIC

The Little Bahamas Bank would appear to be the most unpromising of dive sites – a vast patch of featureless, shallow sand bank. One animal has, however, made this area irresistible to divers. Dolphin encounters here are uniquely memorable.

SHALLOW SEA

The Little Bahamas Bank lies between the islands of Grand Bahama and Great Abaco, two of the larger islands of the 700 that make up the Bahamas archipelago. The northern end of the bank lies 113km (70 miles) east of the Florida coast, allowing access to the region from mainland USA as well as the Bahamas. The bank is relatively featureless, consisting of shallow white sand dotted with low-lying reefs and the occasional wreck. Marine life is relatively

WILD ENCOUNTER
Spotted dolphins have frequented the Little Bahamas Bank for many years, and these inquisitive animals freely interact with snorkellers in the shallow waters of the Bank.

sparse compared to other regions in the Bahamas, although there is the possibility of encounters with some enormous barracuda, several species of turtle, and a number of shark species.

STARS OF THE SEA

Both bottlenose and spotted dolphins visit the bank, but it is the guaranteed encounters with the latter that have made the site famous. These wild pods of dolphins have been interacting with divers for 20 years, and now a booming industry has grown up round these wonderful animals. Although only snorkelling is permitted with the dolphins, divers who have the privilege to encounter them in these clear, shallow seas take away life-long memories.

ESSENTIAL INFORMATION

WATER TEMPERATURE 24–28°C (75–82°F)

ECOSYSTEM Tropical

WHEN TO VISIT Year round, but hurricanes may strike later in the year.

MUST SEES Spotted dolphin snorkelling encounter; The Bull Pit (shark dive); the Sugar Wreck.

Bonaire

DUTCH ANTILLES

For conservationists, Bonaire is a beacon of hope in the Caribbean. More than 40 years ago, the island's authorities realized that good reef management could promote tourism and boost the local economy. Bonaire is particularly noted for fine shore diving.

FORWARD THINKING

Bonaire is the most eastern island in the group that makes up the Dutch Antilles. It has always demonstrated an enlightened attitude towards conservation, with protective laws first passed in 1961 (to protect turtles), followed by a steady stream of additional measures over subsequent years that eventually resulted in the establishment of a Marine Park that now encircles the island. This extends down to a depth of 60m (197ft).

SANDY SHORES

Bonaire offers a wealth of shore diving possibilities. Many divers simply turn up on the island, hire a car and go exploring. The spontaneity of this kind of diving has a charm all of its own. As well as splendidly pristine reefs, Bonaire also has two notable wrecks in the *Hilma Hooker*, a freighter lying at 30m (100ft), and the *Red Slave*. Diving under the Town Pier at Kralendijk, and Salt Pier (on the other side of the island), is also very rewarding.

ESSENTIAL INFORMATION

WATER TEMPERATURE 25–29°C (77–84°F)

ECOSYSTEM Tropical

WHEN TO VISIT There is year-round diving on Bonaire, but hurricane season begins in the later part of the year.

MUST SEES Town Pier at Kralendijk; the wreck of the *Hilma Hooker*.

LEISURELY PACE
Divers join a turtle in a tour over the lush reefs of Bonaire's shallow coastal waters.

Cayman Islands

SOUTHERN CARIBBEAN

The Caymans are three low-lying islands 240km (150 miles) south of Cuba. Views of the islands above the water belie the riches that lie beneath – steep walls, fine reefs, and a very shallow dive that is famed amongst the diving fraternity.

CLEAR WATERS

The Cayman Islands have two key characteristics that make them a classic dive area: they lack any mountains or large rivers, and the limestone bedrock absorbs water. Consequently, there is very little sedimentary run-off from the land when it rains, which ensures that the visibility underwater is excellent.

Added to this are steep walls, sandy lagoons, and 18 protected marine life reserves that ensure excellent diving.

REEFS AND RAYS

The underwater environment is typified by shallow fringing reefs extending some way from shore, leading to busy reef crests and steep drop-offs. Large pelagics, such as mantas, eagle rays, and several species of shark, drift past walls characterized by healthy fish populations and rich coral and sponge growth. The Caymans are famous for one particular stingray feeding site in North Sound, Grand Cayman, where as many as 200 stingrays cluster around divers in the shallows.

ESSENTIAL INFORMATION

WATER TEMPERATURE 27–29°C (81–84°F)

ECOSYSTEM Tropical

WHEN TO VISIT Diving takes place in the Caymans all year round, although hurricane season starts late in the year.

MUST SEES Stingrays in North Sound; the mantas of Bloody Bay Wall.

CLOSE ENCOUNTER
Stingrays gather to be fed at North Sound. Contact with them should always be on their terms.

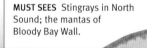

Turks and Caicos

BAHAMAS, NORTHERN CARIBBEAN

These two tiny island groups at the southeastern end of the Bahamas chain offer the diver true variety within a small area – from safe, shallow lagoons to steep walls and strong currents – with big-animal encounters always possible.

DIVE PARADISE

The Turks and Caicos consist of two small clusters of islands either side of the abyssal Turks Island Passage. To the west are the Caicos Islands, epitomized by shallow lagoons and gentle slopes. To the east the smaller Turks Islands offer access to stunning drop-offs only a short boat ride from shore – although both sets of islands do have a range of dives within these broad categories, catering for the tentative beginner through to the hardened veteran.

PROTECTED STATUS

There are 33 protected areas within the Turks and Caicos, and these islands were the first in the entire Caribbean to ban spearfishing. Consequently, the marine life here is very impressive, with healthy reefs dotted with huge sponges, and impressive pelagic activity in the form of dolphin encounters, grey reef, bull, and tiger sharks, as well as three resident species of turtle. In additon to these

THRIVING REEFS
A diver inspects growths of colourful tube sponges, which are a common sight on the reefs of the Turks and Caicos region.

animals, large migrants also create excitement. From December through to April, the entire humpback whale population of the Atlantic passes through Turks Island Passage.

For wreck fans, the remains of the *Endymion* – a British warship that ran aground in 1790 – offer a fascinating glimpse into naval history. Cannonballs and other relics can still be found on the seabed around the site. The wreck lies in shallow water 30km (18 miles) south of Salt Cay; the site is readily accessible by boat.

ESSENTIAL INFORMATION

WATER TEMPERATURE 27–30°C (81–86°F)

ECOSYSTEM Tropical

WHEN TO VISIT Visit the Turks and Caicos between November and August

MUST SEES Humpback whale migration; dolphin encounter; Northwest Point dives; the Tunnel; *Endymion* wreck.

Giant squirrelfish

Cuba

WESTERN ATLANTIC

It did not take long for Cuba's developing dive industry to draw the attention of the international diving community. Certain classic sites have been well known for years, but Cuba's vast and varied coastline has much more to offer travelling divers.

GIANT COASTLINE

Cuba is a huge island 154km (90 miles) south of Florida, with 5,632km (3,500 miles) of coastline bordered by the Gulf of Mexico to the west, the Atlantic to the north, and the Caribbean to the south. The scale of the island is such that each of the three reefs along the coast of Cuba exceed the length of the entire Florida Keys.

MARINE DIVERSITY

A recent survey noted over 1,000 fish species around Cuba – tremendous diversity for this part of the world. There are also some excellent big-animal

ESSENTIAL INFORMATION

WATER TEMPERATURE 24–27°C (75–81°F)

ECOSYSTEM Tropical

WHEN TO VISIT Diving continues all year round in Cuba, but hurricane season begins late in the year.

MUST SEES The Isle of Youth; bull shark dive at Santa Lucía; *Cristóbal* wreck.

encounters to be experienced here, including some classic shark dives and large groups of tarpon.

CLASSIC CUBAN DIVES

Cuba has an abundance of riches in terms of dive sites, and some consider the diving here to be the best in the world. Diving on the Isle of Youth is particularly popular, but Santa Lucia, Guardalavaca, and Santiago de Cuba also offer excellent dives. The last of these boasts a particularly fine shore dive with the wreck of the *Cristóbal Colón*. This former Spanish warship was attacked by the US navy in 1898, during a brief conflict between the two countries provoked by the sinking of a US ship in Havana harbour. The *Cristóbal Colón* was run aground by her commander, and is now a splendid historical dive site.

SOFT OPTION
Soft corals and sponges grow in profusion in Cuban waters. which enjoy unusually high diversity in marine species.

Cenotes

YUCATAN PENINSULA, MEXICO

A network of flooded caves filled with crystal clear water, the Cenotes offer the novice a chance to dive caverns in relative safety. For the more intrepid, and appropriately trained, the honeycomb of tunnels and passages offers advanced exploration opportunities.

GEOLOGICAL WONDER

In Mexico's Yucatan Peninsula, the best dives are not at the coast but take place some distance inland, within the honeycombed heart of the Earth itself. The term Cenotes (from the Mayan word *tzonot*) refers to the entrances to the network of flooded passages and caverns that riddle this region.

Over 60 million years ago, this entire region was beneath the sea, creating rock strata of limestone from compressed coral and marine organisms. In the intervening period, this soft rock

INNER SPACE
A diver surveys the eerie interior of the Cenotes cave network. Though the system offers difficult technical challenges, it also has easier dives.

has been shaped by rain and river, creating one of the finest cave and cavern diving locations on Earth.

DIVING THE CENOTES

Although explorations are still ongoing in the Cenotes, many of the systems are accessible even for novice divers, with guides taking groups into vast caverns where an exit to the surface is always available if required. Sea diving at Cancun and Cozumel is available nearby.

ESSENTIAL INFORMATION

WATER TEMPERATURE 19–25°C (66–77°F)

ECOSYSTEM Freshwater cave

WHEN TO VISIT The best time to dive the Cenotes is between the months of November and March.

MUST SEES Gran Cenote; Car Wash Cenote; coastal resorts nearby.

SAFETY LINE
Specialist equipment helps ensure safe, enjoyable diving in caverns (*see pp.186–87*).

Belize Barrier Reef

BELIZE, CENTRAL AMERICA

Belize is a small Central American country that has the good fortune to have a true natural marvel off its coastline. The Belize Barrier Reef is the longest in the northern hemisphere, and offers a vast range of diving possibilities for all skill levels.

SECLUDED COUNTRY

Belize covers around 23,000 sq km (8,880 sq miles) and has only 220,000 inhabitants. The country is renowned for its marine life, and due to the efforts of various voluntary organizations and its government, over 40 per cent of Belize has been classified as a nature reserve.

THE BARRIER REEF

Belize also boasts a World Heritage Site – the Belize Barrier Reef. Extending for 280km (174 miles) and ranging from 14km (9 miles) to 30km (19 miles) offshore, the reef offers a huge variety of divable sites to explore. Three of the four atolls in the Caribbean are found

ESSENTIAL INFORMATION

WATER TEMPERATURE 25–28°C (77–82°F)

ECOSYSTEM Tropical

WHEN TO VISIT Diving in Belize takes place all year round, but the hurricane season begins around October.

MUST SEES Whale sharks at Gladden Spit, Blue Hole, Shark Ray Alley.

along the length of the reef. An atoll is a circular island that surrounds a lagoon, and is formed when coral reefs grow around the perimeter of a collapsed volcano. Linear sand and coral islands – known locally as Cayes – also run along

the length of the Barrier Reef, and provide a base for much of the area's dive activity. Of these, Ambergris Caye is the most popular location.

DIVING HIGHLIGHTS

Around 500 fish species swarm over the reef, including five different species of butterfly fish. Some larger animal species can also be seen, including huge jewfish and manta rays on the outer reef, and stingrays and nurse sharks at Shark Ray Alley. There are also healthy populations of reef sharks, as well as manatees (*see p.219*) in the shallow inshore waters and estuaries of the country.

While the most famous site in Belize is undoubtedly the Blue Hole, the area has a great deal more to offer, with classic reef dives, magnificent spur and groove reef formations, and some notable seasonal gatherings of big animals. At Gladden Spit in the south of the country, large numbers of whale sharks meet in feeding aggregations during the early part of the year. These huge ocean-going plankton-feeders grow to as much as 18m (59ft) in length.

THE BLUE HOLE

Perhaps the most famous site in Belize is the Blue Hole. Famously explored by Cousteau in 1972, this vast cavern lies 80km (50 miles) off the east coast of Belize in the middle of Lighthouse Reef. Its perfectly circular entrance measures some 300m (984ft) in diameter, with the cavern plunging away to a depth of 125m (410ft) beneath. The resident population of bull and lemon sharks in the interior of the Blue Hole is an eerie sight for divers visiting the stalactite formations found 40m (131ft) below the surface.

Aerial view of the Blue Hole

CYCLE OF LIFE
Whale sharks come to Belize to feed on the vast numbers of eggs generated by the mass spawning of a number of reef fish species, such as dog and cubera snappers, in spring.

Fernando de Noronha

WESTERN ATLANTIC

Fernando
de Noronha
Natal●
BRAZIL
SOUTH
AMERICA

Rising up from the wild waters of the Atlantic, 400km (250 miles) off the eastern coast of Brazil, is Fernando de Noronha. This tiny group of volcanic islands plays host to one of the largest resident pods of dolphins on the Earth.

ATLANTIC TREASURE

The stark island group of Fernando de Noronha was for many years a well-kept secret amongst the Brazilian diving fraternity. The sea around the islands plunges to depths of over 700m (2,300ft), creating rich upwellings and swirling currents.

CLOSE ENCOUNTERS

Although the reefs here are relatively bare – only 95 fish species have been recorded on them – it is the big-animal encounters that have made the site famous. Stories of extraordinary interactions with the huge resident pods of spinner dolphins around the islands

have attracted divers who now travel here from around the world. Some 14 species of shark, including nurse sharks and grey reef sharks, cruise over dark ridges, and two turtles are commonly sighted, one of which – the hawksbill – actually breeds here. The islands have been a World Heritage Site since 1981, a well-deserved status for this exciting site.

ESSENTIAL INFORMATION

WATER TEMPERATURE 21–26°C (70–79°F)

ECOSYSTEM Subtropical

WHEN TO VISIT Diving is best at Fernando de Noronha between the months of September and March.

MUST SEES Spinner dolphins at Baía dos Golfinhos; grey reef sharks at Laje dos Dois Irmãos.

WILD BEAUTY
Green, nutrient-rich Atlantic waters break against the rocky shores of Fernando de Noronha, a remote group of islands.

Cocos and Malpelo

EASTERN PACIFIC

Considered by many to be among the finest big-animal dive sites on Earth, the two volcanic islands of Cocos and Malpelo sit several hundred miles from land amidst the wild currents and big swells of the eastern Pacific ocean.

DOUBLE IDENTITY

Although Cocos and Malpelo are generally referred to in the same breath by divers, the two islands are actually 400km (250 miles) apart – Cocos off the coast of Costa Rica, and Malpelo off the coast of Colombia.

MARINE SANCTUARY

Rising from the deep waters of the Pacific in a series of serrated volcanic reefs and craggy pinnacles, the two islands provide a fantastic opportunity to experience larger marine animals at close quarters. Schooling hammerheads, hunting white-tip reef sharks, patrolling silky and Galapagos sharks – are all virtually guaranteed. Spotted moray eels are present in huge numbers, and itinerant visitors include whale sharks, mantas, and a number of bill-fish species. Both islands have a protected status – Cocos is a World Heritage Site, and Malpelo a Colombian Flora and Fauna Sanctuary.

MEETING PLACE
Sharks of many species congregate in numbers off Cocos Island. Use of a rebreather (*left*) allows close approaches.

TOUGH CONDITIONS

Diving on Cocos and Malpelo is demanding, with big swells, swirling currents, occasional limited visibility, and stark reefs. The rewards for braving the challenging conditions, however, are immense, given the ample opportunities for big-animal encounters. Some shark species, especially hammerheads, are naturally wary of divers, but a careful approach can work wonders. Specialist equipment can help too – rebreathers (*see pp.82–83*), which do not create bubbles, allow the diver to make an unobtrusive approach and so give the best chance for close encounters.

ESSENTIAL INFORMATION

WATER TEMPERATURE 17–24°C (63–75°F)

ECOSYSTEM Subtropical

WHEN TO VISIT Conditions are best from December to September.

MUST SEES Hammerhead schools; spotted morays in Malpelo; white-tip reef sharks hunting prey.

Roca Partida

COLIMA STATE, MEXICO

This stark volcanic pinnacle rises from the depths of the Pacific 320km (200 miles) off the tip of the Baja Peninsula. This is truly wild diving, with powerful swells, big currents, and large marine species at one of the most isolated dive sites in the world.

SHEER DIVING
The most remote outcrop of the Archipelago of Revillagigedo (a group of four islands), Roca Partida rises starkly from the wild surface of the Pacific Ocean, its rugged silhouette reflecting the characteristics of the reefs beneath. Steep walls plunge into deep, dark water, with very little life encrusted on their barren surfaces.

BOUNTIFUL SEAS
The rich upwellings from deep water around Roca Partida provide plentiful nutrients and oxygen for circling fish shoals, including huge black jacks and dense schools of barracuda. These in turn attract silky, white-tip, silver-tip, and hammerhead sharks in great numbers. What makes this dive site so special, however, are the manta ray encounters,

ESSENTIAL INFORMATION

WATER TEMPERATURE 19–25°C (66–77°F)

ECOSYSTEM Subtropical

WHEN TO VISIT Roca Partida has good, year-round diving, but cooler winter water is best for shark diversity.

MUST SEES Manta rays; sleeping white-tip and silver-tip sharks; black jacks.

which are among the best to be had anywhere; these magnificent animals almost seem to seek out divers, resulting in some extraordinary interactions.

The reputation of Roca Partida is spreading, and it is rapidly becoming an iconic site in the diving world. Divers willing to make the journey to this remote and wild location will find themselves amply rewarded.

SHARK ENCOUNTERS
Divers at Roca Partida can count on being buzzed by many different sharks, such as the normally shy scalloped hammerhead.

Hawaii

CENTRAL PACIFIC OCEAN

The underwater terrain of Hawaii reflects its volcanic origins, with twisted lava formations and steep drop-offs into abyssal depths. The oceanic island group is world renowned for its surfing, but offers exceptional diving too.

ISLAND PARADISE

Hawaii is the world's longest island chain, extending more than 2,400km (1,500 miles), and situated over 4,000km (2,500 miles) from the mainland. It comprises eight main islands – each the top of a submerged volcano – as well as another 124 tiny areas of uninhabited land that amount to no more than 8 sq km (3 sq miles). The stark ridges and bizarre rock formations that epitomize Hawaii's terrain above sea level extend beneath the water's surface, offering exciting dive opportunities, and great wildlife encounters. Hawaii's extreme isolation means it is visited by nomadic species from the vast expanse of the Pacific Ocean. The most notable of the pelagic animals are humpback whales, pygmy pilot whales, manta rays, and oceanic white-tip sharks. Humpbacks have been hunted globally almost to extinction, and have become rare even in the waters around Hawaii. Excellent dive sites can be found on the island of Hawaii – or Big Island – at the eastern end of the island chain, as well as Maui, Kauai, and Oahu.

ESSENTIAL INFORMATION

WATER TEMPERATURE 24–27°C (75–81°F)

ECOSYSTEM Tropical

WHEN TO VISIT All year round, but winter months at this busy site are less crowded.

MUST SEES Manta rays at Kona Beach; pygmy pilot whales; Shark's Cove, Oahu; Molokai; Long Lava Tube, Big Island.

WAVE-SWEPT COASTLINE
Hawaii lies at the same latitude as central Mexico. Clean waters, pure sands, and a tropical climate add to its appeal as a dive destination.

Catalina Island

CALIFORNIA, UNITED STATES

Lying only 35km (22 miles) off the coast of California is a spectacular island of dramatic scenery above the water, and tremendous beauty beneath. Catalina Island has been a nature reserve since 1974, with huge rewards for the diver.

PROTECTED ISLAND

Catalina Island is 32km (20 miles) in length and 13km (8 miles) wide, and has been owned by the Wrigley family since 1919. Keen conservationists, they have consistently refused permission for development on the island, and now 86 per cent of it is an established nature reserve. The rugged topography of the island extends below the waterline, with tremendous diving on craggy reefs and steep underwater pinnacles.

RICH SEAS

The island is swept by the cold waters of the Californian Current as it moves down from British Colombia. This creates oxygen-rich waters where kelp forests flourish – some of the larger specimens stretch from surface to seabed 30m (100ft) below. Cruising these underwater forests is a wide range of fish species, the most famous of which is the garibaldi. Fiercely territorial, these brightly coloured fish will stand

FOREST BENEATH THE WAVES
A rich variety of marine life is supported by the giant kelp stands of Catalina Island. Garibaldi fish are familiar residents of the kelp.

their ground as divers approach – a photographer's dream. The kelp forests are also home to huge black sea bass, eagle rays, Californian morays, and two-spot octopuses. The black sea bass is a particularly welcome sight as it was once heavily overfished, but is now making a comeback. Larger residents include Californian sea lions, a species known for its curiosity and willingness to approach divers. The occasional blue shark can be encountered off Catalina's shores, rounding off an exhilarating list of animals waiting to be discovered here.

ESSENTIAL INFORMATION

WATER TEMPERATURE 12–20°C (54–68°F)

ECOSYSTEM Temperate

WHEN TO VISIT Diving takes place all year round at Catalina, but winter diving can be very cold.

MUST SEES The Casino Point Underwater Park; The Farnsworth Banks.

Californian sea lions

The Outer Banks

NORTH CAROLINA, UNITED STATES

Famed in seafaring lore as the graveyard of ships, the Outer Banks are thought to be the site of up to 5,000 shipwrecks. Big ocean currents and an abundance of large pelagic animals combine to make this region one of the most exciting in the diving world.

HISTORIC WATERS

The Outer Banks are identified by a dramatic chain of islands and sandbars that extend for 209km (130 miles) up the coast of North Carolina. Within this barrier is a vast area of estuary, shallow lagoons, and enclosed water. This ecological gem is a crucial breeding ground for many fish species, and 70 per cent of the region enjoys protected status. The Outer Banks beyond the island chain are the real draw for the diver. With three great ocean currents meeting off this coastline, and the continental shelf only 64km (40 miles) to the east, this is dramatic diving

territory. The Outer Banks are littered with wrecks – many of them the result of sinkings by U-boats in World War II. Many of these are home to some of the larger residents of the banks, including numerous sand tiger sharks (also known as ragged-tooth sharks). These fierce-looking animals are in fact quite approachable if not provoked.

ESSENTIAL INFORMATION

WATER TEMPERATURE 12–24°C (54–75°F)

ECOSYSTEM Temperate

WHEN TO VISIT For the most favourable diving conditions, visit the Outer Banks between July and September.

MUST SEES Wrecks of the *Papoose* and *Proteus*; sand tiger sharks.

FEARSOME APPEARANCE

Despite its looks the sand tiger shark is relatively docile. However, like all large predators, it should be treated with respect.

The Great Lakes

CANADA/NORTHERN USA

Straddling the border between Canada and the USA, the five Great Lakes make up the largest expanse of fresh water on Earth. Conditions in the lakes can be demanding, but the reward is access to some of the best-preserved wrecks in the diving world.

WORLD-CLASS WRECKS

The Great Lakes cover an area of 246,000 sq km (95,000 sq miles), and offer a range of diving experiences and conditions. Many of the more densely populated regions around the lakes have always been significant industrial zones and have suffered through pollution and over-exploitation. The water is cold, and visibility can be limited, although in the lower lakes it has improved through the accidental (and in all other respects unwanted) introduction of the zebra mussel – a voracious filter-feeder that has cleaned the lakes of algae. There are many wrecks on the various lake beds. The very low temperatures and the lack of salt in the water have kept metal hulls relatively free of rust, while wooden vessels and even rope can be found in a remarkably good state of preservation.

FRESHWATER OASIS
The pine-flanked shores of Lake Michigan, where nine preserves protect sensitive underwater resources.

ESSENTIAL INFORMATION

WATER TEMPERATURE 0–18°C (32–64°F)

ECOSYSTEM Temperate

WHEN TO VISIT Year-round, but northern dives may be under ice in winter.

MUST SEES Sea caves along Lake Superior coast; the *Arabia* and other well-preserved wrecks.

PRESERVING THE PAST

In the early days of diving the lakes, numerous artefacts were plundered from otherwise pristine wreck sites. This malpractice was quickly stamped out through the establishment of a number of preserves. Michigan alone has nine such special areas, covering 4,920 sq km (1,900 sq miles). Notable wrecks throughout the lakes include the *Arabia*, a sailing vessel sunk in 1884 and still perfectly intact; the *Bermuda*, sunk in 1870; and the more contemporary *Mesquite*, sunk in 1989.

Vancouver Island

BRITISH COLUMBIA, WESTERN CANADA

CANADA
British Columbia
●Vancouver
USA

The cold waters and strong tides around Vancouver Island create a glorious mix of wildlife, and there are also vessels sunk as artificial reefs to add extra interest for the visiting diver. Some of the most popular dives lie between the island and the mainland.

CHANNEL CROSSING

The standard means of reaching Vancouver Island is via a ferry from the city itself, a 90-minute journey that gives you a glimpse of the abundant waters of this region. Cold waters are rich in oxygen and nutrients, and the channel between the island and the mainland is no exception. The addition of strong tidal movements creates an irresistible draw for marine plants and animals, and although the diving can be demanding at times, for example in the fast-running Dodds Narrows channel, there is much to make the experience worthwhile. One of the most famous residents of these waters is the inquisitive giant octopus, although more elusive wolf eels, harbour seals, various whale species (including orcas), and huge numbers of salmon may also be encountered at the right time of year.

EXTRAORDINARY ENCOUNTER
A diver makes contact with a giant octopus, a fascinating species that thrives in the nutrient-rich waters.

ARTIFICIAL REEFS

The vessel *Saskatchewan* was sunk in 1997 as an artificial reef, and has proved a real hit with both local and visiting divers. It is just one of a number of decommissioned warships, all well worth a dive, sunk off the coast by the Artificial Reef Society of British Columbia – a society formed by a group of underwater archaeologists in 1990 to turn warships into dive sites.

ESSENTIAL INFORMATION

WATER TEMPERATURE 9–18°C (48–64°F)

ECOSYSTEM Temperate

WHEN TO VISIT Year-round, but winter can be chilly.

MUST SEES Giant octopuses; whales; wreck of the *Saskatchewan*; Dodds Narrows channel.

Galápagos Islands

EASTERN PACIFIC

The Galápagos were known as the Enchanted Isles by early mariners, baffled by the currents that swirled around them. The name has changed, but the experience remains the same for divers fortunate enough to visit this unique archipelago.

RUGGED AND REMOTE

The Galápagos Islands are named after the Spanish word for saddle – *galápago* – after the shape of the giant tortoise shells that provided a food source for the early explorers and whaling ships that visited the islands. The island group consists of 13 main islands situated 970km (600 miles) off the west coast of Ecuador. These stark islands, only a few million years old, still show the contorted rock formations – twisted reefs and pitted ridges – caused by their volcanic birth. These provide an excellent substrate for busy marine communities, replenished by the seven ocean currents that converge on this island group from all directions.

ESSENTIAL INFORMATION

WATER TEMPERATURE 16–27°C (61–81°F)

ECOSYSTEM Temperate

WHEN TO VISIT Diving continues all year round in the Galápagos.

MUST SEES Hammerheads and white-tips at Wolf and Darwin; whale sharks; sea lions; marine iguanas; penguins.

MARINE LIFE

Although there are only 13 reef-building species of coral in the Galápagos, meaning that the reefs are stark affairs clinging to the dark volcanic rock, the life that swarms over them is spectacular.

The fame of the Galápagos as a dive site lies in its gatherings of large marine animals, including magnificent schools of scalloped hammerheads. Sadly, overfishing has had a serious impact on shark populations in the waters around the islands, and unless circumstances change, such sightings may become increasingly rare. Groups of cow-nosed rays and eagle rays are regularly sighted off the more exposed reefs, as well as gatherings of manta rays and the occasional whale shark.

UNIQUE SPECIES

A visit to the Galápagos offers animal encounters that cannot be experienced elsewhere. The islands have evolved in isolation, and are home to a number of remarkable species. Perhaps the most famous of these is the marine iguana, although the islands also have colonies of the most northerly penguin species on Earth – the tiny Galápagos penguin. It is possible to snorkel with both of these species if accompanied by a knowledgeable local guide and with the right sea conditions.

WILD GALÁPAGOS

Visiting Californian sea lion

It is unsurprising that the Galápagos Islands provided inspiration for Darwin's theory of evolution – they are rich in all kinds of life. There are well over 300 fish species in the region, including 30 species of shark. Larger residents include nearly 80,000 seals and sea lions. There are also 600 species of mollusc and 100 different types of crab! Larger visitors include sperm whales, humpbacks and brydes whales, as well as many species of dolphin. The islands are a naturalist's paradise.

BARREN APPEARANCE

The bleak contours of the Galápagos Islands might seem to suggest a region devoid of life. The appearance is deceptive, however, as life thrives here both above and below the green waters of the surrounding Pacific Ocean.

Useful resources

PADI: DIVE SAFETY CHECKLIST

- Divers should limit their depths according to their training, certification level and experience.

- Regardless of level of training, any increase in diving depth should be incremental.

- Further training and/or supervision is needed when diving in a new type of environment.

- Avoid overweighting; carry out a buoyancy check whenever using new equipment. Remember to reduce weighting when going from salt to freshwater.

- Ensure all weight systems used have a quick release and that each buddy is familiar with its operation.

- Always review emergency procedures prior to each dive.

- Have regular medical check ups and keep fit for diving.

- If surface conditions, currents or visibility deteriorate, consider aborting dive.

- Consult tide tables where appropriate and seek local advice on prevailing diving conditions.

- Use Surface Marker Buoys and ascent/descent lines wherever appropriate.

- Always inform a non-diver where you are going and when you expect to return.

Visit www.padi.com

PROJECT AWARE FOUNDATION: TEN WAYS A DIVER CAN PROTECT THE UNDERWATER ENVIRONMENT

Divers and snorkellers are obvious ambassadors for the underwater environment. Let's make sure we:

1. Dive carefully in fragile aquatic environments
Although, at first, they may look like rocks or plants, many aquatic organisms are fragile creatures that can be damaged or harmed by the bump of a tank, knee or camera, a swipe of a fin or even the touch of a hand. It is also important to know that some aquatic organisms, such as corals, are extremely slow growing. By breaking off even a small piece, you may be destroying decades of growth. By being careful, you can prevent devastating and long-lasting damage to magnificent dive sites.

2. Streamline yourself
Much damage to the environment is done unknowingly. Keep your gauges and alternate air source secured so they don't drag over the reef or bottom. By controlling your buoyancy and taking care not to touch coral or other fragile organisms with your body, diving equipment or camera, you will have done your part in preventing injury to aquatic life.

3. Continue your education
If you haven't dived in a while, your skills (particularly buoyancy control) may need sharpening. Before heading to the reefs, seek bottom time with a certified assistant or instructor in a pool or other environment that

won't be damaged by a few bumps and scrapes. Better yet, take a diving continuing education course such as PADI Scuba Review, the PADI Adventures in Diving programme, or a PADI Speciality Diver course. AWARE continuing education diving courses provide you with the skills practice and practical application of environmentally sound diving techniques.

4. Consider your impact on aquatic life through your interactions
Very few forms of aquatic life pose a threat to us. In fact, some creatures even seem friendly and curious about our presence. As we become bolder and more curious ourselves, we may even feel compelled to touch, handle, feed and even hitch rides on certain aquatic life. However, our actions may cause stress to the animal, interrupt feeding and mating behaviour, introduce food items that are not healthy for the species or even provoke aggressive behaviour in normally non-aggressive species. Interact responsibly with the aquatic environment.

5. Understand and respect underwater life, resist the urge to collect souvenirs
Through adaptation to an aquatic environment, underwater life often differs greatly in appearance from life we are used to seeing on land. Many creatures only appear to look like plants or inanimate objects. Using them as 'toys' or food for other animals can leave a trail of destruction that can disrupt a local ecosystem and rob other divers of the pleasure of observing or photographing these creatures. Consider taking part in a Project AWARE programme to become more familiar with the importance of, and the interdependent nature of, worldwide aquatic

ecosystems. Dive sites that are heavily visited can be depleted of their resources in a short time. Collecting specimens, coral and shells in these areas can strip their fascination and beauty. If you want to return from your dives with trophies to show friends and family you may want to consider underwater photography instead.

6. Be an ECO-Tourist

Protected areas, such as parks, reserves and sanctuaries are one of the best tools for conserving the aquatic environment. Support the creation of protected areas, follow all local laws, and learn to appreciate that all aquatic habitats (such as grass beds, mangroves and rubble zones) are important and interesting environments. Do not confine your diving only to sites highlighted in brochures and articles. When planning a diving trip, choose ECO Tour Operators involved with ECO-resorts and ECO-operators. Make informed decisions when selecting a destination and support the Project AWARE Go ECO environmental campaign.

7. Respect the underwater cultural heritage

Divers and snorkellers have the privilege to access dive sites that are part of our cultural heritage or maritime history. You should help preserve these sites for future generations by obeying local laws, diving responsibly and treating wrecks with respect. Wrecks can serve as important habitats for fish and other aquatic life.

8. Report environmental disturbances or destruction of your dive sites

Divers and snorkellers are in a unique position to monitor the health of local waterways, lakes and coastal areas. If you observe an unusual depletion of aquatic life, a rash of injuries to aquatic animals, or notice strange substances or objects in the water, report them to your local authority or similar organisation.

9. Be a role model

As a diver or snorkeller, you realise that when someone throws a plastic wrapper or other debris overboard, it is not out of sight, out of mind. You see the results of such neglect. Set a good example in your own interactions with the environment, and other divers and non-divers will follow suit.

10. Get Involved

There are plenty of opportunities to show your support of a clean aquatic environment, including local beach clean-ups, surveys and attending public hearings on matters that impact local coastal areas and water resources. Divers' skills in particular are always needed and appreciated by many environmental organisations.

Visit www.projectaware.org for more details

USEFUL CONTACTS

Training organizations

International groups offering both basic and specialized dive tuition, including training organizations based on an amateur footing.

Professional Association of Dive Instructors (PADI)
www.padi.com

PADI Americas: 30151 Tomas Street, Rancho Santa Margarita, CA 92688-2125, USA

PADI Europe: Oberwilerstrasse 3 CH-8442, Hettlingen, Switzerland

National Association of Underwater Instructors (NAUI)
Worldwide headquarters: PO Box 89789, Tampa, FL 33689-0413, USA
www.naui.org

British Sub Aqua Club (BSAC)
Telford's Quay, South Pier Road, Ellesmere Port, Cheshire, CH65 4FL, UK
www.bsac.com

Sub Aqua Association
Space Solutions Business Centre, Sefton Lane, Maghull, Liverpool, L31 8BX, UK
www.saa.org.uk

Scottish Sub Aqua Club
The Cockburn Centre, 40 Bogmore Place, Glasgow, G51 4TQ, UK
www.scotsac.com

Scuba Schools International
2619 Canton Court, Fort Collins, CO, 80525-4498, USA
www.ssiusa.com

World Underwater Federation
Viale Tiziano, 74 00196, Roma, Italia
www.cmas2000.org

Technical Diving International
18 Elm Street, Topsham, Maine, 04086, USA
www.tdisdi.com

International Association of Nitrox and Technical Divers
5609 Power Road, Ottawa, Ontario, K1G 3N4, Canada
www.iantd.com

USEFUL CONTACTS (CONTINUED)

National Association for Cave Diving (NACD)
P.O. Box 14492, Gainesville, FL, 32604, USA
www.safecavediving.com

Governing bodies
Organizations promoting and regulating recreational diving activities:

World Underwater Federation
Viale Tiziano, 74 00196, Roma, Italia
www.cmas2000.org

International Association for the Development of Freediving (AIDA)
Rue du Petit-Beaulieu 4
CH 1004 Lausanne, Switzerland
www.aida-international.org

Freediving Regulations and Education Entity (FREE)
7480 NW 175 St., Miami, FL, 33015 USA
www.divingfree.com

International Association for Handicapped Divers
http://www.iahd.org

Conservation and heritage organizations
Charitable and non-profit organizations promoting marine wildlife conservation, and groups involved in preserving maritime heritage.

Coral Cay Conservation
40-42 Osnaburgh Street, London,
NW1 3ND, UK
www.coralcay.org

World Wildlife Fund
1250 Twenty-Fourth Street, N.W.
P.O. Box 97180, Washington,
DC 20090-7180, USA
www.worldwildlife.org

Marine Conservation Society
Unit 3, Wolf Business Park, Alton Road,
Ross-on-Wye, Herefordshire, HR9 5NB, UK
www.mcsuk.org

British Divers Marine Life Rescue
Lime House, Regency Close Uckfield,
East Sussex, TN22 1DS, UK
www.bdmlr.org.uk/donate

Marine Fish Conservation Network
600 Pennsylvania Avenue, SE, Suite 210,
Washington, DC 20003, USA
www.conservefish.org/site

Nautical Archaeology Society
The Nautical Archaeology Society,
Fort Cumberland, Fort Cumberland Road,
Portsmouth, PO4 9LD, UK
www.nasportsmouth.org.uk

Whale and Dolphin Conservation Society
Brookfield House, 38 St Paul Street,
Chippenham, Wiltshire, SN15 1LJ, UK

The Shark Trust
National Marine Aquarium, The Rope Walk
Coxside, Plymouth, PL4 0LF, UK
www.sharktrust.org/sharkconservation.html

Historical Diving Society
Historical Diving Society USA , PO BOX 2837,
Santa Maria, CA 93457, USA
www.hds.org

Historical Diving Society UK
www.thehds.com

Maritime Archaeological and Historical Society
P.O. Box 44382, L'Enfant Plaza, Washington,
D.C 20026, USA
www.mahsnet.org

Diving medicine and safety organizations
Expert advisory groups on diving medicine and safety issues.

Divers Alert Network (DAN)
The Peter B. Bennett Center, 6 West Colony
Place, Durham, NC 27705, USA
www.diversalertnetwork.org

British Diving Safety Group
West Quay Road, Poole, BH15 1HZ, UK
www.bdsg.org

London Diving Chamber
Hospital of St John and St Elizabeth,
60 Grove End Road, St John's Wood,
London, NW8 9NH, UK

Glossary

ABSOLUTE PRESSURE The total *pressure* acting on a body, equal to the sum of *atmospheric pressure* and *gauge pressure*.

A-CLAMP FITTING A *regulator first stage* that attaches to the *pillar valve* of a *cylinder* by means of a yoke that clamps it securely in position.

AIR CONSUMPTION The depletion of oxygen in air through respiration; the rate at which air is used by a diver during the course of a dive.

ALTERNATE AIR SOURCE A redundant source of air supply, either in the form of an *octopus second stage*, or a completely independent *cylinder* and *regulator*.

AMBIENT PRESSURE The total *pressure* acting on a body at a given depth. See also *absolute pressure*.

ANCHOR LINE A rope, cable, or chain that attaches a ship to its anchor.

ANOXIA A medical condition caused by a lack, or severe deficiency of, oxygen in the human body.

AQUA LUNG The first underwater breathing apparatus to use compressed air and a two-stage *regulator*, designed by Emile Gagnan and Jacques Cousteau.

ARCHIPELAGO A group or chain of islands.

ARTIFICIAL REEF A man-made object deliberately scuttled to create a haven for marine life, and for the enjoyment of divers.

ASCENT Returning from depth to the surface at the end of a dive. This must always be performed carefully to avoid *decompression sickness*.

ATMOSPHERIC PRESSURE The *pressure* exerted by the gases in the atmosphere. At sea level, this is equal to 1 bar (14.7psi).

ATOLL Circular *coral reef*, often surrounding a lagoon, that has formed around a submerged extinct volcano.

BALLAST Lead weights carried to offset the inherent *buoyancy* of the diver's *exposure suit*.

BENDS See *decompression sickness*

BEZEL A rotatable, notched, or marked outer ring on instruments, such as watches and compasses, used to mark key datum points, such as a bearing.

BLOCK SHIP A vessel sunk deliberately across the approaches to a naval harbour to bar entry to hostile submarines and surface ships.

BOMMIE An isolated outcrop of coral growth on the seabed.

BOYLE'S LAW Physical law stating that at a constant temperature, the volume of a gas is inversely proportional to the *pressure* exerted on it.

BRACKISH Water that is not as salty as seawater, but that has a higher salt content than freshwater.

BREATH-HOLD DIVING See *freediving*

BUBBLE CHECK A precautionary visual inspection of another diver's kit (conducted underwater) to determine if it has any air leaks.

BUDDY A diver who assumes an informal duty of care over the other member of their assigned "buddy pair" during diving.

BUDDY LINE A safety line for tethering a *buddy* pair together.

BUOYANCY An upward thrust exerted on an immersed object, which is equal to the weight of the water that has been displaced by the object.

BUOYANCY COMPENSATION DEVICE (BCD) A jacket that can be inflated and deflated to allow the diver to control their *buoyancy*.

BUOYANCY CONTROL Manipulation of *buoyancy* through the use of devices such as a *BCD*, and the breathing cycle.

CAISSON A pressurized, watertight chamber used to undertake construction work underwater.

CERTIFICATION CARD Accreditation proving that a diver has achieved a certain level of dive training with one of the recognized agencies.

CORAL HEAD Protrusions on a *coral reef* formed by a colony of living coral polyps feeding and growing.

CORAL ISLAND Portion of a *coral reef* that is permanently out of water, its surface usually eroded to a flat top of white coral rock and sand. May occur in a chain along a reef.

CORAL REEF A massive, marine, rock-like ridge or outcrop created by the gradual accretion of the skeletons of generations of coral polyps.

CYLINDER A steel or aluminium container designed to hold compressed gas.

CYLINDER CONTENTS GAUGE An instrument that displays the remaining quantity of air or other breathing gas in a diver's *cylinder*. Also known as a submersible pressure gauge (SPG) or pressure gauge.

DATUM LINE A line used as a fixed reference to aid in an accurate survey of an area.

DECOMPRESSION To return to conditions of normal *atmospheric pressure* by controlled means.

DECOMPRESSION SCHEDULE A plan describing the number, duration, and depth of *decompression stops* required for a given dive.

DECOMPRESSION SICKNESS (DCS) A potentially dangerous medical condition resulting from the formation of bubbles of nitrogen in the bloodstream and tissues of a diver's body. Also known as decompression injury (DCI) and the bends.

DECOMPRESSION STOP A scheduled pause in a diver's ascent to allow nitrogen to pass from body tissues back into the blood at a safe rate.

DEHYDRATION A medical condition resulting from excessive loss of water from the body.

DELAYED SURFACE MARKER BUOY (DSMB) Marker buoy deployed just before ascent. It is inflated underwater, then released to indicate where a diver will surface.

DEMAND VALVE See *second stage*

DEPTH GAUGE An analogue or digital gauge that measures *ambient pressure*, and uses this to give a reading of depth.

DESCENT Travelling from the surface to depth.

DIN FITTING A screw-thread fitting for attaching a *regulator first stage* to a compatible *pillar valve*. Allows higher working pressures than *A-clamp* fittings.

DISPLACEMENT The displacement of water that occurs when an object is submerged in it.

DISTANCE LINE A line fastened to a submerged feature and deployed from a *reel* as a navigational guide, especially in areas of low visibility.

DIVE CENTRE A commercially run diving school and kit-rental centre, frequently offering organized trips and guides to local *dive sites*.

DIVE COMPUTER A digital device that provides the diver with a range of information, such as depth, time, and ascent rate.

DIVE CONSOLE An instrument panel incorporating a *cylinder contents gauge*, *depth gauge*, and sometimes also a compass, or a *dive computer*.

DIVE GUIDE An employee of a *dive centre* or school who guides qualified divers around local *dive sites*.

DIVE LEADER The diver in a *buddy* pair who is designated (by agreement) as the principle pace-setter and decision-maker underwater.

DIVE MARSHAL A senior diver whose role on a dive trip is to allocate *buddy* pairs, approve

dive plans, ensure that complete records of dives are kept, and to initiate and direct rescue efforts in the event of a diving accident.

DIVE PLAN The outline of a proposed dive, including its depth, duration, intended goals, entry and exit points, signalling conventions, and contingency plans.

DIVE SITE Any location where diving is conducted.

DIVE SLATE A plastic tablet used for making notes underwater.

DIVE TIME The duration of a dive, starting at the moment the diver leaves the surface and ending with their return to the surface.

DIVEMASTER A person qualified to act as a *dive guide*, assist diving instructors, and oversee the organization of dives for paying customers.

DIVING CLUB An organization offering diving tuition and social events on an amateur basis (UK usage). This term can also refer to continental European diving centres offering tuition on a commercial basis.

DIVING SCHOOL A centre for tuition in diving skills (usually on a commercial basis).

DPV (DIVER PROPULSION VEHICLE) A propulsion device either ridden or clung to by a diver to minimize swimming effort or aid in the exploration of large *dive sites*.

DRAG Frictional resistance to the motion of an object through a fluid.

DRIFT DIVE A dive in which the diver is propelled along a route by undersea currents.

D-RING A D-shaped ring of metal or plastic used as an anchor point for tethering equipment to your *BCD* during a dive.

DROP-OFF A falling-away of the ground or seabed, such as a *reef wall* or rock shelf that descends steeply.

DRYSUIT An *exposure suit* designed for use in very cold waters, in which trapped air is the principle insulating medium and that offers a high degree of thermal protection.

DSMB (DELAYED SURFACE MARKER BUOY) A tubular buoy designed to be deployed at the end of a dive to aid *ascent* and alert observers at the surface.

DUMP VALVE One-way valve used to release air from an inflatable device.

DYE MARKERS A fluorescent dye designed to be released into the water to alert rescue craft to the position of a drifting diver.

ECOSYSTEM The interactions between a community of living organisms and the environment they inhabit.

EL NIÑO A warming of the eastern tropical Pacific occurring every few years that has a pronounced effect on both the local and wider climate. Often occurs around Christmas time – "*El Niño*" in Spanish refers to the Christ child.

EQUALIZATION The process of "clearing" the ears and sinuses until the pressure within them matches the pressure of the water surrounding the body. See also *Valsalva Manoeuvre*.

EXPOSURE SUIT Any suit worn by a diver in order to prevent excessive loss of body heat. See *wetsuits*, *semi-dry suits*, and *drysuits*.

FILTER FEEDER An aquatic animal that feeds by straining minute organisms and other suspended food particles from the water.

FINNING Kicking the feet rhythmically while wearing fins to achieve forward motion.

FIRST STAGE A major component of the *regulator* that reduces the *pressure* of air from the cylinder to 8–10 bar above *ambient pressure*, then allows it to pass to the *second stage* for inhalation by the diver. It also supplies air for inflatable kit items such as the *BCD*, and to *pressure gauges* displaying the remaining contents of the *cylinder*.

FOOD CHAIN A sequence of organisms, each depending on the next as a source of food.

FOOT POCKET A style of fin shoe that covers the whole of the foot.

FREE ASCENT An *ascent* that is carried out without the use of a line or any other point of reference.

FREEDIVING A form of diving in which divers do not carry an air supply but remain underwater only as long as they can hold their breath.

GAUGE PRESSURE The surrounding water pressure, as measured by a gauge that does not take *atmospheric pressure* into account.

GLOBAL POSITIONING SYSTEM (GPS) A navigation system that uses satellite signals to determine an exact longitude and latitude position.

HELIOX A mixture of helium and oxygen, used for diving beyond *recreational diving* limits.

HYDROSTATIC TESTING A method of testing a *cylinder* for serviceability by filling it with pressurized water.

HYPERVENTILATION A medical condition caused by rapid or deep breathing, resulting in lowered carbon dioxide levels in the blood.

HYPOXIA A medical condition caused by a deficiency of oxygen in the human body.

INFLATOR VALVE A manually operated valve that admits compressed air into the buoyancy bladders of a *BCD*, or into a *drysuit*.

KELP FOREST A marine *ecosystem* based around dense growths of seaweed belonging to the kelp family.

LIVEABOARD A recreational diving vessel equipped to conduct extended diving trips without returning to port.

LOG BOOK A record containing the details of individual dives made by a diver.

LONGSHORE CURRENT A current running parallel to the shoreline.

MANGROVE Assorted coastal tree and shrub species with aerial roots that grow in dense thickets along tidal shores in the tropics.

MARINE PARK An area of sea or coastline in which marine species are protected by government legislation.

MASK FOGGING Misting caused by the accumulation of oils on the lens (or lenses) of a diving mask, permitting moisture to condense there more readily.

MASK SQUEEZE Discomfort caused by increasing water *pressure* acting on the diver's mask, pressing its frame into the face.

MUCK DIVING Informal term for diving in areas where the bottom sediments are dark and coarse but where small marine species proliferate (such as Sulawesi's Lembeh Straits).

NEAP TIDE The point in the monthly cycle of tides where the gravitational influences of the Sun and Moon are least aligned, resulting in the lowest high tides and the highest low tides.

NEOPRENE A synthetic rubber fabric with good heat insulation properties used to make *wetsuits*.

NITROGEN NARCOSIS Intoxication caused by breathing nitrogen at elevated *partial pressures* (such as during deep dives), resulting in the impairment of reasoning and motor skills, feelings of irrational anxiety or elation, and perceptual narrowing.

NITROX Any mixture of nitrogen and oxygen prepared for use as a breathing gas, but normally one containing a greater percentage of oxygen than that found in air.

OCTOPUS SECOND STAGE A redundant *second stage*, carried by divers as a contingency against failure of the main second stage, and to enable air-sharing with a diver whose own air supply has been depleted.

OFF-GASSING The gradual release of gases (especially nitrogen) that have accumulated in a diver's body during the course of a dive. Off-gassing occurs as *ambient pressure* decreases during *ascent* and at the surface.

OPEN WATER A body of water that is not sheltered from the influence of naturally developing weather conditions and currents, and whose depth may exceed safe training limits.

O-RING A ring-shaped gasket, used to seal interfaces between one pressurized piece of equipment and another, such as in the *pillar valve* of a *cylinder*.

OVERHANG A projection from the face of a reef, cliff etc.

OVERHEAD ENVIRONMENT Any diving environment where direct access to the surface is restricted, such as inside a cave or under ice.

OXYGEN TOXICITY Acute nervous system dysfunction caused by breathing oxygen at elevated pressures. Can cause loss of consciousness and convulsions.

PARTIAL PRESSURE The *pressure* of a single gas in a mixture of gases, measured as if that gas alone were present (the total pressure of a gas mixture being the sum of the *partial pressures* of its constituent gases).

PELAGIC ANIMALS Creatures that dwell in the *open ocean*, rather than coastal waters.

PILLAR VALVE The valve that transfers gas from the diver's *cylinder* to the *regulator first stage*.

PLANKTON Minute free-floating plant and animal organisms inhabiting seas and lakes, which form the basis of the *food chain* in many environments.

PLB (Personal Locator Beacon) A submersible device that emits a radio signal on an internationally-recognized search-and-rescue homing frequency, enabling emergency services to pinpoint its location.

POLAR SEAS The cold seas at the polar extremities of the planet, varying in temperature from -1.8–10°C (29–50°F).

PONY CYLINDER A small *cylinder* of breathing gas with an independent *regulator*, intended for emergency use if the diver's main breathing apparatus fails.

PRESSURE The exertion of force by one surface, substance, or gas onto another.

REBREATHER A breathing apparatus that recycles exhaled gas by filtering out carbon dioxide and replacing any oxygen metabolized by the diver.

RECOMPRESSION CHAMBER A pressure chamber used in the treatment of divers suffering from *decompression sickness*.

RECREATIONAL DIVING Sport diving that takes place within certain depth and environmental limitations, as defined by the various training agencies.

REEF WALL A vertical face of coral growth, often descending into deep waters.

REEL A spooling device used to store and deploy line.

REFRACTION The change in the velocity of light (or any propagating wave) that occurs when it passes from one medium to another (e.g from air to water).

REGULATOR The mechanism that supplies breathing gas from the *cylinder* to the diver via a two-stage process of *pressure* reduction. The regulator is made up of two parts: the *first stage* and the *second stage*.

RIB (Rigid Inflatable Boat) A fast utility boat characterized by a V-shaped hull with an inflatable tube running round its upper edge.

RIP CURRENT A fast-moving current running perpendicular to the shore, caused by the action of incoming waves.

RULE OF THIRDS, THE Rule of thumb used when calculating air requirements for a dive, especially one requiring a conservative approach, such as a cavern exploration.

SAFETY STOP A precautionary pause in a diver's *ascent* to prevent the formation of nitrogen bubbles in the bloodstream. Its purpose is as a failsafe against *decompression sickness* even when no scheduled *decompression stops* need to be made.

SALINITY The salt content of a measure of water.

SCUBA Acronym for Self-Contained Underwater Breathing Apparatus.

SECOND STAGE The part of the *regulator* that regulates the *pressure* of a diver's gas supply to the same pressure as its immediate environment.

SEMI-DRY SUIT A thick *neoprene exposure suit*, similar to a *wetsuit*, designed for use in cold waters.

SHELTERED WATER A shallow body of water protected from currents and weather conditions, used for training divers in a controlled environment.

SHOTLINE A line with a weight at one end and a buoy at the other, chiefly used to mark the position of wrecks and provide a guideline for descending and ascending divers.

SILTING A rapid reduction in underwater visibility that occurs when fine sedimentary particles are stirred up.

SKINSUIT A thin *exposure suit*, typically made of Lycra, designed for use in tropical waters.

SLACK WATER A period of reduced water movement that occurs between incoming and outgoing tides.

SMB (Surface Marker Buoy) An inflatable buoy designed to be towed behind a diver to indicate their position to observers on the surface.

SNORKELLING Swimming face-down at the surface using a short, curved tube to draw breath.

SPG (SUBMERSIBLE PRESSURE GAUGE) See *cylinder contents gauge*

SPRING TIDE The point in the monthly cycle of tides when the highest high tides, and lowest low tides occur. Spring tides occur when the gravitational forces of the Sun and the Moon are aligned.

SPUR AND GROOVE REEF FORMATION A typical growth structure of coral reefs, in which outcrops of coral are separated by linear depressions.

STANDING CURRENT A continuous directional movement of water generated by prevailing weather, sea, and climatic conditions.

STROBE A beacon that emits high-intensity flashes of light at short intervals.

SUBTROPICAL SEAS Warm seas within a loosely-defined zone between *temperate* and *tropical* climatic conditions.

SWELL The undulating motion of surface waters in areas of open sea.

SWIM-THROUGH A submerged arch, or short passage of rock, where direct access to the surface is restricted, but in which the exit is clearly visible at all times.

TECHNICAL DIVING The use of special breathing-gas mixtures, such as *Nitrox*, *Trimix*, and *Heliox*, to extend depth limits and dive durations beyond *recreational diving* limits.

TEMPERATE SEAS Seas of an intermediate temperature between *tropical* and *polar*, typically 10–20°C (50–68°F).

TEST DATE The date when a compressed gas *cylinder* was last subjected to *hydrostatic testing*.

THERMOCLINE A layer in a body of water in which temperature changes rapidly with depth. This is usually between a warm surface layer and colder deep water.

TIDAL CURRENT A current generated by the action of the tides.

TIDAL CYCLE The cyclic rise and fall of shoreline sea level, caused by the gravitational influence of the Moon and Sun.

TOPOGRAPHY The shape or form of a region of land or seabed.

TRIMIX A mixture of oxygen, helium, and nitrogen commonly used as a breathing gas for dives deeper than 50m (164ft).

TROPICAL SEAS The seas found within the boundaries of the 20°C (68°F) isotherm – a band of warm equatorial water.

VALSALVA MANOEUVRE A method of manually increasing *pressure* on the inside of the eardrum by closing the nasal passage and exerting expiratory effort, forcing air through the Eustachian tubes into the inner ear.

WATER COLUMN The zone of water between the surface and the bottom of a lake, sea, or river.

WEIGHT SYSTEM The means by which a diver's lead *ballast* is secured.

WETSUIT An *exposure suit* made of *neoprene* rubber, which traps a thin layer of water against the skin as an insulating medium.

WICKING The absorption of moisture into a fabric by capillary action.

WORKING PRESSURE The normal *pressure* at which an equipment item is designed to operate.

WORLD HERITAGE SITE An area of natural or cultural importance protected by a United Nations treaty.

WRECK Remains of ships, aircraft, or other vehicles found on the seabed.

INDEX

A

ACKNOWLEDGMENTS

Authors' Acknowledgments

Monty Halls (www.montyhalls.co.uk) would like to thank: Oceanic, Gates Housings, Fourth Element, Ed Poore of Poseidon Diving, the Hilton Hotel in Dahab, Dave Moore – the finest diver I have ever met – and in particular Dr Antje Steinfurth.

Miranda Krestovnikoff would like to thank: Bristol University Sub Aqua club for introducing me to the world of diving, and Damian Wozniak and Tim Walsh for their thorough training and inspiration; DIVER magazine for giving me opportunities to visit exotic diving destinations and for publishing the resulting articles; and Dave Shaw, Dive Services UK, Phil Bullen, and Richard Bull for attentive and solid buddy support when diving commercially. Both Monty and I would like to thank Dan Burton for his spectacular photography in this book and for making initial contacts with DK to make it all possible. Thanks also to the editors for working with Monty and me, taking our abstract scribbles and turning them into this dive guide. Most importantly, a huge thank you to my husband, Nicholas, who has been immensely patient and supportive during book writing and for my baby daughter, Amélie, who waited to emerge until after my deadlines were met!

Publisher's Acknowledgments

Dorling Kindersley and cobalt id would like to thank the following for their invaluable help with this book: Dr Kim Bryan, Christine Heilman, and Letitia Luff for editorial assistance; Hilary Bird for indexing; and Stephen Dye for specialist advice. Special thanks to Poseidon Divers (www.poseidondivers.com) for their generous provision of diving equipment and expert advice during the photographic shoot in Dahab, and for the help of Mark Rogers, Katie Rogers, and Sophia Crook, who kindly agreed to act as models; and to Dan Burton for technical guidance throughout the production of this book. Many thanks also to John Womack of Otter Watersports (www.drysuits.co.uk) for allowing us to use his products and premises for photographic purposes; Vicky Boateng and Catwalk Model Management; the team at PADI UK for kindly arranging permission for us to reprint PADI advisory texts; Coral Cay for providing images of their work in marine conservation; and Fraser Bathgate for advice on, and images of, adaptive training techniques.

We also extend our thanks to the following manufacturers who kindly contributed images and products for the production of this book: Mares, Tabata USA (TUSA), Aqua Lung, Apeks Marine Equipment, AP Valves, Delta P Technology, Seemann, Diving Unlimited International Inc., Bob Evans Designs Inc., Mazin Submersible Technology Inc., SpecialFins Ltd, Northern Diver, Inon Inc., Sea & Sea, Canon Inc., Pentax, DZ Active Systems, HydroOptix LLC, Ocean Reef, Nikon Corporation, McMahon Precision Engineering Ltd, Ambient Pressure Diving Ltd, Bright Weights, Fujifilm, Ikelite, and Underwater Kinetics. Jetboots™ are manufactured by Mazin Submersible Technology, Inc. (www.jetboots.com). Force Fins are manufactured by Bob Evans Designs Inc. (www.forcefin.com).

Picture credits

The publisher would like to thank the following for their kind permission to reproduce their photographs:

Abbreviations key: t = top; b = bottom; l = left; r = right; c = centre; rh = running header.

4 Dan Burton; **6–7** Kevin Davidson; **8–9t** Kevin Davidson; **8cr** Dorling Kindersley/Dave King/Courtesy of the North Wind Undersea Institute, New York; **9cl** iStockphoto/Andy Lim; **9cr** iStockphoto/Ian Scott; **10–19rh** Dan Burton; **10bl** Linda Pitkin; **10c** Alamy/POPPERFOTO; **11b** Ross Armstrong; **11tr** Dan Burton; **12–13b** Tony White; **13br** Ross Armstrong; **13tl** Dan Burton; **14** Dan Burton; **15bl** Linda Pitkin; **15tr** Dan Burton; **16b** Dan Burton; **16tl** Dan Burton; **16tr** Kevin Davidson; **18** Linda Pitkin; **19b** Kevin Davidson; **19tl** Kevin Davidson; **19tr** Linda Pitkin; **20–21** Getty/Hulton Archive/Fox Photos; **22–29rh** Dorling Kindersley/Dave King/Courtesy of the North Wind Undersea Institute, New York; **22cl** Mary Evans Picture Library; **23c** Alamy/POPPERFOTO; **23tr** Mary Evans Picture Library; **24c** Mary Evans Picture Library; **24tr** Mary Evans Picture Library; **25c** Corbis/Bettmann; **26c** Dorling Kindersley/Alex Wilson/Courtesy of the Charlestown Shipwreck and Heritage Centre, Cornwall; **26tl** Mary Evans Picture Library/Dr David Lewis Hodgson; **27t** Corbis/Bettmann; **28c** Kevin Davidson; **29tr** Dan Burton; **30–31** Dan Burton; **33tr** Dorling Kindersley/John Davis; **34–35b** Dan Burton; **34c** Kevin Davidson; **35tr** Kevin Davidson; **38–39b** Dan Burton; **38tc** Fraser Bathgate; **39br** Alamy/David Fleetham; **40–41** Dan Burton; **45t** Dan Burton; **46–47b** Kevin Davidson; **47b** Mares; **47c1** Mares; **47c2** Northern Diver; **47c3** Ocean Reef; **47c4** Ocean Reef; **47t1** Mares; **47t2** Mares; **48cr1** Tabata USA (TUSA); **48cr2** Aqua Lung; **49c1** Mares; **49c2** Tabata USA (TUSA); **49c3** Tabata USA (TUSA); **49t1** Aqua Lung; **49t2** Bob Evans Designs Inc. (Force Fin); **51bl1** Tabata USA (TUSA); **51bl2** Tabata USA (TUSA); **52bc1** Mares; **52bc2** Mares; **52t** Dan Burton; **54br** Diving Unlimited International Ltd; **54tr** Nataliya Chervyakova; **55cr2** Mares; **56b** Dan Burton; **58c** Kevin Davidson; **58t** Kevin Davidson; **59l1** AP Valves; **59l2** Mares; **59l3** Mares; **59l4** Tabata USA (TUSA); **59l5** Aqua Lung; **59r1** AP Valves; **59r2** Mares; **59r3** Apeks Marine Equipment; **59r4** Tabata USA (TUSA); **59r5** Aqua Lung; **60b** Kevin Davidson; **61br** Aqua Lung; **63br** Kevin Davidson; **63tr1** Tabata USA (TUSA); **63tr2** Aqua Lung; **63tr3** Mares; **63tr4** Apeks Marine Equipment; **63tr5** Aqua Lung; **64bc** Mares; **64bl** Mares; **65b** Corbis/Todd Gipstein; **65tr1** Apeks Marine Equipment; **65tr2** Mares; **65tr3** Apeks Marine Equipment; **65tr4** Mares; **66b2** Mares; **66b3** Tabata USA (TUSA); **67cl** Mares; **68c** Dan Burton; **69b** Kevin Davidson; **70br1** Seemann; **70br2** Mares; **70cr1** Mares; **71bl** Bright Weights; **72tr3** Kevin Davidson; **74b** Alamy/GUILLEN PHOTOGRAPHY; **75bl1** AP Valves; **75bl2** AP Valves; **75bl3** AP Valves; **75t** Dorling Kindersley/Demetrio Carrasco/Rough Guides; **76c** Dan Burton; **77b** Dan Burton; **77cl1** Aqua Lung; **77cl2** AP Valves; **79br1** Mares; **79br2** Mares; **79br5** Apeks Marine Equipment; **79cr** Alamy/Jack Sullivan; **80b** Dan Burton; **81br** Mares; **81c** Alamy/GUILLEN PHOTOGRAPHY; **82bl** Alamy/Stephen Frink Collection; **82c** HydroOptix LLC; **82tr** Ocean Reef; **83bl** Dan Burton; **90–91** Dan Burton; **92–103rh** iStockphoto/Dennis Sabo; **92bc** Alamy/Chris A Crumley; **95bc** Kevin Davidson; **97cr** Kevin Davidson; **98cr** iStockphoto/Daniel Gustavsson; **99c** Kevin Davidson; **100tc** iStockphoto/Dennis Sabo; **101tc** Kevin Davidson; **102tc** iStockphoto/Kevin Bergen; **103bc** Kevin

Davidson; **109br** iStockphoto/Joe Gough; **109tr** Alamy/ Nick Hanna; **113bl** Dorling Kindersley/Brian Pitkin; **117br** Mares; **122bl** Kevin Davidson; **125tc** Linda Pitkin; **129tl** Dan Burton; **132tr** Dan Burton; **135tc** Paul Reid; **136bc** Kevin Davidson; **137tc** Kevin Davidson; **141tr** Dan Burton; **152-153c** Kevin Davidson; **152tr** Dorling Kindersley/John Davis; **153tl** Dorling Kindersley/John Davis; **153tr** Dorling Kindersley/John Davis; **154cr** Dorling Kindersley/Sian Irvine; **154tc** Dorling Kindersley/Andrew Whittuck; **156-157** Dan Burton; **159cl** Nataliya Chervyakova; **160b** Ross Armstrong; **160tc** Marek Walisiewicz; **161br** Nataliya Chervyakova; **161tl** Poseidon Divers; **162c** Marek Walisiewicz; **163t** Dan Burton; **164bl** Dan Burton; **165tl** Dan Burton; **166bl** Kevin Davidson; **166tc** Kevin Davidson; **167** Linda Pitkin; **168t** Kevin Davidson; **169b** Dan Burton; **169tr** Dan Burton; **170b** Alamy/Stephen Frink Collection; **171br** iStockphoto/Lara Seregni; **171tl** Alamy/POPPERFOTO; **172tc** Coral Cay Conservation; **173b** Kevin Davidson; **173tr** Coral Cay Conservation; **174b** Coral Cay Conservation; **175b** Alamy/Sarkis Images; **175t** Dan Burton; **176bl** Ross Armstrong; **176tr** Tony White; **177b** Dan Burton; **177tr** Kevin Davidson; **178bc** Pentax; **178bl** Nikon Corporation; **178br** Fujifilm; **178tr** iStockphoto/ Dennis Sabo; **179c** Inon Inc.; **179cl** Pentax; **179cr** Inon Inc.; **179t** Sea & Sea; **180bl** Canon Inc.; **180br** Canon Inc.; **180tc** Alamy/Roger Munns; **181b** Dan Burton; **181tc** Sea & Sea; **181tl** Sea & Sea; **181tr** Sea & Sea; **182b** Kevin Davidson; **182tc** Kevin Davidson; **184bl** Sea & Sea/ Underwater Kinetics; **184tr** iStockphoto/Rob New; **185t** Dan Burton; **186bl** Dan Burton; **186cr** Tabata USA (TUSA); **187t** Ross Armstrong; **188bl** Dan Burton; **188c** Mares; **189c** Dan Burton; **189t** Dan Burton; **190bl** Dan Burton; **190c** Mares; **190cr** SpecialFins Ltd; **191br2** Dorling Kindersley/Michael Moran; **191** Dan Burton; **192-193b** Dan Burton; **192bl** Alamy/Hugh Sitton Photography; **193tl** Dan Burton; **194bl** Dan Burton; **195br** Dan Burton; **195t** Dan Burton; **196-197b** Dan Burton; **196bl** Alamy/Henry Owen; **197tl** Dan Burton; **197tr** Corbis/The Cover Story; **198-199** Dan Burton; **200-233rh** iStockphoto/Johnny Lye; **200tc** Tony White; **201b** Kevin Davidson; **201tr** Kevin Davidson; **202bl** iStockphoto/Dan Schmitt; **202tr** iStockphoto/Steven Tulissi; **203b** Linda Pitkin; **203tr** Kevin Davidson; **204cr** Alamy/STOCK IMAGE/PIXLAND; **205** Linda Pitkin; **206b** Dorling Kindersley/Demetrio Carrasco; **206tr** Alamy/GUILLEN PHOTOGRAPHY; **207bc** Alamy/Reinhard Dirscherl; **208-209b** Dan Burton; **209br** Dorling Kindersley/Kim Taylor and Jane Burton; **209tr** iStockphoto/Sue Loader; **210b** Ross Armstrong; **210tr** Alamy/Robert E. Barber; **211** Linda Pitkin; **212-213b** iStockphoto/vera bogaerts; **212bl** Dorling Kindersley/ Harry Taylor; **212tr** iStockphoto/sandra minarik; **213tr** Nataliya Chervyakova; **214-215b** Linda Pitkin; **214cl** Alamy/Michael Patrick O'Neill; **215tr** Tony White; **216bl** iStockphoto/George Hoeylaerts; **216c** Dorling Kindersley/ Jerry Young; **216tr** iStockphoto/Vera Bogaerts; **217** Alamy/Visual&Written SL; **218b** Dorling Kindersley/Ken Findlay; **219br** Dorling Kindersley/Frank Greenaway; **219t** Alamy/George McCallum Photography; **220-221tc** Tony White; **220bl** Kevin Davidson; **221br2** Dorling Kindersley/ Frank Greenaway; **222-223b** Kevin Davidson; **223tr** Kevin Davidson; **224b** Kevin Davidson; **224c** iStockphoto/ Steffen Foerster; **225t** Kevin Davidson; **226bl** Alamy/ Reinhard Dirscherl; **226tr** Tony White; **227** Kevin Davidson; **228bl** Linda Pitkin; **228cr** Tony White; **229bc** Kevin Davidson; **230bl** Tony White; **230tr** iStockphoto/ Simon Edwin; **231** Kevin Davidson; **232-233b** Ross Armstrong; **232tc** Tony White; **233br** Linda Pitkin; **234-**

235 Linda Pitkin; **236-327rh** Dan Burton; **236-237b** Dan Burton; **236cr** Nataliya Chervyakova; **237tr** Dan Burton; **238bl** Mares; **238t** Dan Burton; **239b** iStockphoto/Lisa Kyle Young; **239tr** Dan Burton; **240b** Dorling Kindersley/ Frits Solvang; **240tr** Dorling Kindersley/Francesca Yorke; **241** Dan Burton; **242b** Dan Burton; **243bc** Alamy/ Wolfgang Pölzer; **243cr** Dorling Kindersley/Ian Aitken/ Rough Guides; **244cr** Alamy/Reinhard Dirscherl; **245b** iStockphoto/Dan Schmitt; **246bc** Alamy/Worldwide Picture Library; **247tr** Dan Burton; **248bl** Alamy/ Worldwide Picture Library; **249bc** Dan Burton; **249tr** Corbis/Bettmann; **250bl** Dorling Kindersley/Frank Greenaway; **250c** Alamy/Trevor Smithers ARPS; **251b** Alamy/David Lyons; **252cr** Dan Burton; **253b** Dorling Kindersley/Linda Whitwam; **254b** iStockphoto/Nancy Barr-Raper; **255cr** Nataliya Chervyakova; **256bl** Dan Burton; **256c** Linda Pitkin; **257** Linda Pitkin; **258c** Tony White; **259b** Dan Burton; **260b** Dan Burton; **260c** Alamy/ Peter Pinnock; **261c** Tony White; **262-263b** Dan Burton; **263tr** Dan Burton; **264b** Linda Pitkin; **265c** Alamy/Jon Arnold Images; **266c** Dan Burton; **267b** Dan Burton; **268tr** Dan Burton; **269bc** Dan Burton; **270bl** Dan Burton; **271bc** iStockphoto/Chartchai Meesangnin; **271tr** Ross Armstrong; **272-273c** Dan Burton; **273tr** Dan Burton; **274tr** Alamy/Reinhard Dirscherl; **275bc** Dan Burton; **276br** Linda Pitkin; **276c** Ikelite; **277bc** Tony White; **278bl** Linda Pitkin; **279bc** Ross Armstrong; **280bl** iStockphoto/ Erik de Graaf; **281br** Kevin Davidson; **281tc** Alamy/F. Jack Jackson; **282bl** Dan Burton; **282tc** Glen Edney; **284bl** Dan Burton; **285bc** Alamy/Iconsinternational.Com; **285tl** Dorling Kindersley/Alan Williams; **286bc** Dan Burton; **287tr** Dan Burton; **288bc** Tony White; **289bc** Andy Salmon; **290bc** Dan Burton; **291br** Glen Edney; **291tc** Glen Edney; **292tr** Corbis/Greenpeace/Sygma; **293br** Dan Burton; **294-295c** Dan Burton; **294bl** Dan Burton; **295tr** Kevin Davidson; **296br** Dan Burton; **297** Kevin Davidson; **298bl** Dan Burton; **299bc** Corbis/Claude Rives/Mer Images; **299br** Alamy/POPPERFOTO; **300b** Alamy/Chad Ehlers; **301br** Dan Burton; **302bl** Dan Burton; **303** Dan Burton; **304bc** Alamy/Stephen Frink Collection; **304cr** Alamy/David Fleetham; **305b** Tony White; **306b** Alamy/Chris A Crumley; **306c** Linda Pitkin; **307** Linda Pitkin; **308c** Dan Burton; **309b** Dan Burton; **309cr** iStockphoto/Wayne Johnson; **310c** Alamy/Stephen Frink Collection; **311b** Linda Pitkin; **312b** Dan Burton; **313bc** Alamy/ImageState; **313cr** Alamy/OceanPix.com; **314bl** Linda Pitkin; **315c** Alamy/Gavin Newman; **316-317b** Alamy/Brandon Cole Marine Photography; **317cr** Alamy/Brandon Cole Marine Photography; **318b** Alamy/ Andre Seale; **319c** Ambient Pressure Diving Ltd; **319cr** Alamy/Jeff Rotman; **320b** Alamy/Wolfgang Pölzer; **321b** Dorling Kindersley/Rob Reichenfeld; **322bc** iStockphoto/ William Smith; **322cr** Linda Pitkin; **323b** Tony White; **324b** Alamy/Visions of America, LLC; **325br** Alamy/ Wolfgang Pölzer; **326-327b** iStockphoto/Dan Cooper; **327tr** Linda Pitkin.

All maps on pages 200, 204, and 242–326 are Mountain High Maps® copyright © 1993 Digital Wisdom, Inc.

Every effort has been made to trace the copyright holders. The publisher apologizes for any unintentional omissions and would be pleased, in such cases, to place an acknowledgment in future editions of this book.

All other images © Dorling Kindersley
For further information see **www.dkimages.com**